THE
BULLIES

UNDERSTANDING BULLIES AND BULLYING

DENNIS LINES

Jessica Kingsley Publishers
London and Philadelphia

First published in 2008
by Jessica Kingsley Publishers
116 Pentonville Road
London N1 9JB, UK
and
400 Market Street, Suite 400
Philadelphia, PA 19106, USA

www.jkp.com

Library of Congress Cataloging in Publication Data
Lines, Dennis.
  The bullies : understanding bullies and bullying / Dennis Lines.
    p. cm.
  Includes bibliographical references and index.
  ISBN-13: 978-1-84310-578-7 (pb : alk. paper) 1. Bullying. I. Title.
  BF637.B85L56 2008
  302.3--dc22
                          2007031850

British Library Cataloguing in Publication Data
A CIP catalogue record for this book is available from the British Library

ISBN 978 1 84310 578 7

Printed and bound in Great Britain by
Athenaeum Press, Gateshead, Tyne and Wear

Contents

Preface

The theme for this book emerged from my therapy work with young people in secondary school. In listening to the stories of teenagers facing parental separation and family conflict, there appeared new narratives of their parents' own struggles in managing life and their own relationship battles voiced through them. After I invited the parents to come into school, I found they were keen to offload their own anxieties about their past, present and future. Therapy with parents over their offspring's management therefore reinforced for me the almost inescapable cyclic nature of family difficulties.

A second factor was a rising concern over child protection. For some years I had served my school as the designated teacher for child protection and children in public care, and over that period there were trends in policy change and practice that I felt uncomfortable with. One was an over-the-top reaction to parental 'over-correction' when tempers were raised with adolescents over their challenging behaviour. I had witnessed young teenagers or their parent or step-parent removed from the family home in order to secure protection from an 'abusing' adult, when what was wanted was the behaviour to stop, not a person removed. Although I recognize the difficulty in managing child protection in a media-hungry, 'holier-than-thou' age, it appeared to be a 'back-covering' exercise of social workers to avoid culpability. What I felt some families needed was support and guidance, not prosecution. And whenever I saw child protection inquiries being completed with no charges brought against the perpetrator and the authorities swiftly moving out and closing the file, I thought more understanding was required, not more legislation.

Acknowledgements

I thank all the headteachers I have served under – and particularly my current headteacher, Dave Firman – for their support over the years in recognizing the therapeutic needs of pupils at a time when education has become so competitive and where resources are so stretched to reach academic targets. I thank also my young clients and their parents for allowing me to enter their private worlds of trouble and despair. I am particularly grateful to three major contributors to this book for granting me permission to tell their stories, albeit anonymously, and many more who have shared their insights and experiences. Finally, I express gratitude to my friend Wendy Oldfield-Austin for inspiration to begin this book.

I am grateful to Jean Barley and Steve Fitton for their artwork, and to The M. C. Escher Company for granting permission to use Escher's 'Relativity'. Throughout the book the text is illustrated with photographs of typical bullying situations. I am grateful to my peer counsellors and their parents for allowing me to publish these pictures. I have to stress that these were not real situations but were simulated events that the students put together. I also have to say that although this book covers school bullying, all the evidence routinely collected has given me an assurance that bullying is a minimal problem in the school where I counsel, thanks to a vigilant management team led by a headteacher who places the need for an ethos of anti-bullying high on the school agenda. Finally, I am grateful to Stephen Jones, commissioning editor at Jessica Kingsley Publishers, for advice in steering this book through to completion.

Introduction

A pupil at school told me of his 15-year-old friend who punched himself hard in the face and head-butted the bus shelter simply because he had missed the last bus home that would have prevented him from getting a beating from his dad.

I once counselled a 13-year-old girl whose grandmother told her that as a babe in arms she was held over a balcony and threatened to be dropped during a domestic quarrel between parents. I have wondered over the years how such a negative view of self embedded in the mind might affect relations with others.

Bullying behaviour occurs in many areas of social life, including school, the family and the workplace. There are many group contexts where some individuals seek to exercise domination and control over weaker people, and the reasons for this are not as clear as is often supposed. Rules and procedures to curb school bullying, domestic violence and 'institutional bullying' are so obviously in tune with Western democratic values that they hardly need justifying. But a paradox exists in many cultures in that, whereas political and humanitarian values decry bullying behaviour, legislation and civil rights manifestos do not of themselves reduce the possibility of bullying in the home, the school or the workplace. Whilst behaviour may be modified to some extent by legal codes, morality is another matter.

From the classic narratives of *Tom Brown's Schooldays* in English literature to cartoon characters like Popeye and Bluto or Tom and Jerry, the Persian story of Ali Baba, and the biblical drama of Jacob and Esau, bullying of the weak by the strong appears so universal that it is wondered whether sublimating lesser fellows is not essential for social functioning. We laugh at Road Runner thwarting Coyote's painstaking plans to catch him because the drama speaks of the human condition of having to avoid threat, sharpen up one's defences and acquire the skills necessary for survival, but then we wonder who really is in control of whom.

This book is written to give insight into some of the complexities and intricacies of bullying behaviour amongst people who are in close relationships. It is not principally a work designed for practitioner competence, or to provide strategies and methods to reduce bullying, but rather to inform on how such measures may be shaped through more enlightened understanding.

There is no shortage of victims' stories expressing various bullying plights in social and domestic situations. What is not common is to find accounts of perpetrators or sentenced individuals who have committed crimes of physical assault against colleagues, 'friends' or members of their own family. In this book, I am not interested in the hardened criminal committed for murder or grievous bodily harm against an unknown person, or in those who revel in football or turf-war violence who may view street fighting as social amusement. My interest is in those who arguably are 'drawn into' aggressive behaviour, almost helplessly, as a reaction to relational conflict. We shall consider primarily those who are judged harshly by senior staff through exclusion or dismissal, or by society through the criminal justice system and periods of internment for violence against friends, family or colleagues.

When bullies victimize their subjects voyeuristically and unjustifiably, the injured parties clearly need redress. The imbalance of power and the inability of the sufferer to defend himself or herself require the strong arm of law to maintain justice. In such matters, there are normally few shades of grey that cloud the issues of necessary restitution. This book will argue, however, that in many cases of bullying in school, in the family and in the workplace, and even in the armed services – where fighting and 'man-power' are unequivocally part of the training programme – the issues are not always so clear-cut. In attempting to unearth a rationale for relational bullying and violence, we shall discover that power-hierarchies are not unified entities but quite complex processes.

I will reason that we will not understand the dynamics of bullying behaviour by paying too close attention to characters involved in extreme violence. Neither can we fully grasp the meaning of bullying behaviour by looking at some forms of trivial teasing as occurs regularly in schools and in adult social groupings, since this is a form of social interaction that may serve, paradoxically, to cement relationships together and result in tighter social bonding. It is the much larger and more commonplace area of relational bullying that will occupy our attention, particularly where it is conceived that an acceptable form of banter and horseplay has overstepped the mark or resulted in unintended violence and aggression between parties who are in a personal or professional relationship.

In the pages that follow, narratives will be presented to illustrate that the typical construct of *bad bully* and *innocent victim* is not always as clear-cut as people might think. I shall have cause to examine commonplace bullying behaviours, both in terms of causal factors and justifying principles from a holistic perspective, and shall question common tendencies amongst the public and some professionals to demonize provocateurs (normally men) and pathologize victims (normally women).

The title of this book might suggest that it is a further onslaught on bullies designed to reinforce the plight of 'innocent victims', but this is not the case. Bullying at school, within the family or at work, in whatever manifestation, is *relational* behaviour and it is within this framework that the problem must be analysed if it is going to be understood and reduced.

Book structure

Definitions of bullying are reviewed in the first chapter to see what scope a definition might offer in understanding conflict in close-knit relationships. Shortcomings of definitions are considered before broadening an understanding of bullying behaviour through common manifestations like aggression, dominance and control. Chapter 2 considers whether bullying derives from an 'animalistic' side of human nature and whether to dominate, fight, maim or even kill another human being is a 'natural' impulse of human biology and evolutionary function. One question posed here is why do some of our near and not-so-near animal relatives have to be aggressive and yet sometimes appear to behave altruistically. Some research into neuroscience will have relevance in understanding human rage and aggression. In Chapter 3 the argument extends to consider the social influences of dominant and over-controlling behaviour that is often regarded as bullying, principally through what is known from genetic and environmental studies of identical twins and fostered and adopted children. It covers the classic nature–nurture debate of human behaviour and heredity, and considers the implications of attachment theory.

The next two chapters examine how judgements are made on commonplace bullying. Here research is fairly limited in that much of what is known has arisen from international research into bullying in schools. Chapter 4 asks whether it is possible to draw up a profile of 'the bully' from types of observable behaviour. There is an extensive continuum from teasing to murderous behaviour that has to be included in definitions for applying to regular situations that arise in school and beyond. Chapter 5 is the theoretical centre of the book that offers a range of ways to view what is observed when children exercise undue control over weaker peers, when adults become violent with their partners and children, and when powerful bosses and managers flex their muscles with employees and members of their teams. In providing templates for understanding bullying behaviour there is scope to translate the remaining chapters of narrative material.

Chapters 6 to 9 cover bullying in school, in the family between partners and parents/guardians and children and in the workplace – where professions like teaching, the prison service and the army are considered in place of manual labour (the rationale for this selection is that such institutions more closely resemble schools where most research has been carried out). Each chapter comprises three sections: namely, what commonly happens in the social context, how it is made sense of and what perpetrators have to say to justify their behaviour. It is this third theme that is of greatest importance in understanding the 'meaning' of bullying, in that it grants an opportunity to enter the mind of the particular provocateur to see how bullying and dominating behaviour is rationalized. These chapters close with a concluding comment while at the same time avoiding making a definitive judgement, to encourage reflection on the bullying behaviour described. I am keen for the reader of this book to approach the material with an active and open mind.

These chapters present a range of narratives of young people and adults accused by others and/or the legal system of being bullies in various social and professional contexts. You will hear the voices of adolescents in secondary school, a man convicted for domestic violence against his wife, a released man who attempted to 'strangle' his step-daughter, an employer of a weddings business and a recruiting NCO in the army. I am grateful to these participants, and where relevant their parents, for granting me permission to publish their interviews. Although their stories are related anonymously – removing identifiable details from the scripts – and under pseudonyms, even so the participants have to some extent laid their necks on the line. It has not been an easy task finding such candidates for obvious reasons, but I regard the effort well worth the trouble because I have learnt so much in that I have been challenged, as I hope you will be, to examine my own preconceived ideas about bullies and bullying.

I am keen to let my contributors' voices speak for themselves rather than embellish their stories with over-interpretation or steering. Such accounts in writing can never give the whole impression that is received by the listener, where the greater percentage of communication is unspoken. Even so, I have avoided giving emphasis, pausing, inflexion and other body language codes as customarily given in narrative analysis (apart from obvious comments like 'crying' or 'laughing') for fear of translating what is spoken from my subjective stance. In keeping with professional and ethical standards, all published material in context has been shown to and approved by each respondent before going to press, with tapes erased after transcribing. For those students interested in qualitative research and methodology, the presented narratives are not selected from a batch – they are the only recordings I made. The only selection exercise was in removing extraneous or repetitive material so as to let the text speak to the point without monotony.

Chapter 10 explores the social implications arising from this book, in terms of how society deals with bullies and provocateurs of domestic violence. Lock them up for the protection of their victims, or rehabilitate offenders to get them to reform and behave non-aggressively, are the options that divide opinion and draw out people's prejudices and – as in other social concerns where costs and benefit have to be balanced – political agendas will often override evidence of effectiveness.

I am conscious that, in the argument which unfolds, the prejudices and assumptions of many may be challenged, as indeed mine have been. This book will in no way minimize the plight of bullied victims. I am aware of the lowering in self-esteem – of the pain, hurt and prolonged suffering inflicted on both the victims of bullying and their families. The acknowledgement of the pain caused by bullying should not preclude efforts to ensure that perpetrators are made to feel responsible rather than simply blamed. In presenting a rationale of bullying behaviour, I have not written this book with an unawareness of my gender as male.

My interest in listening to the voices of perpetrators of bullying and domination is to shift attention from blame towards a mediatory function which views bullying and over-control as relationship issues. This book seeks to dilute conceptions of discord and rivalry – like 'bully–bullied', 'abuser–abused' and 'dominator–dominated' – in favour of those that promote restorative justice and a holistic approach to conflict. Whether bullying takes place amongst children in school, within the family or at the workplace it is normally a complex behaviour of parties known to each other: *it is a relationship problem which requires a relationship solution.*

Chapter 1

What Is Bullying?

In a book titled *The Bullies* it seems inevitable that we should have to ask the question 'What is bullying?' How can any discussion move forward into examining the relational aspect of abusive behaviour unless such a question is answered? Since it is largely an observable activity amongst people, we need first to distinguish clearly between behaviours that constitute 'bullying' and those that may be considered as understandable reactions of defence or of letting-off-steam. We begin then by looking at classical bullying definitions to see what scope exists for drafting a particular definition to help understand the particular characteristics of bullying that underlie inter-relational conflict. This chapter will draw attention to two correlates of typical bullying behaviour, which are aggression and a drive to dominate the weak through an abuse of power.

Defining the nature of bullying

When I have asked pupils in school to define bullying, apart from some generally agreed aggressive responses (punching, kicking, slapping and pushing about), there are often as many different views on the incidentals of bullying behaviour as there are people. Whilst deliberate and unjustified physical violence will be universally accepted as bullying, other more covert behaviours that are insidious and spiteful, such as name-calling, mickey taking, or being isolated, ignored or rejected from the friendship group, whilst viewed as unpleasant, are not universally accepted as bullying. This is the problem with bullying definitions: it is trying to find a suitable definition that encompasses all recognizable bullying activity. There are a considerable number of bullying definitions and it would be beyond the scope of this book to examine these in any detail, other than to illustrate the emphases and intended purposes of some put forward by leading theorists working in the field of bullying research.

I led a whole-school working party a few years back to draw up an anti-bullying policy and gathered together representatives of senior and teaching staff, sixth-form students, parents, lunchtime ancillaries, caretaking staff, an education social worker and a school governor. We needed a definition of bullying that would be comprehensive yet simple to understand by 'every pupil', direct but not over-wordy. I presented for preliminary consideration a range of definitions from the literature:

1. Bullying can be described as the systematic abuse of power...
   Power can be abused: the exact definition of *abuse* will depend on
   the social and cultural context. (Smith and Sharp 1994)

2. Bullying is a wilful conscious desire to hurt another and put
   him/her under stress. (Tattum and Tattum 1992)

3. A student is being bullied or victimised when he or she is exposed,
   repeatedly and over time, to negative actions on the part of one or
   more other students. (Olweus 1993)

4. Bullying is longstanding violence, physical or psychological,
   conducted by an individual or a group against an individual who is
   not able to defend himself in the actual situation. (Roland 1989)

5. Bullying is a special case of aggression which is social in nature.
   (Bjorkquist, Eckman and Lagerspetz 1982)

6. Bullying is behaviour which can be defined as the repeated attack –
   physical, psychological, social or verbal – by those in a position of
   power, which is formally or situationally defined, on those who are
   powerless to resist, with the intention of causing distress for their
   own gain or gratification. (Besag 1989)

7. Bullying happens when one person or a group tries to upset
   another person by saying nasty or hurtful things again and again.
   Sometimes bullies hit or kick people or force them to hand over
   money; sometimes they tease them again and again. The person
   who is being bullied finds it difficult to stop this happening and is
   worried that it will happen again. It may not be bullying when two
   people of roughly the same strength have a fight or disagreement.
   (Mellor 1997)

8. Bullying is repeated oppression of a less powerful person, physical or psychological, by a more powerful person. (Farrington 1993)

From these definitions we constructed a group definition:

> *Bullying behaviour is continual physical, psychological, social, verbal or emo-tional methods of intimidation by an individual or group. Bullying is any action such as hitting or name-calling that makes you feel angry, hurt or upset.*

Much of the research carried out on bullying has been conducted within a school context and Ken Rigby (2002, p.51) has built upon earlier research to present a comprehensive definition that could hardly miss any category:

> Bullying involves a desire to hurt + hurtful action + a power imbalance + (typically) repetition + an unjust use of power + evident enjoyment by the aggressor and generally a sense of being oppressed on the part of the victim.

Common themes in bullying definitions

Some definitions of bullying deliberately attempt to be general and non-specific (e.g. 'the exact definition of abuse will depend upon the social and cultural context': Smith and Sharp 1994), whilst others attempt to encompass every facet of intimidation by spelling out in detailed covert and overt terms (e.g. Mellor 1997), though few mention social isolation and ignoring a person; it is perpetrated by an individual or a group. What interests me about these defi-nitions is that many of them state or imply that bullying is systematic ('re-peated') misbehaviour that is a regular and deliberate form of abuse, almost as though it were *organized* by perpetrators. As such, bullying can be a planned attempt to hurt another individual. Many of these definitions involve the abuse of power, and the differential of power between bully and victim forms a major component in most understandings of threatening or aggressive behaviour, whether stated or not. Some bullying behaviour, whatever the definition used, suggests that the 'bully' plans to hurt his or her victim for sadistic pleasure, as though it is voyeuristic behaviour similar to that of a cat catching a bird for no other reason than to play and torment it whilst it suffers needlessly. Such bullying by an individual or group may reveal a baser instinct that lies poten-tially in all of us and that links us in some respects to predatory animals – a point I address in Chapter 2.

More developed forms of definitions, like Rigby's, attempt to reveal internal processes between the injurer and the injured, such as an intent to hurt as opposed to accidentally bringing pain to another person ('evident enjoy-ment by the aggressor': Rigby 2002; 'a wilful conscious desire to hurt another': Tattum and Tattum 1992); and one wonders whether bullying can be rightly used as the classifying term if the victim against whom a particular action has been malevolent and spitefully intended is unreceptive to what has taken place. But this would rule out intentional behaviour directed towards those who are immune to provocation generally, such as, possibly, some children with autism, who may not register the subtle social gestures that malicious individuals might direct towards them. The problem with centring attention too much upon intent is that it is not always easy to diagnose, and is open therefore to misinter-pretation, or misjudgement, by an overseeing adult or manager – 'Oh, come on, he was only joking!' Labelling bullying only from an 'intent to hurt' basis, as opposed to an observable behaviour that is wrong in itself without question, denies the observer a necessary role in teaching youngsters what is appropriate and inappropriate behaviour. Some children will need to be taught that particu-lar behaviours constitute bullying, and this would require common agreement of a bullying definition.

Three of the above definitions recognize the inability of victims to defend themselves and which see this factor as being central to bullying activity (Besag 1989; Mellor 1997; Roland 1989). Most of the definitions cover explicitly or imply the social characteristics of bullying behaviour. Along with my school's definition (constructed to meet the requirements of the school community), three of the cited definitions cover psychological bullying as well as the physical elements (Besag 1989; Farrington 1993; Roland 1989); and whilst some may imply that emotional intimidation is bullying, it was only the school's definition which included it specifically.

One definition of workplace bullying has been composed to support employees by Amicus-MSF, a British trade union:

> Persistent, offensive, abusive, intimidating or insulting behaviour, abuse of power or unfair penal sanctions which makes the recipient feel upset, threatened, humiliated or vulnerable, which undermines their self-confi-dence and which may cause them to suffer stress. (cited on Bully OnLine n.d.)

This definition is clearly designed to suit a specific work context and adds nothing new apart from condemning behaviour that undermines self-confi-dence and leaves a recipient in a state of stress, the latter recognized by theorists above (Besag 1989; Mellor 1997; Tattum and Tattum 1992).

It is fair to say that most definitions are drafted to meet the requirements of the institution for which they were composed. The underlying question is *What is the bullying definition required for and for whom should it be composed?* Alternatively, *What is the audience and what series of behaviours is the definition attempting to regulate?*

Relational aspects in bullying definitions

Some of the above definitions centre wholly upon 'the activity' with little to no relevance to 'the quality of relationship' that is affected by the activity. The emphasis is upon behaviour regulation, justice and fair play. A definition that may serve the purposes of a professional association or a trade union will be designed to protect subordinates from superiors in a vertical line management structure; it is not designed primarily to regulate the behaviour of employees with each other on a horizontal plane, as is the case with pupils with their peers in school. In a school setting, there is need to regulate the behaviour between peers, because this is central to what a school is all about – cooperative learning in a friendly and wholesome community. Each school will have an ethos centred upon quality relationships within the organization, and indeed inspectors see this as a relevant indicator when measuring the performance of the school and the effectiveness of the leadership team.

Since I am concerned with the relational aspects underlying bullying behaviour, it is evident that the definitions mentioned above will not suffice, but then it is legitimate to ask what is meant by bullying within a relational context. In what follows, I do not think it appropriate to shape a definition of bullying that will suit my purpose to reveal the dynamics of relational conflict. My emphasis throughout is to listen to the voices of the perpetrators of aggression within close-knit relationships, whether at school, in the family or in the workplace; and in order to gain insight into why some people become aggressive or violent I think it would be distracting and misleading if we were to fit each interview within a limited framework that aims to be comprehensive in scope, which bullying definitions tend to be. While I loosely term such people within relationships as 'bullies', I wish to say at the outset that this would not be my preference as a general label. Whilst society may judge at a distance a typical range of behaviours as bullying *per se*, I hope to show in the pages that follow that this might not be the case. In order to amplify what I mean, let's look at the shortcomings in general bullying definitions.

First, the 'intention to cause harm' will not be central within a relationship where all parties choose to live together. This is not to say that harm might not result from thoughtless and inappropriate behaviour, but it is to recognize that this is not the principal intention. Provocateurs behaving in a certain manner may have another goal in mind than one of causing harm. Oppressive chastisement may be regrettable behaviour – such as when a father impulsively reacts when drunk, or has been sacked from work, or been bereaved of someone close – but other parental disciplinary measures may be mistimed or misjudged. For example, a father may violently beat his son for being 'lippy' and leave him bruised after coming in high on heroin. His main aim, arguably, may be to 'correct' his son and divert him from a life of drug dependence and all that that may involve; it is not to bully him. Although a power differential will exist, and in spite of informed parenting commending that a display of physical aggression might not be necessary or indeed helpful, the underlying purpose of the behaviour, however unpleasant to the observer (and to the son), is not to cause harm. In modern times, where human rights laws will more readily bring violent incidents between peers in school and partners in the home to court, incidents of brutality in the playground and domestic violence, not to mention child protection, could well render perpetrators liable to prosecution for physical assault. In such cases, underlying 'intentions' carry little weight in criminal law.

This kind of rule could be applied to psychological and emotional bullying as well as to physical maltreatment. But emotional and psychological intimidation and violence is difficult to determine and legislate for through bullying definitions; and given that psychological and emotional factors may be more prevalent in relational conflict than physical violence and aggression, any bullying definition may not be sufficiently inclusive to be informative.

Underlying intentions can only be understood fully through listening to the views, or the rationale, of the principal players demonstrating covert or public forms of bullying. Whilst society's view might be to consider every wildly aggressive means of managing children and young people, or handling relational conflict between partners, as 'bullying', I hope to show through the discourses which follow that this is not necessarily the case. Should such people be termed 'bullies' then, as the title of this book might suggest? Well, if an aggressive act is judged to be 'bullying' then the person delivering it must be termed 'a bully'. But this kind of thumbnail categorization is misleading and not very informative – labels and watertight definitions do not help us look beneath the surface of relational conflict.

Domination within relational conflict

Much violence and aggression that can be observed in school, such as when boys and girls fight, is not necessarily bullying (even where there is an initial power differential), since it involves two willing partners becoming engaged in combat. Aggression is a serviceable tool for individuals seeking to bully weaker peers, whether or not they are in a close relationship, and in Chapter 2, 'Bullying in Nature', the role of aggression within social groupings will be considered in greater detail. But I'd like to briefly examine here one other form of social behaviour that is often associated with bullying – the wish to dominate or subjugate a 'lesser' person. Dominating behaviour amongst peers may be classed as bullying, whether accompanied by violence or not, since intention is not difficult to establish with unguarded youngsters, but what about those who are 'friends' or who are in a close relationship, whether adults or teenagers?

Why do some particular individuals seek to dominate and apply excessive control over their friends or close loved ones? I shall examine in Chapter 5, 'Interpreting Bullying Behaviour', typical traits that characterize adolescent behaviour through puberty and beyond. In Nick Luxmoore's (2000) book, *Listening to Young People in School, Youth Work and Counselling*, he presents the case of Chloe, a youngster in school who frequently fell out with her personal friends. In that case he demonstrates the hustles and tussles occurring in close-knit friendships where youngsters frequently test out their different roles through trust and betrayal and regular infighting. Such behaviour, he argues, and I fully agree with him, is an unconscious psychological need to experiment with attachment and separation at such a time that each adolescent is moving away from the parent towards the peer group. It has been my regular experience that such squabbles are common in school, particularly amongst girls, and become the source of fierce battles and intense bullying behaviour if not managed competently. This indicates for me the inextricable link between the most hostile bullying and the betrayal of friendship. As youngsters in school group together and form separatist identities, the impregnable fortress walls of their loyalty, as the in-group, has the effect of barring the rest, the out-group, and often by the most despicable means, which can be truly designated as bullying. Some pupils, as we shall see, will use power and subtle controlling techniques to exercise dominion as a means of bolstering their own self-esteem and status amidst the group.

Subtle controlling manoeuvres of adults with their partners may also illustrate an immature means of winning control in insecure and fragile relationships, as we shall see later on. Over-controlling behaviour can be seen in friendships as in transactional relationships in contained settings like school and the workplace, both for youngsters and adults, and this ubiquity suggests that this behaviour may in some way fulfil a psychological need.

There is one other feature of controlling and dominating behaviour I would like to introduce at this point, which is the 'role of the victim' in the reciprocal process of dominant relational behaviour. For one to dominate another requires that other to be dominated, or at least to willingly remain within that relationship of domination, and acknowledging this in a definition of bullying can only help us move forward in understanding the internal dynamics of a relationship. Family systems theory highlights this in the reciprocal nature of family and close-knit relations.

It is for these reasons that I think that the definitions of bullying introduced at the start of this chapter only serve as rough guides of classification, and that in particular relational conflicts they can prove to be obstacles for understanding the nature of intentional motivations.

Conclusion

It seems reasonable at the outset to identify 'the bully' as he or she who displays any form of overt or covert bullying behaviour. Definitions of bullying are usually coined to suit a particular social context, so while it may initially appear profitable to utilize or modify some common bullying definitions to help guide us through the process of understanding the mind of the bully in particular institutional settings, they are less helpful when examining the nature of conflict and overly aggressive behaviour within close-knit relationships. Definitions are useful tools for identifying the act of bullying, as opposed to the intention, but they offer little insight when seeking to make sense of the internal dynamics of tension and conflict within close or loving relationships. It seems fitting, therefore, when penetrating the surface of observable bullying behaviour within familial social contexts, to understand it through active listening of the often silent voice of the perpetrator – a technique that avoids prescriptive definitions getting in the way of full understanding.

Chapter 2

Bullying in Nature

This chapter seeks to place bullying in context by looking at biological and evolutionary impulses. Why do particular people become excessively violent towards weaker individuals? Why do some want to dominate others? How is such behaviour rationalized and justified? It will consider the degree to which aggressive people are genetically predisposed to act violently, and by extension appear to 'need' to dominate and bully others. Is it a token of our animalistic nature that we impulsively have to counter threat by physical means? As well as exploring the 'natural' behaviour of aggression, it also considers evidence in nature of contrasting behaviours like caring and altruism, which have evolved to meet very different goals. Answers to these questions will provide the necessary groundwork from which to interpret aggressive behaviour that is sometimes identified with bullying.

Nature 'red in tooth and claw' versus altruism

In Richard Dawkins' controversial book *The God Delusion* (2006), he expresses regret that his seminal work *The Selfish Gene* (1976) has often been misunderstood by writers and commentators. His original thesis was not to suggest that organisms have to be selfish to exist in the struggle for life, but that their genes 'appear' to function in a selfish manner. Human beings – as well as animals and plants – are highly efficient machines that have evolved to preserve and propagate their genes into the next generation. With human beings and most animals this occurs by sexual reproduction in which half of the organism's genes are carried over into the offspring.

This may seem a somewhat bleak picture of the purpose of life, and indeed many have rejected this grim portrayal of how life on our planet functions. There is a suggestion in the selfish gene theory that the sole goal of life is hedonistic barbarism. Perhaps it is a moot point of difference to suggest that genes are different from *gene machines*, but as we look around in the animal kingdom it is not easy to come away with any other impression than that nature functions ruthlessly 'red in tooth and claw'. Without getting too embroiled in gene theory, it may serve as a useful starting point to examine human behaviour through how animals behave in order to survive.

Predatory carnivores

Predators of the air (such as eagles, hawks and buzzards) and of the land (such as lions, leopards and hyenas) are unconsciously programmed to make decisions when developing their hunting strategies. They will rarely find the healthy adult of their prey but will instead go for the injured or the young. In the fight to preserve their genes they will not risk injury from a fight with an 'able' opponent, but by going after the weak a nutritious meal can be enjoyed at little relative cost. Lions don't hunt lions for their meat, but they attack antelopes. The lion 'wants' the meat of the antelope's body, but the antelope has very different plans for its body. Lions' genes 'want' meat as food for their survival machine, but antelope genes 'want' meat as working muscle and organs for their survival machine.

As Dawkins concludes, these two uses for meat are mutually incompatible; there is a conflict of interests. Although lions are the only social member of the cat family, they will attack other lions to take over control of the pride, just as stags do in the Scottish Highlands, and whilst stags will not kill their young a male lion will attack and kill a competitor and will even kill the cubs of his rival's pride. Since the new champion will then mate with the females of the pride, it seems that the motive is not to obtain food but to wipe out the genes of the previous lion king and perpetuate his own in his stead. This is not the case with polar bears...

Cannibalism

A lone female polar bear struggles hard against a changing environment to nurture and bring up her cubs, and if she by chance meets a solitary male her youngsters are in danger of ending up in his stomach. This apparently 'cruel' behaviour is prompted by the shortage of food and there is nothing that thwarts resulting cannibalism even if the cubs are his offspring.

Other carnivores illustrate cannibalistic behaviour. We may have to stand by in frustration at times when we notice a magpie snatching a chick from the

Figure 2.1 'Lions' sketched by Jean Barley

nests of blackbirds or great tits rather than seek carrion from elsewhere, but they don't eat their own. Some seabirds, however, particularly black-headed gulls, will cheat on their own species in the fight for life. Some opportunist gull of the same species will wait until her neighbour has left her nest and will swoop down and snatch a chick of its own kind and swallow it whole. In preserving its own genes she has expended little energy and safeguarded her own in the process. As Dawkins acknowledges, there is a balance to be struck between *cost* and *benefit* in the struggle to preserve the species. A barn owl chick will swallow whole his smaller brother or sister when the parent brings insufficient food due to wet conditions, and it seems as though 'nature' has equipped this species for such a contingency by 'programming' a delay in egg laying and incubation to allow varied physical growth to make this possible – one larger chick amongst smaller siblings.

Perhaps the best example of cannibalistic behaviour amongst insects is that of the praying mantis. The praying mantis is a carnivore which lives by eating insects, but when the male attempts to copulate by mounting on his mate's back the female will attempt to bite off his head for a nutritious meal, either before, during or after copulation. The ability to mate is not restrained if the male loses his head; in fact there is some evidence that inhibitory nerves are severed which may cause the male to be more fertile once beheaded.

Needless to say, cannibalistic behaviour has also been recorded amongst peoples of Africa and South America, yet it is difficult to ascertain whether such tribal behaviour stems from religious beliefs, rather than the need for food, and whether accounts have been exaggerated due to political motives of Western Europeans. This is a one-sided picture of animal behaviour, however, for there are examples of 'altruism' amongst our near and not-so-near relatives in spite of the common evolutionary requirements of survival.

Altruism 'for the good of the species'

One useful question to ask is whether or not there is evidence of altruism amongst animals. It may be inappropriate to use the term 'altruism' since we see it as a human value of caring and self-giving, and, indeed, Dawkins is keen to stress that when he speaks of 'selfish' and 'altruism' he is not thinking in moral terms as we understand them. Nevertheless, he gives examples of animals that appear to demonstrate self-sacrificial behaviour 'for the good of the species'.

Particular groups of penguins in the Antarctic have been observed grouping together on the edge of the ice waiting for one to enter the water first.

The hazard is very real in that a seal may be lurking under the water in the hope of catching a delicious meal. The penguins are hungry and at some point one will volunteer to plunge into the water, appearing to surrender his life for the good of the species. There is no way his genes can be reproduced through to the next generation if his life is forfeited for the group. Birds like lapwings have been observed fluttering on the ground, or dragging their wing to mimic injury. It is as though genes have selected this behaviour as the most efficient means of luring away a fox or similar predator from the chicks nested on the ground.

Behaviour for a common good is evident amongst birds in instances where there is a predator around. If a hawk flies overhead, or a cat is on the prowl in the garden, an 'alarm call' is sounded and birds take cover or gang together to chivvy the intruder. Whilst the predator may be seen off, there is great risk to the bird that first gives the alarm. Whilst Jackdaws dominate to establish their seniority, they check squabbling amongst the younger birds. Their genetic reason to establish superiority is that when they sound an alarm the rest will take notice. In this way their aggression can be said to benefit the species (Rigby 2002).

Some creatures living in colonies, such as ants, appear to demonstrate altruistic behaviour in nature. Ants will care for aphid eggs inside their own underground nests, feed their young and finally, when they are grown, gently carry them up to the protected grazing grounds. This is a relationship of mutual benefit between members of different species and is called 'mutualism' or 'symbiosis'. Symbiotic relationships of mutual benefit are common among animals and plants.

In some of these examples, however, it will be argued that parents are merely protecting their young, and thereby in the long run are preserving their own genes through their offspring, and that most living creatures behave this way. But there is much agitation and upset witnessed when predators carry off another creature's young. Altruistic behaviour amongst troops of monkeys and schools of whales has frequently been reported. Whales and dolphins drown if they are unable to breathe air. Baby whales and individuals who are injured and who cannot swim to the surface have been seen to be rescued and held up by companions in the school, and it is not certain whether they know who their relatives are. The altruism is worth the cost. There are even examples where a dolphin has rescued drowning humans and brought them to the surface.

Dawkins discusses many examples of apparent 'altruism' and recognizes a slight contradiction with his selfish gene theory. His solution is to reason that such creatures are probably acting out unconscious behaviour of a genetic rule which runs like this (in the case of dolphins): 'rescue long things thrashing about and choking near the surface'. Male baboons have also been known to risk their lives by defending the rest of the troop against predators such as leopards. It is probable, argues Dawkins, that adult male baboons have a fairly large number of genes tied up in other members of the troop. A gene that says, in effect, 'body, if you happen to be an adult male, defend the troop against leopards', could become more numerous in the gene pool. Conclusive evidence of such instinctive behaviour is obviously going to be difficult to find if it is based upon deductive observation, and causes will therefore remain as interesting but speculative.

Group 'caring' behaviour

However the selfish gene theory is evaluated, there can be no serious doubting the genuine caring nature of some animals for others, and not only from motives of profiting their own species. There are many examples of creatures which foster parasites within their body and not only to benefit themselves. It has often been remarked that elephants illustrate a particularly caring nature. Although enormous creatures, they show incredible sensitivity and have been known to shed tears at the death of one of their own or the stillbirth of one of their family members. Domestic animals, such as dogs and horses, demonstrate particular caring behaviour for their owners, and will appear at times as though they will 'sacrifice' their own well-being in the process.

The wild dogs of Botswana and the emperor penguins of the Antarctic strongly suggest that some animals have evolved a corporate sense of community support by looking after one another for the benefit of the group. Unlike competitive behaviour amongst a pride of lions, the wild dogs of the woodlands of Botswana have cultivated organizational skills of group behaviour in order to survive. They hunt as a pack and appear to have quite complex communications when hunting their prey, since they have to keep continually on the move. To avoid predators the lean dogs must continually run and this is only halted when one female is selected for breeding. She is particularly vulnerable at this point, but the rest of the group protect her until after she has delivered her pups. Other males than the father provide her food and defend her from predators. Often when injured, wild dogs have been observed licking each other's wounds rather than leaving their fellow injured to die and be a liability for the group – which might better serve their genes' interests. Survival for all depends on *group support*, not the 'survival of the fittest'.

The emperor penguins of the Antarctic are another good example. They travel to a pre-selected area covering nearly one hundred miles across the frozen sea at the critical time. After choosing a partner and mating, the mother's egg is reluctantly given over to the father. Producing the egg has taken so much energy from her that she cannot incubate it but must make the return journey for food. The male safeguards the egg in his warm pouch. The male must preserve the egg through a very harsh climate of hurricane winds and extreme temperatures of up to −60° and for over a month. During this bleak period hundreds of males have to survive by collective support of the group. They shuffle around with their eggs in a curious style of packing tightly together in order to keep out the cold. They assemble and reassemble in different formations so that those on the outside are now left to take on the severe conditions, but receive in turn their time in the centre. The chick just hatches before the mother returns to provide a belly full of fresh fish. But some mothers fail to return and therefore leave their chick orphaned. So strong is the maternal instinct that other chick-less females charge after an orphan – often crushing it to death in the process. It seems as though they are driven to adopt another's chick and to continue genes which are not their own.

What is of interest when looking at the behavioural characteristics of many species is that the notion of 'nature red in tooth and claw' only presents one facet of the natural world. Animal group caring and nurturing, for whatever survival purposes, seems as natural as predatory behaviour. Animals are programmed to fight and kill, just as they are programmed to preserve and support, not only within their species but also beyond them. A more fitting analysis of the natural world, therefore, is to view nature as in balance and harmony, where all behaviour is reciprocal and interdependent. The behaviour of the lion as predator only has meaning within a particular survival context of the behaviour of the antelope as its prey. Nature is truly in balance, and understanding the meaning of one species makes little sense without a consideration of the context of its whole environment, shifting though that balance will be over time and through altering environmental factors. As the argument proceeds later on to examine human behaviour, I think we shall understand more fully the behaviour of the bully once we have understood the reciprocal nature of the behaviour of the victim. Rival behaviour amongst species in the struggle for survival in essence appears to be complementary in the animal world, and it remains to be seen whether the same is true in human relations. If genetic programming amongst animals might operate in predatory and altruistic behaviour for the benefit of the group, what purpose does aggression serve in individual and group behaviour?

Animal aggression

Aggression is similarly observed amongst animals and humans, and perhaps it is the one trait that links us so indisputably with our animal ancestry. We shall have cause to examine human aggression from a psychological perspective later, but at this point let us ask the question: what is the role of aggression according to Darwinian theory? What purpose does aggression have in preserving the stability of the species?

Let's look at what can be learnt from studying chickens and crickets. The behaviour of chickens in the pen as they establish their pecking-orders of superiority is well known and has been observed through time by most communities. When a batch of hens who have never met before are introduced to each other there is normally a great deal of fighting. But this fighting dies down in time as each learns their place in the community. Whilst in this agitated and aggressive state, hens appear unsettled and, as far as the farmer is concerned, are unproductive in terms of egg yield. It is not good for the group as a whole when energy is expended in fierce fighting. Biologists often speak of the advantage or 'function' of 'dominance hierarchies' as being to reduce overt aggression in the group, but this is the wrong way to put it, argues Dawkins. A 'dominance hierarchy' cannot be said to have a function in an evolutionary sense, since it is a property of a group, not of an individual.

Dominance hierarchies when viewed at the group level might be said to have 'functions' in terms of evolutionary stable species, in asymmetric contests where there is individual recognition and memory. For example, it is known that when crickets fight they preserve a memory of 'being a victor' from earlier trials. This serves them in deciding whether to become more 'hawkish' or 'dovish' in other battles, to preserve or to use up energy for survival. Crickets do not recognize each other as individuals and consequently can constantly become involved in fighting if they have won most past encounters.

Unlike crickets, monkeys do not exhibit ongoing aggressive behaviour. If a monkey has been defeated in an earlier encounter it will preserve the memory of that particular contest and the particular individual, and the dominant genetic response is likely to register caution next time around. Better not challenge a victorious opponent a second time. The best strategy is to be relatively dovish towards an individual who has previously defeated you.

The behaviour of boys in the playground resembles monkeys in some respects and hens in others, in that memory of a previous encounter will influence a boy's decision to further take on his opponent (exceptions can occur with renewed confidence during puberty), but in the new social mix at transition to a new school the wish for status will prompt battles for dominance to secure social cohesion. One interesting 'purpose' for this aggression, therefore, might be to establish a 'dominance hierarchy', which, paradoxically, may be directed towards establishing stability within the group. This may be an interesting explanation for gang and turf warfare and street bullying behaviour – more of this later.

Organized aggression by human communities resembles that of groups of animals that battle over territory where resources of food and other valuable commodities are in scarce supply. It is possible to draw maps of territorial boundaries for robins and great tits, and these exist within species rather than between them. The characteristic friendliness of the garden robin delights the gardener weeding the soil, but this apparent 'socialization' is more likely to be a sign of the robin marking her patch and symbolizing the area of her domain rather than a gesture of playful curiosity. More severe examples of territorial aggression amongst animals include the group behaviour of monkeys and chimpanzees living in the rainforests. In these areas there is a competition for food and fig trees offer a staple diet for many creatures throughout the year. Siamang gibbons, for example, stake their claim to the treetops by grouping together in a frenzied activity and a cacophony of calls which carry for over a mile. Their message is clear. They are saying to any poachers: *this is our patch, you'd better keep out!*

In the search for food in the African jungle, groups of chimpanzees organize themselves as a regimented army, moving effortlessly among the trees of the canopy to establish their territory. Figs are a vital part of a chimpanzee's diet, but when a rival group moves into their domain they organize themselves with military precision. They orchestrate a menacing cry as a prior warning before patrolling towards the enemy. Once the invading troop is in sight, the cavalry charges towards the unsuspecting. They scream aloud and drum on fruit boughs and with menacing aggression attack their intruders, regularly taking an enemy and in a grisly manner will sometimes tear its body apart and devour it, sharing it amongst all members of the troop. Killing a captive makes sense to protect your food supply, but why they cannibalize them is not fully known. It may simply be an opportunity for extra protein. Animal cannibalism is, however, relatively rare. The reason why tigers don't hunt tigers is that it risks instability in the population – the tiger would not otherwise become an evolutionary stable species.

Likewise, antelopes run away from lions because it risks evolutionary instability. There is too much danger involved in retaliation because the contest might result in injury and this would not serve as an advantage for the species. Each organism has to strike a balance between cost and benefit with a predatory or an escapist behaviour in the interests of becoming an evolutionary stable species.

For Dawkins, evolution continues in the modern world not so much through biology but through culture – true 'altruism' is not a product of our biology but is *something that is taught through culture*. He writes that with the influence of culture more than biology, evolution continues through what he calls 'memes': memes are tunes, ideas, catchphrases, clothes, fashions, ways of making items and of building constructions, and so on.

> Just as genes propagate themselves in the gene pool by leaping from body to body via sperms or eggs, so memes propagate themselves in the meme pool by leaping from brain to brain via a process which, in the broad sense, can be called imitation. (Dawkins 1976, p.192)

Summarizing the contents of this chapter it would be reasonable to conclude that parallels between some animal and human behaviour may be found of such a kind that could be regarded as bullying, but to reason for a direct link would stretch the evidence. It would depend on where we look and how we evaluated typical patterns of observed behaviour. Rigby's (2002) assessment draws upon the work of Konrad Lorenz (1969) in which he saw three distinct advantages of animal aggression towards their 'inferiors': the bullies had the best chance of mating, bullying could maintain a hierarchal social structure that contributed to stability and viability of the group, and intra-species aggression provides for the group the necessary space in order to avoid exploiting limited local resources.

As Rigby concludes (2002), some animal bullying appears 'evil' and unnecessary for survival, whilst other bullying appears necessary to meet a particular goal:

> We can find support for a variety of views: that bullying is good for us; that bullying is an unspeakable evil; that bullying is the means by which we can, and sometimes do, protect ourselves from 'outsiders' and preserve the purity of the group. (p.22)

As I have shown above, some creatures are particularly altruistic and caring (wild dogs of Botswana), even to those of another species (ants towards aphids, dolphins), whilst others can be particularly aggressive even to their own kind (praying mantis, chimpanzees), including their siblings (barn owl chicks). Many creatures become particularly hostile towards those not of their group, and here we may find parallels in group social behaviour with outsiders, both in school and in the workplace.

Neuroscience and physiology

The study of neuroscience has made giant strides in aiding our understanding of human aggression and its relation to the electro-chemical processes of the brain. Daniel Goleman, in his revolutionary book *Emotional Intelligence*, draws attention to the physiological states accompanying emotions like anger and fear. When a person experiences anger, blood flows to the hands, making it easier to grasp a weapon or strike at a foe, and with fear blood goes to the large skeletal muscles, such as in the legs, making it easier to flee. The physiology of reactive behaviour through 'fight or flight' is grounded in brain chemistry. We have two minds, says Goleman, an emotional mind and a rational mind, which operate in tight harmony, but the emotional mind is pre-cognitive and evolved first. It develops earlier in child brain development, long before the rational brain, the neocortex.

The limbic system is the part of the brain involved in emotion, motivation, and emotional association with memory. It influences the formation of memory by integrating emotional states with stored memories of physical sensations. The limbic system includes the following brain areas:

- amygdala – this signals the cortex of motivationally significant stimuli such as those related to reward and fear

- hippocampus – this forms long-term memories

- hypothalamus – this regulates the autonomic nervous system via hormone production and release, affecting and regulating blood pressure, heart rate, hunger, thirst, sexual arousal, and the sleep/wake cycle

- thalamus – this is the relay station to the cerebral cortex.

The amygdala is well developed at birth and is the first part of the emotional brain to mature; as the American neuroscientist Joseph LeDoux would say:

'When you see a twig on your path that looks like a snake, you jump back fear-fully, or freeze – you act first, think later' (cited in Gerhardt 2004, p.33). The hippocampus and the amygdala are the two key parts of the primitive 'emotional mind' – the cortex and then the neocortex of the rational mind evolved at a later stage (see Figure 2.2.). This evolutionary sequence is paralleled in the way the brain processes stimuli:

> Research has shown that sensory signals from eye or ear travel first in the brain to the thalamus, and then – across a single synapse – to the amygdala; a second signal from the thalamus is routed to the neocortex – the thinking brain. This branching allows the amygdala to begin to respond *before* the neocortex, which mulls information through several levels of brain circuits before it fully perceives and finally initiates its more finely tailored response. (Goleman 2006, p.17)

4. Neocortex (conscious brain) receives slower but accurate image to process for a more calculated reaction

1. Thalamus receives image which is shunted instantly to the amygdala and more slowly to the visual cortex

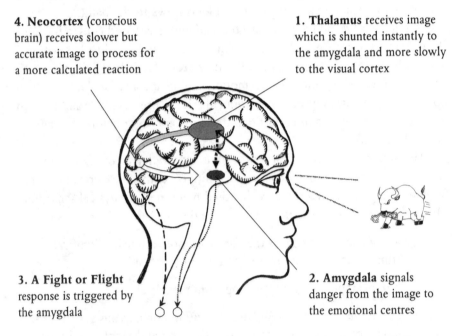

3. A Fight or Flight response is triggered by the amygdala

2. Amygdala signals danger from the image to the emotional centres

Figure 2.2 Drawn by Steve Fitton. The mental process of learned emotional rage through an active amygdala: (1) A visual (heard, smelt, touched) fear stimulus reaches the thalamus; (2) a recalled emotion is registered at the amygdala within an instant for a less-precise reaction; (3) a fight or flight response occurs through increased heart rate and blood pressure for muscular quick reaction; (4) the larger signal goes to the visual cortex, where it is analysed for a more considered response - shall I continue to run or should I fight the threat? It is as important for survival to have to respond instinctively as to reflect seconds later on the best course of action.

The route from eye or ear to thalamus to amygdala is crucial because it saves time in an emergency when an immediate response is required. This direct route is reckoned in thousands of a second. The longer route through the neocortex allows for a better response that avoids the kind of catastrophe like a shock killing through an impulsive reaction. Goleman gives an example of a 14-year-old girl named Matilda Crabtree who played a practical joke on her father by jumping out of the closet and yelling, 'Boo!' Not expecting her to be at home, her father thought someone was in the house and entered tentatively with his gun. As he went into the bedroom to investigate, Crabtree shot her in the neck, and Matilda Crabtree died 12 hours later.

The prefrontal lobes just behind the forehead serve as the brain's damper switch for the amygdala. For animals this amounts to 'attack' or 'run', but for humans, apart from running or fighting, it amounts to the decision to placate, persuade, seek sympathy, stonewall, provoke guilt, put on the facade of bravado, be contemptuous, and so on through the whole repertoire of emotional wiles. The neocortical response is slower in brain time than the unthinking amygdala because it involves more circuitry. Circuits from the limbic brain to the prefrontal lobes mean that the signals of strong emotion – anxiety, anger, and the like – can create 'neural static', sabotaging the ability of the prefrontal lobe to maintain working memory. Individuals can become highly charged emotionally by over-reacting or by reacting inappropriately – 'I just didn't think' – when faced with a perceived threatening situation that triggers an early memory of a frightening event. It is during those moments that impulsive feelings override the rational and it is the amygdala that is pivotal for this mental processing.

The significance of this work cannot be underestimated in terms of helping people manage their anger and aggression. The impulsive reaction to 'flee or kill' in the face of perceived threat is the result of an immediate chemical signal of rage received at the amygdala. The slower signal to the neocortex that prompts more reflective anger, allowing a more reasoned and cautious response, should, ideally, override rage, and in helping youngsters to manage their anger and avoid a similar impulsive response, like that of Matilda's father, the rage signal must be dampened or the signal via the thalamus to the neocortex has to be developed through learning.

Much of the early work on discovering the key role of the amygdala in the emotional brain was carried out by Joseph LeDoux, a neuroscientist at the Center for Neural Science at New York University (LeDoux 1993). Other studies in neuroscience have examined the neurology of empathy, and other more developed social-emotional responses like sadness, shame, guilt, love, pleasure and happiness, revealing some interesting results (Turner 2000). Greenfield (2004) cites evidence to suggest that six basic emotions of fear, surprise, anger, happiness, disgust and sadness are universal feeling states that occur across all cultures and that can be read from facial expression. Robert Levenson, a psychologist at the University of California at Berkeley, studied married couples and their varied capacities to detect and empathize with the emotions of their spouse. After recording and playing back videotaped feelings during heated discussions on family matters, the most in-tune partners were able to track accurately the other's feelings through the physiological matching of an elevated sweat response and drop in heart rate, which accurately matched that of their partners in the moment-to-moment incidents during replay. In other words, in-sync spouses were mimicking what their partner was feeling (Levenson and Ruef 1992). It is recognized that as children get older they are more able to empathize, and recent findings in neuroscience illustrate that empathy leads to a firing of 'mirror' neurons in the watcher (the child) and these appear to be the exact same neurons that are fired in the subject (the mother). There is an imitation through learnt behaviour from observation of empathy that is matched in the brain (Rothschild 2005).

Children with Asperger syndrome are often mistakenly thought of as being incapable of showing empathy and of displaying bullying behaviour at times, but Dubin (2007) has discounted this. What they are really displaying is anxiety about a need to have control in a social situation, which is misunderstood as an inability to empathize with others. According to neuroscience, people with Asperger's are extremely reactive due to an enlargement in the amygdala, which along with the hippocampus is the emotional centre of the brain.

From an understanding of the role of neuroscience and physiology, it becomes clear that both rage and empathy can be traced to neuron activity in the brain (Gerhardt 2004), and that the internal mind of a person has as much relevance to bullying behaviour as their social environment. Whilst intense anger and aggression in human behaviour may be an automatic impulse to maintain stability within the dominance hierarchy to meet particular social needs, it is difficult to conceive that an emotion like empathy has any value in meeting the same goal, and suggests that taking a purely biological view of human bullying does not tell the whole story.

Conclusion

This chapter has looked at the nature of aggressive and altruistic behaviour amongst animals in an attempt to understand their roles according to evolutionary theory. Some animals, particularly carnivores, need to fight and kill for their food, and perhaps exercise domination over others in order to compete for a scarce resource. Others establish pecking-orders of superiority, but it is not always clear what evolutionary purpose this behaviour serves. There is evidence in nature of behaviour that we might term altruism, even though this may not be the best description. In practice, animals do exhibit behaviour for the 'benefit of the species', not solely, it would seem, to preserve their own genes.

When we relate this to the nature of bullying behaviour and the motivations behind it within relationships, there are obvious links. It seems reasonable to conclude that people are not merely rational beings; they have animalistic impulses which will become just as evident in tightly bonded relationships as in other more formal friendships. When tempers are raised in family fights and peer-group conflicts, the rage that is experienced, and the aggression that inevitably follows, may stem from unconscious ancestral drives. At the flashpoint of conflict, there may be traces of an archaic impulse to dominate another person in order to reach stability – an automatic and largely redundant behaviour that can lead to friendship infighting, even though this may not be wanted at a conscious level.

A more extensive discussion looked at the role of aggression observed in animals. It is not clear whether animals derive a macabre pleasure from aggression as opposed to seeing it as necessary behaviour to achieve goals essential for survival, and in this respect we may find human behaviour different at times.

The type of language we use to depict human behaviour – such as aggression, domination, caring and altruism – does not effectively translate when talking about animal behaviour – it is difficult to deduce motives and intentions from observing animal instincts, since to speculate with creatures that have not acquired language leaves us prone to making interpretations from human perspectives.

Having said that, the link between human aggression and typical animal fury is undeniable, and it remains to be seen through the rest of this book whether human aggression towards other people is simply an inherited biological impulse or whether it serves other, more psychological, needs and goals.

Chapter 3

The Nature–Nurture Influence on Behaviour

Social hierarchies exist in all forms of human groupings, whether at an international, national, community or family level, and what appears to secure stability in all of these contexts is power and control.

Although bullying is a dual or group activity, we first need to understand it at the individual level, and whilst attention is customarily given to victims this book focuses in particular on the motivations of those who are the protagonists. In this chapter, I question whether some individuals are predisposed towards violence and dominant behaviour owing to their genetic makeup, or whether social conditions cause them to be so. This question centres upon the nature–nurture debate. Is there evidence that the genetic makeup of particular individuals inclines them more than others towards bullying behaviour? Or is it all to do with upbringing?

The nature–nurture debate

The apparent opposite influences on behaviour of genetics and environmental factors has been the subject of much medical and psychological research and debate. An early awareness of the debate was reflected in one of Shakespeare's plays, *The Tempest*, in which Prospero speaks of Caliban as 'A devil, a born devil, on whose nature / Nurture can never stick'. But the principal importance of the dual influence of nature and nurture has been the need to identify particular genes that determine characteristic personality traits or diseases to which individuals may become prone to suffer. Studies of personality also depend upon an understanding of the genetic makeup and the environmental nurturing of the particular individual. My interest in the basis of aggressive behaviour is not merely to reflect on how we become who we are, but to ask some searching social questions about how aggressive people should be dealt with for the smooth running of society. For example, if it can be determined that particular individuals are not responsible for their aggressive behaviour because their genetic makeup causes them to be this way, is it morally acceptable to punish them for such wrongdoing?

The majority view amongst psychologists and social scientists is that no one factor – nature nor nurture – is solely the cause of a particular behaviour. This was evident in our previous considerations of the 'selfish gene' and altruism, that although the drive of life according to evolutionary theory might be understood as the need for genes to replicate themselves in gene machines, copies of genetic makeup as they become formed in the next generation are not reproduced as carbon replicas, but will become subject to modification – although infinitesimally slight – with changing environmental conditions. Genes therefore are influenced by the environment in which the 'gene machine' has to function, in the sense that the environment will either facilitate or negate the tendency for the gene to mutate advantageously (Gerhardt 2004; James 2003).

With individuals, particular genes influence the development of a trait in the context of a particular environment. If we were to measure the degree to which a trait is influenced by genes versus environment, it will depend on the particular environment and the particular genes that we choose to examine. Although genes will make a substantial contribution to determining psychological traits, such as intelligence and personality, these traits may be largely influenced by the environment, which can either foster these genes or limit their potential. A child may be particularly gifted in having a high IQ, but if that child suffers from environmental deprivation, or excessive and continual stress, it is likely that that level of intelligence will be adversely affected (Goleman 2006).

In medicine, the importance of genetics in relation to certain conditions or illnesses is taken for granted, and medical scientists have made great progress in being able to predict particular conditions by studying parental susceptibilities. There are many diseases that have been strictly identified as genetic, such as Huntington's disease, diabetes, Crohn's disease, cystic fibrosis, sickle-cell anaemia, cardiovascular conditions, cystic fibrosis and certain forms of cancer, in which it is possible in some cases to avert the disease, or to treat patients beforehand to offset their vulnerability to the disease, on the basis that the condition commonly ran in the family. Mental illnesses brought about largely by environmental factors include: minor depression, addictions, personality disorder, eating disorders, neuroses, and hyperactivity (ADHD); and mental illnesses with a significant genetic component include bipolar disorder, schizophrenia and major depression (James 2003). Although schizophrenia is genetic, its appearance and management is affected by environmental factors, notably the presence or absence of a discouraging and negative home situation.

Genetic predisposition for violence

Sue Gerhardt (2004) weighs the research evidence of genetic predisposition for violent behaviour and concludes from the meta-analysis carried out by Hyun Rhee and Waldman (2002) that the heritability of antisocial behaviour may be overestimated. When examining the methodology of various studies more closely, there seems to be a much more modest heritability than early studies indicated. Whilst there is evidence that genes in human beings contribute to the likelihood of committing property crimes, this is not necessarily the case for violent crimes. Violent offending is more likely to be linked to birth complications combined with maternal rejection in the first year of life (Raine, Brennan and Mednick 1997); and according to Michael Bohman in Sweden (1996), the influence of alcohol rather than genes may be a greater determining factor. For many geneticists, whilst genes will influence features such as blue eyes or brown hair, they do not and cannot code for socially defined behaviours. In summary:

> There is no 'aggression' gene or 'criminal' gene, although there may be other inherited factors that make an individual susceptible to particular environmental pressures. In any case, there aren't enough genes to specify all of the connections in our brain and nervous system in advance, so the role of genes is much more to provide the basic structures of behaviour such as knowing how to cry or how to be afraid, but not *what* to be afraid of or how to relate to a particular person. (Gerhardt 2004, p.170)

In other words genes do not act independently of environments, but respond to them in quite a flexible way by switching on and off when required, often within minutes or hours. For example, it is possible that a risk-taking gene might equally find expression in criminal activity or in great creativity depending on the environment in which it is nurtured (Rutter 1996).

Gerhardt's own contribution to the debate is to reason that there seems to be a blind spot in that much of the findings fail to recognize the importance of pregnancy and the first year of life in shaping future behaviour. The research that has become of particular interest to those wanting to understand the nature–nurture determinants of personality and behaviour is the study of identical twins and adopted children.

Study of identical twins

It is possible with animals to set up experiments that have rigid controls that isolate and test the two influences of nature and nurture. It is only by eliminating one or the other that the researcher can distinguish the prime influences upon particular outcomes, and indeed such studies have been done. These controlled experiments would be unethical for human research, however, but well-designed studies that monitor the behaviour and personality types of identical twins from childhood into adulthood have resulted in a significant body of research that has opened our understanding of the nature–nurture debate.

Identical twins reared apart share identical genes but have not been nurtured in the same environment. Studying such twins, researchers are therefore able to eliminate genetics as a cause of any behavioural differences between them. Such differences do exist, so they must be due to nurture. More useful though are the comparisons that can be made between groups of identical and non-identical twins (who each share only half of their genetic makeup). Because the precise genetic similarities are known within each group, comparing them can reveal the degree to which physical and behavioural traits are inherited ('heritability').

Some personality traits like extroversion and emotionality prove to be 40 per cent heritable, whilst others like sociability and creativity prove to be only 25 per cent heritable for both, with genius being totally environmental in origin (Plomin, DeFries *et al.* 1997). The propensity to violence or personal romantic preferences or degree of masculinity or femininity show very little heritability (Plomin, DeFries *et al.* 1997). Recent studies of identical twins show that differences between them must be environmental in origin. According to Craig Venter (Venter *et al.* 2001), one of the researchers heading the Human Genome Project, human diversity is not hard-wired in our genetic code, it is our environment that is crucial, and Robert Plomin, a leading authority on the subject, consistently argues that human behavioural variability is largely environmentally influenced (e.g. Plomin and Daniels 1987; Plomin, Fulker *et al.* 1997).

Study of adopted children

Research is still divided on whether adopted children develop similar cognitive abilities as their biological parents or their new adopted ones. Earlier adoption studies suggested that genetic heritability was significant (Goodhart 1995), and whilst some psychologists (Thomas, Bouchard and McGue 2002) still claim that psychological differences are moderately to substantially heritable, particularly when measured over time (say, by middle age), the general thinking of late has swung in favour of environmental influence (Plomin 1990; Turkheimer and Waldron 2000). A range of factors will be instrumental, such as age when adopted and high parental expectation. It seems that 'children from low-income homes who are adopted into affluent ones in infancy tend to do as well on IQ tests or at school as the biological children of their adopting parents', and further that when it comes to guaranteeing career success, individual motivation is the principal factor since children with massive IQs are no more likely to be high achieving adults than those with average IQs of the same social background (James 2003, p.275).

Linda Mealey (1995) has carried out a research overview of the nature/nurture influences through childhood. Examining twin studies she reasons that a 'substantial' genetic effect on criminal behaviour is evident (60 per cent heritability), that childhood aggression predicts adult criminality, and that there is also evidence gathered by behavioural geneticists (Cadoret *et al.* 1995; Gerhardt 2004) that children of antisocial parents have a greater likelihood of becoming antisocial, even when adopted into another family.

Other research questions this in claiming that adopted children whose biological parents were convicted of crimes are only half as likely as them to be convicted of crimes themselves. Despite often having come from homes with parents who are prone to criminal behaviour, the crime rates of the adopted child tends to change to reflect the more stable homes in which they have been brought up (Bohman *et al.* 1982; Mednick, Gabrieli and Hutchings 1984), particularly where the mental health is more sound in the adopting mother than the biological one (Horn *et al.* 1975).

A large number of studies have compared what happens to children adopted when young with children who endure a series of different foster homes, who live permanently in children's homes or are returned to their biological parents. These are critical comparisons because these children may have been born to parents who were unstable, mentally ill or criminal, so if there is any genetic risk attached to the kind of care received it should not make much difference (Roy, Rutter and Pickles 2000). The results clearly indicate that it is the kind of care that is decisive, not the genetic stock. Children adopted in early infancy are no more at risk of mental illness or criminality than children who are raised by stable, law-abiding biological parents. By contrast, fostered children do worse than those adopted. However, very tellingly, when fostered children and those who are permanently institutionalized are compared, the fostered ones do better, but those that do worst of all are the children who are returned to their (usually disturbed and disturbing) biological parents. So the amount of damage correlates closely with the quality of care received, not with the genetic stock (James 2003).

In general, permanently institutionalized children are more likely to suffer depression, become delinquent and fail at school than those brought up by their biological parents (Quinton and Rutter 1988). A major shortcoming of many adoption studies is their failure to specify clearly the age at which adoption occurred, leaving open the possibility that the child who is adopted may already have developed an oversensitive stress response and even have acquired particular behavioural strategies, such as being aggressive or violent, by the time he or she is adopted (Gerhardt 2004).

The general conclusions of all these studies seem to point to the dual influence of both environment and genetic makeup, with the pendulum swinging towards the former as being most influential. According to Susan Greenfield, human development results from

> the endless interaction between the individual and the external world 'out there' that drives a ceaseless configuring and reconfiguring of brain connections, through the switching on and off of genes. So a gene is simply a tool, one cog in the sophisticated biochemical machinery that translates each influence from an external environment into a physical shift in the pattern of brain connections. It is therefore impossible to label an emergent behaviour with a nature–nurture provenance. (Greenfield 2004, p.253)

The central problem, however, is that it is impossible to engineer completely an identical environment for the nurturing culture of two separate individuals so as to measure this variable completely. Let me elaborate.

Even identical twins reared together turn out to have very different personality types, skills and predispositions in their thinking, feeling and behaviour. Differing traumas during the birth process, different associations and friendships and vastly different experiences of occupying space and time with a multitude of variable stimulants will mean that no two environments can ever be entirely the same (see box below for an example). Second, identical twins are not two encapsulated entities living within tight boundaries where it might be possible to engineer identical stimulants and measure resultant traits or behaviours. Identical twins are not only reacting with each other, they are reacting with their parents quite differently. Their perception of how the world treats them and how they make sense of the manner in which they have been loved and cared for is a further variable. The dynamics of family life are not merely responsive, they are inter-responsive.

Malcolm and Robert attend the nursery. Malcolm picks up a cold virus and feels pretty miserable, whilst Robert is lively in spirit after having enjoyed a good breakfast. Ali, another boy at the nursery, rejects Malcolm and plays instead with Robert, being attracted by his jovial, playful nature. Malcolm may internalize the response as rejection and may, indeed, interpret his carer's gestures as reinforcing a self-construct that says, in effect, *I am not as attractive as my brother as a playmate* upon the shaky foundations that he has been whisked away from the group to get on with some painting by himself because he is irritable and keeps crying. When they get home and talk about matters of the day, if Malcolm misconstrues his mother's attempts to placate his misery as an indicator that he will never be as popular as his brother, then Malcolm's self-construct is going to develop quite differently to that of Robert's. Having then shaped the template of his experience, he will not only interpret further gestures and behaviours according to the template, his construct will influence behaviours towards him as self-fulfilled predictions.

Nurture predisposition for violence

A study of British murderers found that one third subsequently committed suicide (West 1965). Was this due to genetics or to the lack of nurturing received in prison? If it is genetics that predisposes some to become violent and aggressive and to dominate others, what has happened to the gene-pool to account for the 45-fold increase in police reported crime in England and Wales over a 50-year period – 6000 crimes of violence in 1950 compared with 258,000 in 1998 (James 2003)? The peak occurred in 1995, but then began falling, according to 2005/6 figures (Walker, Kershaw and Nicholas 2007); and while public confidence in police reported crime has not been high in recent times, it seems that violent crime has more to do with nurture and social change than genetic heritability.

There are strong grounds for doubting that genes play as much of a role as mental illness and the social environment in most violent crime, and perhaps we should look at other factors of violent criminality. The findings of an official survey on mental health (Singleton, Meltzer and Gatward 1998) established that 90 per cent of criminals were found to have had a mental illness with two thirds having had a personality or neurotic disorder, depression or a serious drug problem. One third of British prisoners have spent some time in a local authority care institution at some point during their childhood, 50 per cent of which for sexual or physical abuse, and the vast majority of children in care have suffered early emotional deprivation.

James (2003) endorses a view of some who regard social changes and the rise in inadequate childcare, particularly in responding to children's immediate needs as opposed to fitting them into 'convenient regimes' to suit over-taxed single parents or professional mothers, as the cause of rising delinquency and violence in Western society, but this is not easy to prove. A more likely interpretation is one that looks into what it is that is missing for children who grow up to be violent than to find blanket explanations like social and economic factors.

Goleman (2006) sees aggressive behaviour as arising from a lack of 'emotional caring' during those early mother–toddler experiences of intimate facial interactions known as 'attunement'. Gerhardt (2004) translates this necessary early mother–infant bonding inter-reaction by saying that during this period touching and physical contact are essential, particularly the power of a smile together with other cues received by facial reading. The baby's brain is growing rapidly in the first year where it doubles in weight owing to increased glucose metabolism triggered by the baby's chemical responses to his mother, facilitating the expression of genes. In other words, social input is essential (Gerhardt 2004). The plasticity of the baby's brain in the early period of development allows each child to adapt to its particular social environment, whether the Brazilian rainforest or suburban Manhattan. Such views take us to the heart of problems to do with attachment and separation.

Attachment and separation

If the environment of two youngsters brought up within the same family cannot be identical, this does not imply that it is plausible to then deduce that the more measurable influence and determinant of personality must centre upon nature. There may be environmental factors to do with childcare that are measurable, at least observable, that may be indicative of creating angry and violent young people and adults later on.

What we do know is that a lack of empathic care from birth to three years old creates angry, belligerent boys and predicts violence in later life (Lerner *et al.* 1988; Luxmoore 2006; Panskepp, Siviy and Normansell 1985). Research has also shown us that the costs of having too little 'emotional intelligence' during the early years will have a detrimental effect upon infant brain development (Schore 1994).

Psychoanalytical therapists account for challenging behaviour in the neighbourhood and school as being due to unresolved attachment issues where youngsters unconsciously seek out in their streets and schools 'transitional attachment figures', but find in reality the same projected 'insecure', 'anxious', 'avoidant' or 'resistant' attachments that they have experienced in the home (Bowlby 1969, 1973, 1980). Bowlby, the key figure in attachment, states: 'The prolonged deprivation of a young child of maternal care may have grave and far reaching effects on his character and so on the whole of his future life' (cited in Holmes 1993, p.37).

When studying the effects of 'maternal deprivation' it is important to draw a distinction between privation (the absence of something which is needed) and deprivation (the removal of something that was previously there). Anyone looking at the awful images of those children living in the orphanages of Romania during the 1990s could not fail to see the damaging effects that emotional deprivation had on development through an absent maternal figure, but it is also recognized that maternal deprivation refers not only to the time that the mother spends or does not spend with her child but also with the quality care that is given (Oakley 1981). For a busy mother who responsibly has a carer for part of her day, whether father, grandmother, childminder or *metapelet* in a kibbutz, and who in spite of a busy schedule still provides for her child the 'quality of care' that is needed, then there is less harm done than would be the case with a mother who is not 'emotionally available' to her child in spite of being physically there 24 hours a day (Chodorow 1978).

For a child, to be held close to her mother, to feel the warm contact of her skin, to feel safe and comforted and to be held in security, is intensely pleasurable, and from such a reliable anchorage the child is sufficiently relaxed to be able to 'get on with things' and to explore a wider and larger world. If such an experience has been repeated and is known to be dependable then the child feels safe to separate, but if there have been long periods of separation, continual withdrawal of affection and contact, or a serious and significant change from one to the other, then the anxious state will leave the child with permanent attachment anxieties which will affect her the rest of her life. Naturally, children once separated protest through crying, screaming, shouting, biting or kicking, and in itself this not harmful, but if this becomes extensive, then the child becomes increasingly insecure (Ainsworth *et al.* 1978). Equally insecure is the child who experiences ambivalent or avoidant care and physical contact.

A piece of research relevant to observing insecurity in children is Ainsworth's Strange Situation experiment, which involved a mother, her one-year-old infant and a third party in a 20-minute session in a playroom (Ainsworth *et al.* 1978). The mother is first asked to leave the room for three minutes and to return leaving the child with the third party, after which both leave the room for a further three minutes, leaving the child on her own. Mother and child are then once again reunited. The whole sequence is video-taped and rated focusing particularly upon the responses of the child to separation and reunion. If the child is *securely attached*, she will feel slight distress on separation, but on being comforted on reunion will continue to play contented. If there is an *insecure-avoidant attachment*, the child will show few overt signs of distress on separation and ignore her mother on reunion, remaining watchful but inhibited in her play. With an *insecure-ambivalent attachment*, the child will be highly distressed on separation but will not be easily pacified on reunion. She will seek contact but then resist by kicking, turning away and squirming, refusing offered toys to help pacify her. Finally an *insecure-disorganized attachment* relates to a small group of children who illustrate a diverse range of confused behaviours including 'freezing' or stereotyped movements when reunited with their parents (Holmes 1993).

Luxmoore (2006) articulates later effects of insecure attachment through school-based examples. He presents a challenging exchange between a child called Richard and his teacher, which illustrates how a surface conversation may operate on deeply felt but largely unspoken (unaware) levels of consciousness as befits psychodynamic processes of attachment theory (pp.67–68). Richard is challenged for not wearing his correct uniform (the unspoken thoughts behind the words are given in italics).

Richard: What's wrong with these trainers, Miss? I don't see why we have to wear uniform anyway! (*I have mixed feelings about attaching myself to this family.*)

Teacher: Look, Richard, if you're going to be at this school you have to wear the uniform. Same as everyone else. (*I want this to be a straightforward transaction, without feelings.*)

Richard: But other people wear trainers and they don't get told off! (*You love other people more than you love me.*)

Teacher: That's not true. We treat everyone the same. (*I have no particular feelings for anyone and I don't expect anyone to have feelings for me.*)

Richard: So how come Scott was wearing trainers the other day and you never told him? (*You love Scott and not me.*)

Teacher: I didn't see Scott wearing trainers and if I had seen him I would have told him. (*I feel nothing for Scott.*)

Richard: You didn't see because you didn't look! (*You love Scott and not me! I hate you!*)

Teacher: [Long-suffering silence.] (*Honestly, I don't love Scott.*)

Richard: I haven't got any other shoes anyway. (*If you won't love me, I'm going to fight you!*)

Teacher: In that case, I'll write a letter home and tomorrow I'll expect to see you in different shoes. (*If you fight with me, you will have to leave this family.*)

Richard: What if I haven't got any? (*That scares me. Don't make me leave!*)

Teacher: That's for you to sort out at home. (*Find somebody else to love you. Not me.*)

Attachment theory describes the way we instinctively and immediately seek to attach ourselves to someone who will keep us safe. Without attachments we cannot survive. At birth, a baby immediately attaches to its carer, normally its mother, but as we normally venture out into the world from the safety of our first attachments we will seek to attach to other figures for comfort, stimulation and safety. Attachment theory proposes that the quality of new and different attachments will relate directly to the quality of the earlier ones. These attachments are not necessarily people, for pupils can be attached to their new school just as an adult can be attached to her work. In this sense, the school and the workplace have become an internalized 'mother', and the instinctive drive through life is to continually seek to be 'mothered'.

I can relate to this through my own experience with a 13-year-old boy I fostered who I shall call Joseph. For the first three months Joseph settled in well and continued his normal routines of schooling and socializing with his best friend Brian. But after this honeymoon period, he began to fix himself resolutely in the home and avoid going out to friends, or wanting them to come to him. He would remain sitting on the carpet playing with model cars and be quite content with my company only, thus avoiding any external mixing with a larger outside world. He sabotaged every attempt I made to invite Brian home to play with him, and it ended up with explosive arguments of shouting and slamming of doors, which led me to take Brian home for his safety.

Another curious feature of his behaviour was a daily ritual of moving the furniture around in his bedroom, including a heavy wardrobe and bed. It was as though he could not be content without altering his surroundings to test out whether he felt safe in an altered room in order to create a new comfort zone. Having been separated when very young from his mother and having been in care since the age of two suggested that he could only make insecure attachments to people. At an unconscious level he seemed to keep attempting to recreate a distant childhood through immature play, resisting me helping him move on, and feeling compelled to search for that mourned-for 'mother–son attachment' through perpetually altering his personal surroundings.

Psychologists have shown that how we relate to someone depends on how we perceive them (Goleman 2006). If we think someone does not like us, or if we imagine they are being critical through veiled insults, we will react to them very differently from the way we will if we assume they like us or find us friendly. Aggressive young people have great difficulty in assessing 'mistakes' and 'accidental collisions' from 'cheating' and 'deliberate threats'. Genes play very little role in this respect, since we base our impressions on how others view us, on our expectations of their future behaviour and on our past relationships, especially the accumulation of early childhood experiences. James (2003) observes a similar tendency that has great significance when thinking about bullying behaviour: 'confronted by a stranger, we impose on their identities from our original family script. What is more, having invented them as ghosts from our past, if they do not behave in this scripted manner we try to manipulate them to do so' (p.280).

How to raise a bully

A study that confirms the phenomena of learnt behaviour was carried out on 870 children from upstate New York. It was a longitudinal study that examined the outcome of particular parenting styles (Huesman, Eron and Warnicke-Yarmel 1987). The children were followed from the age of eight until they were 30.

The study found that the most belligerent among the children – those who were quick to start fights and habitually used force to get their own way – were the most likely to drop out of school and by 30 to have had a serious record for crimes of violence. These children received arbitrary though relentless and severe discipline from either the mother or father whom the child had identified as being 'highly aggressive'.

The gender of parent and child made little difference, and along with harsh and violent treatment they experienced regularly being ignored and left alone. At the same time parents of the study gave their children vivid and violent examples of aggressiveness, models of behaviour which they took with them to school and to the playground and on throughout adult life. These children suffered severe punishment if either parent was moody. Such aggressive treatment was capricious – sometimes they could get away with mayhem at home; at other times the slightest mistake would bring down upon them a tirade of verbal and physical abuse. These children were identified throughout school life as bullies and had little sense of empathy for others.

I close this chapter by giving an example of behavioural predisposition from my own experiences of fostering children. In discussions with friends who have also fostered and adopted children, I find that my anecdotal experience is not uncommon, in that when fostering youngsters from ten years upwards it remains difficult when observing aggressive behaviour to determine when bullying is due to genetic or environmental factors; but I remain convinced that issues of attachment and separation lie at the heart of the problem.

An insecure attachment of a boy in foster care

During my early thirties in the 1970s I was asked to manage a children's home. The house parents were being rejected by the young people, most of whom were middle adolescents. The particular problem was that the house parents had been teachers of a primary school and as such their management style was too inflexible for troubled adolescents. There was a need for rules, but healthy adolescent development often requires flexibility of management styles to suit the particular temperaments of each individual young person passing through puberty (Lines 2006a). It seemed as though the managers were adopting an impersonal regime of *stick to the rules otherwise you'll be punished severely* as the controlling enforcement.

I learnt a lot in this short period about the particular plights of young people living in children's homes but became particularly attached to one boy who was 11 and who I shall call Russell in order to preserve his anonymity. He first came into care with his siblings when he was only four years of age. He described how his mother went to the housing department and demanded a larger property that had four bedrooms for herself, her partner and her six children. When this could not be found immediately, she left the children in the office and travelled with her partner to Devon: 'If you can't find me a suitable house, you can have the kids!'

Russell's older brother, Nathan, had previously lived in the same children's home for 12 months, but it was felt that he had such a negative influence upon young Russell that he was moved to another institution. When the time came for me to hand over the home to new house parents, the particular bond I had formed with Russell was evident to all. With his full agreement, and that of his social worker, I began the process of becoming a foster parent, and after receiving preliminary training took Russell with me to live in my new home in the West Midlands. I had bought an old house, and Russell and I spent many happy hours renovating the old building and bringing it up to a comfortable living standard. Russell attended the local school and achieved much of his potential up until his final year.

Over five years I got to know Russell well, understood his temperament, catered for his aptitudes, responded to his needs and attended to his emotional state when feeling particularly low and bereaved of his family – or so I thought!

After leaving school to form a new attachment to work, he began to go off the rails. He ran away from home on two occasions, sometimes for up to three days, not because there was any rift between ourselves but merely to support his girlfriend who had had an argument with her father – she had become the new attachment over me. I don't know where they went, but I was aware that food was being taken from the freezer by Russell entering the house during the day. He got into glue-sniffing and at times I would find him huddled under a coat in the nearby woods high on glue. I found it embarrassing that Russell would choose a form of addictive behaviour on which he was fully aware that I had fairly strong views. Nevertheless, I tried being flexible and to support him, in trying to understand what was leading to this period of insecurity. It was particularly disturbing for me to find out that his father was an alcoholic who would regularly be seen stoned out of his mind in the neighbourhood. But Russell had virtually no contact with his father, so I thought poor role-modelling would not be significant. Then another shock occurred in his family.

Russell's youngest sister Emily, who had been adopted from the age of 11 months, and who had remained totally shielded from all family contact and influence, began to reject her adoptive parents and seek out her own biological family members (attachment issues for her). Russell's social worker judged that since he was 'relatively stable', in relation to his elder siblings, it would be a useful exercise to encourage Russell and Emily to meet regularly, and this they did. But then Russell began to run away with Emily, and whilst I cannot speak for her adoptive parents there were no harsh words that came between Russell and me throughout this testing period – I viewed him as a confused and lost young man. Then a further tragedy hit Russell.

His mother, whom he had not seen since the age of four, and with whom Russell had had no contact at all, had arrived in town at the railway station and had collapsed on the platform with a note around her neck which read: 'I am the mother of Emily, Russell… etc. and I have cancer and want to see my kids before I die.' She was taken by ambulance to hospital and admitted to intensive care where she was kept relatively pain-free on morphine. When I took Russell to the hospital, I shall never forget his reaction. I saw him sitting at her bedside holding her limp hand (she being virtually unconscious) with tears flooding down his cheeks, trying to make contact with the mother who had rejected him as a child, trying to will her to live in order for him to understand fully who he was. It was at this time that I began reflecting on the nature–nurture debate and the cost of insecure attachment.

When she died, it brought Russell and Emily into contact with their other siblings again. I remember attending the funeral and being in the company of the older brothers and sisters and of seeing how identical their mannerisms and behavioural traits were. Although appearing marginally different in physique and facial characteristics, the family personality traits were striking. There was a certain frown and an idiosyncratic swaggering when walking around the room, a nervous laugh when somebody said something funny, an impulsive reaction when being challenged (even with a joke), a fidgety state only calmed by smoking, a particular veneer of pretending to be strong when in reality being quite weak, and a manifest learnt-helplessness and expectation for continual support and nurturing.

The two youngest, Emily and Russell, had virtually no later contact with any of their siblings, but it was clear to all that these were indeed related. What was so discouraging was that all of these children had a predisposition towards a dependency pattern of behaviour upon alcohol and heroin.

I have often reflected on my input into the life of Russell and the outcome. Two incidents spring to mind that suggest a powerful influence of an insecure attachment that was to be repeated through life. On one occasion Russell became uncharacteristically angry in my presence. He had a friend called Paul whose mother felt that her son should no longer befriend Russell. This was because they had been discovered truanting together from school. I went along with her decision. She came out to our house and accused Russell of telephoning her son. Russell exploded, screamed and yelled at her whilst I sat calmly in the chair. I asked her politely to leave when Russell began to punch the door aggressively. He split the wood as he punched harder and harder and became increasingly aroused and violent. I still sat calmly and in a reassuring manner said, 'It's OK Russell; it's OK. Come and sit down.' It took nearly ten minutes to reassure him and calm him down. I eventually rose from my seat and hugged him while he sobbed for a short while – Russell was being separated 'again just like before' (now from Paul, his friend).

The second incident occurred when he had just turned 16. We were going through a difficult patch when the glue-sniffing was at its height. I felt I could no longer provide a safe and caring environment for him and in consultation with his social worker decided that it was best for him to return to a local children's home. I discussed this with Russell and we agreed that this would be a pragmatic course of action. In retrospect, it was pride that made that statement, not his personal wish. He was merely testing boundaries. Perhaps also it was my pride in not being comfortable in being out of control of the situation. Whatever the case, when we arrived at the children's home a particularly menacing sight greeted us. There were five teenagers who appeared to be 'leaders of the pack'. They were leaning from a bedroom window smoking pot, swearing and insulting passers by. I felt intimidated, but what surprised me was the way Russell dealt with the situation. In presuming he was about to enter this environment, he changed in a manner that came as a complete surprise to me. Chameleon-like, he responded to the new situation that looked threatening. He broadened out his shoulders and began his swaggering walk towards the door and called out to them in such a way that was clearly designed to register an aggressive persona: *Don't mess with me otherwise you'll find yourself in trouble!*

I was stunned and taken aback by a response I had never witnessed before and, although he didn't stay within the institution but agreed to come back home and toe the line, it left me bewildered as to whether I really knew Russell at all. I had failed him by being prepared to deposit him in the children's home again because I couldn't cope with the testing – his insecure attachment and view of a rejecting world could remain intact; I had failed his test.

For five years I believed that I had presented Russell with a very different role model to those of his family. I thought I could offset the influences of his family inheritance. I had modelled hard work and industry, particularly with the renovation of the old house (our joint enterprise). I had demonstrated a composed and controlled demeanour in the face of threatening situations. I had hoped that he might emulate my belief system and reinforce the link between hard work, progress and prosperity. As I look back, I cannot see much evidence that these were modelled or had had a significant impact on Russell's personality traits and skills in managing conflict and pressure. Perhaps it's true after all, as the Jesuits say: Give me the child till the age of seven and I'll give you the man. What I do not know is the quality of nurturing childcare that Russell received till the age of four, though it would not be difficult to guess. Perhaps the problem really was the fact that the 'right' influence came along much too late, that indeed the damage was already done. Perhaps the ongoing need through me to find replacement attachments to seek out that blissful world of 'oceanic feeling' between idealized mother and infant was too demanding and unrealistic (Luxmoore 2006).

I have had cause to follow the life histories of Russell and his siblings ever since because we still keep in touch, albeit spasmodically. He settled down with a woman old enough to be his (surrogate) mother but had no children. He's been to prison on five occasions to my knowledge and for each offence it's always the same. He will attempt to drown his sorrows in alcohol or other drugs and then someone will ring the police because he is disturbing the peace, and when a constable arrives to arrest him because of his intoxicated state he will strike out and be charged for resisting an officer from carrying out duties. The inevitable result is another term of imprisonment – another attachment in which to feel safe and protected.

Summary

In attempting to understand the motivations of those who become aggressive with the weak, you cannot underestimate the environmental nurturing influences of those vital early years when the infant's brain is so plastic and open to synaptic registering. While the animalistic side to human nature can be seen in human beings' propensity to become enraged, violent or aggressive in certain social situations, this chapter has focused more on the environment that can increase the likelihood of such rage and aggression manifesting itself in particular social situations. Attachment and separation issues stem from early infant years and continue into adult life, where insecure attachment increases the likelihood of a person being involved in aggressive behaviour and even criminality.

In the case of Russell the damage of being separated from his mother showed itself in an ongoing series of attachment and separation experiences. These were: moving into a children's home, leaving that home to attach to me in a fostering situation, finding a new attachment figure through his girlfriend and running away, being separated from a further attachment figure through his best friend, being taken to another institution when I could no longer manage him and turning to glue-sniffing as a symbolic attachment to release tension and find escape. The point is that with every threat of separation – forced or willed – the insecurity of that first loss of mother is replayed.

I have not outlined Russell's family predicament to illustrate how the chips are down for some fostered youngsters who have not received privileged beginnings in life, but to make my point of the long-term detrimental effects of poor attachments during infancy and deprived early nurturing, and to illustrate how difficult it can be to 'reform' characters, even slightly, if left relatively late in development. I would not say that Russell was 'by nature' aggressive or dominant or an abuser of the weak, or indeed a bully; quite the reverse. It was a predictable and repeated pattern of behaviour that led society to penalize him, a behaviour that *appeared* aggressive but in reality was 'weak', 'nervous' and 'helpless'. Was it genes alone that shaped those particular family characteristic traits of dependency, or poor attachments and inadequate parenting in those vital early years that provided the culture for those genetic predispositions to sprout and take hold? There is no way to tell. What is clear when looking at the majority of troubled young people with aggressive and angry fronts, you are in fact observing individuals with complex and inadequate lives – it is important to look further than superficial appearance.

Attachment theory and separation might help us understand why particular individuals become angry and aggressive, and perhaps become bullies, but such insight does not of itself help to repair the damage – at least unless accompanied by extensive therapy. In the remainder of this book we shall have cause to see how bullying behaviour shows itself in various social encounters of relationship conflict, and so will have to leave attachment theory behind as merely a possible, though likely, hypothesis.

The next chapter asks searching questions about judgements on what constitutes bullying behaviour from casual, and often limited, observation. It considers how aggressive parental role-modelling influences the formation of violent personas of young children and attempts to identify who may indeed become a bully.

Chapter 4

Who Bullies?

Is there a particular type of person who becomes a bully? Whilst traditionally bullying has been viewed as a male activity, with theories linked to the chemical changes of adolescents with the release of testosterone, there is mounting evidence to show that females also engage in extensive bullying (Ness 2004).

This chapter will not attempt to classify 'the bully' by gender, age, race or social class, or to stylize him or her as one particular form of personality or character type, but will examine commonly viewed interactive responses and behaviours that lead people to regard an individual as a bully. Is it possible, as some psychologists maintain, to identify who may become a bully by observing children in the nursery, and so to modify bullying behaviour at an early stage? Should we label an individual as 'a bully', or does the practice of labelling dominant characters in this way merely create the very responses that we anticipate but want to avoid?

These kinds of question are of vital importance for all those interested in bullying reduction. I am interested in this chapter in exploring *Who bullies?* But to answer that we need first to have a clear understanding what behaviours constitute 'bullying' from those which may be considered as understandable reactions of defence or of 'letting off steam'.

In the early period of planning this book, I was visited by an ex-pupil whom I had supported at school. We exchanged pleasantries and I began to tell him of my project and my intention to interview perpetrators of bullying. I was aware he had spent a few years in prison, largely through difficulties giving up heroin. He began to tell me that on the inside prisoners would not willingly speak openly if they were up for remand, or were awaiting sentence or applying for parole. Clearly, they might have something to lose by being too honest with a stranger carrying out research. He also said that what you must remember is that those people in prison for beating women or children will have a hard time. The moral code for those on the inside is commonly formulated along the lines of 'Whatever offence you have committed *you should not strike women or children*'. Such prisoners have to go into protected wings, or even solitary confinement. The other insight he shared with me was that I should not paint the same picture of those serving prison sentences, whatever they have done.

When writing a book, there is a tendency to categorize themes, to structure data within common 'truths' and to look for regularly repeated factors, a tendency that can lead to pigeon-holing people and stereotyping. It is for this reason that I chose to let these people speak for themselves rather than present clever interpretations of their material.

Types of bullying behaviour

Below, I describe the range of behaviours associated with bullies, some of which are certainly bullying behaviours, but others which can depend on context and motive.

Heartless violence

This extreme interpretation of 'the bully' is portrayed by Jonathan Kellerman, a child psychologist and clinical professor of paediatrics at the University of Southern California, in his reflections on violent children, *Savage Spawn* (Kellerman 1999). This brief and informative study examines those who appear to have no remorse and who can kill in cold blood. The conclusion of his thesis is that some individuals are incapable of change and can be identified as young as six years old. He recommends that we should stop searching for causes from media influence of violent movies and gruesome computer games, or from social deprivation.

Early on in the book he speaks of Tim, a referred client by his GP and grandmother – whom he addressed as 'Stupid asshole'. Both his parents were killed in a motor vehicle accident when he was very young. Kellerman was conducting research on the psychological effects of catastrophe, but after meeting Tim, and many of his type, his views radically altered.

He described Tim as tall, muscular, tanned and with clear-cut good looks, but it was his persona that troubled him so deeply, particularly when he began to articulate his view of the world. Early on Tim played the psychotherapeutic game of giving his therapist the answers he felt he required. He proudly showed him his business cards and spoke casually of his pursuits – I deal in 'stuff' and I carry out 'favours'. When asked for clarification, he stretched out like a young lion and said, 'If someone's bugging someone and they want it to stop, I make it stop.'

'And you get paid for it?'

He pointed a finger gun in Kellerman's direction and said, 'Correct.'

There was a turn in the session when Kellerman refused Tim his request to smoke and his whole confident demeanour changed. He yawned, looked at his watch and dismissed his therapist. Kellerman felt uncomfortable as he left the room and made an approach towards him as though he were about to butt him. He recoiled and checked his advance.

'Faked you out,' he said, and in self-assured manner he winked at him and said, 'Bye, Doc.'

What was frightening for Kellerman was his controlling manner, cold with no feeling. He never displayed a whit of anxiety and rarely blinked. He was not a troubled youth but was truly untroubled, as though he were of another species. He moved about in Kellerman's office as though it were his own territory, and it was unbelievable, as he reminded himself, that this young man was only 13 years of age. He writes, 'I was unwilling to believe anyone so young could be so dispassionate, so nakedly cruel.'

The point Kellerman makes so graphically is that there are some hardened young people who are cool, collected and streetwise and yet reasonably bright – *they are scary!* They seem devoid of conscience, as though they have become 'calcified and move in a universe beyond hurt'.

Kellerman reasons that the trouble with understanding those he terms 'psychopathic killers' is that we fail to understand them because we do not think like them. They are not crazy: 'Psychopathic killers are anything *but* crazy' (1999, p.23). Profiles, he says, are based on those who are captured, not on those operating on free licence. Biological theories abound, but there is no chemical that modifies their behaviour. Psychotherapy is useless because it is based upon insight – they have none. Rehabilitation does not work either, because such programmes assume people 'want to change' and 'become like us' conforming individuals (Kellerman 1999).

If most serious violence is committed by males, then it is important to examine the nature of male influence upon young children. How do they learn to manage their own aggression pro-socially without any significant male role model? They learn it from those that can readily be found on the street, or in 'heroes' through the media. Spankings and beatings merely model aggression, whereas self-examination and reflection urges change. 'Might is right' is the psychopath's first commandment.

Kellerman's grim prognosis may only be averted for some individuals if they are removed completely from their families, isolated from guns and other weapons, and targeted before they reach six years of age – the Jesuit principle again. This is because, by the time they reach adolescence, psychopathic killers have proven to be incapable of change.

Counsellors and psychotherapists are essentially in positions of power, whether they acknowledge it or not, and what Kellerman no doubt finds troublesome is that Tim's behaviour was not a normal therapeutic encounter with a young person. Most clients find therapy quite a nervous enterprise initially, particularly when so young. In the example given above, there are clearly illustrated shifting positions of power between two persons, but since we have only the perspective of a well-meaning therapist we have no way of knowing how his client viewed the engagement. We may well ask at this point whether there are examples of young people bullying their parents or teachers in their day-to-day encounters.

Goleman (2006) makes the point that sociopaths or psychopaths are not to be identified with perpetrators of domestic violence, since the former register a frightening and untypical drop in heart rate as they become increasingly angry and will extend their violence outside the family confines. Being a teacher and the school counsellor at the same school for over 30 years has an advantage in that you get an insight into some of the lives that youngsters lead through having known their parents well as adolescents.

When I listen to the stories of young people who have been knocked about by their parents or carers, adults whom I had known from early school days, it has often struck me that few if any of the characters were regarded as tough at the time of being in school; they were not those who appeared to lust after fighting and aggression through adolescence. In fact, I can think of hardly any youngsters who were regularly fighting at school who have turned out in their adult life to be bullies in the classical understanding of the term. By contrast, those who bully their partners or their children, as I recall, were viewed by the school pupils and teachers alike as being quite weak, and they were often bullied themselves by stronger characters – I present one such case at the close of this chapter. It was not fighting and aggression that turned some into bullies in adult life, at least in my experience; it was a wish to control others. We might rush in here too hastily and conclude that the major causal factor for becoming a bully is aggressive and dominating role-modelling, and that the only difference between one who dominates and another who is dominated is that the latter wants to move higher up the power hierarchy, as though life is little more than a relentless and unconscious vying for power. But this is too simplistic, as we shall see.

Whilst not denying Kellerman's experience with those judged to be very serious cases, I do not think we can regard the majority of bullies as psychopathic in the main but as individuals having poor social skills and who are often unpopular. Collectively, they seem to lack a strong sense of individual self and will feel threatened when being questioned or challenged. It is as though they need to have and to exercise control and power over those they regard as being subservient to them. We saw in Chapter 2 how some social animals behave 'for the good of the species', whilst others fight and compete in order to establish their position in the power hierarchy, and it seems, if school playgrounds are anything to go by, that developing children and adolescents appear to resemble chickens and crickets as much as penguins and whales, in the sense that they can be competitive and provocative as much as cooperative and caring.

More importantly, it seems to me that we cannot separate action from motive if we are to fully understand bullying behaviour. If a form of physical aggression is loosely labelled as bullying *per se*, without understanding its underlying motive, in that particular instance we are not going to move very far forward. Many boys will fight in secondary school but will not view their aggression as bullying, not only because bullying is a pejorative term, but simply because they are not selecting someone in combat who is weaker than them so much as one who has become for them a rival. There are further individuals, however, who clearly should be termed as bullies because their psychological or aggressive behaviours are strategically planned or have an underlying motive to abuse someone weaker to achieve a goal other than which the occasion demands, such as a perception of approval by peers, or a desired persona in the eyes of their friends.

The strategic bully

Theorists tend to build into our understanding the notion that bullying should be viewed as a continual, systematic abuse of power. That is to say that bullying is not a one-off impulsive event but a pre-planned and continual harassment, putting a weaker subject down and making them feel humiliated or tormented. You can find countless instances of such ridicule in school. Children are great observers. They will *mimic* someone with a handicap. They will *name-call* endlessly and will *persecute* continually one who is considered to be different from them, one who is not in the in-crowd (Lines 1999, 2001, 2006a).

The premise of much school bullying that currently takes place is that the peer group is exceptionally powerful. All young people enjoy the jibes of calling each other names, and if there is no power differential but a giving and taking, there is little suffering experienced but a general bartering of wit and horseplay. Young people play pranks on each other and set each other up as a joke, and again, if there is no power differential exercised in the process, it is unclear whether this should be classified as bullying. Boys wrestle with each other as a means of testing their newly acquired physical strength and sense of fun, and girls will compete with each other and will sometimes cheat their 'friends' in their romantic relations to establish their pecking-orders of sexual prowess. Again, it is the context which determines whether their behaviours and motives should be classified as bullying. Strategic name-calling is another matter. It is when groups of youngsters all turn against a sole individual with the intention of gross humiliation that bullying occurs.

Photo 4.1 Girls can be particularly hostile where boys are concerned

Much strategic name-calling towards a victim may be said to be done 'just for the fun of it', and when challenged, youngsters often say, 'We didn't mean it; we're just messing about.' But when this happens day-by-day, relentlessly, there is very serious erosion in self-esteem for the victim. Suicide and potential-suicidal victims have recorded in notes and diaries the insidious nature of repeated name-calling that prompted their decision to terminate their lives.

At the other extreme, strategic bullying can show itself in instances of gross violence and physical assault. It is how the group become carried away by herd instinct and appear to have a low sense of personal responsibility, as though the group responsibility diminishes their felt sense of accountability for what they have each done as individuals (Rigby 2002). I remember one occasion where a group of girls tormented a new pupil 'because of her clothes' (see box below). Sadly, our newspapers and news broadcasts inform us on a regular basis of similar cold-hearted examples of barbaric, systematic bullying.

Four girls aged 13–14 persistently harassed Salina around the school, teased her by hiding her school bag, called her a tramp and followed her on the way home, pushing and tripping her, snatching her scarf and prodding her in the back. This happened for many weeks because she was afraid to speak out and to say what was going on. It was brought to a head one chilly December night when she took her dog for a walk in the local park. The group seized the moment and attacked her, punched her violently in the face and kicked her on the floor. She was left severely beaten up. But what was almost unimaginable was that they became like a pack of savage wolves, returned and dragged her towards a brook and left her semi-naked and exposed to the cold night air. If she had been left face down, she would have drowned in the shallow water. When she was found, she had little recourse but to disclose to the authorities all that had happened, and the consequence was that her assailants were given custodial sentences.

Bullying for kicks

A recent study has drawn attention to a pattern that has been observed regularly by youth workers for years. Research carried out by Trevor Bennett and Fiona Brookman (Wright, Brookman and Bennett 2006) on British youth showed that many muggers had a desire for brutal violence rather than financial gain. The study concluded that robbers increasingly carry out their vicious attacks for 'kicks' and street credibility rather than cash. Up to a third of sentenced criminals questioned – some arrested on more than 50 occasions – said they were involved in gangs or criminal groups. The researchers recognized that the amount and severity of gratuitous violence used in street robbery had increased in the UK, and some subjects commented with statements like:

> It weren't even for money. I had money. It was more like the buzz you get from doing things.

> It's for the fun. 'Cos the point of street robbery is to get them to fight back, innit? I'd give him a couple of slaps and tell him to fight back. If he won't fight back, we just give him a kick and go.

> I picked a fight with someone on the street. They were the first people I come across. I started hitting one of them and calling him names and said 'What are you looking at?' and stuff like that.

The authors said that one element in the excitement felt by the violent offenders came from overpowering the victim and obtaining dominance. This report reminded me of similar behaviour I have come across with some youngsters at school who had only become involved with joyriding and stealing cars after leaving school. Vehicle theft is prompted by teenagers not for profit, as might be the case with professional teams, who target prestige models for cloning or shifting across to the continent, but for the thrill of the chase. Having established trust in the community of my school by working with many young people, I quite frequently hear tales of misfortune where 'at risk' teenagers have served time in prison for regular car theft. I asked one young man why someone known to us both had chosen to steal cars in spite of the police being aware of his activities.

'That's the point,' he said. 'It's for the "kicks" of being chased by the police.' The police are not a deterrent but a stimulant, by unconsciously setting up the conditions of the chase. Although car theft may not be considered to be bullying, the same factors of control and dominance are at play when car chases are involved. Escaping from the police draws on a primitive human instinct of the thrill of the chase, a primordial drive stimulated by a rise in adrenalin to compete male with male, together with the typical trait of rebellion against authority that arises through puberty (Lines 2006a), a behaviour which asks a significant question of who really is in charge, as this is a fundamental basis of bullying behaviour.

Bullying for approval

Some youngsters in school engage in bullying because they want to be popular (Lines 2006a). Winning self-approval appears to be a human drive that is 'hard-wired' into our systems (James 2003). Children seek the approval of their parents and teachers, adults seek the approval of their managers, and we all feel immensely proud if a person we regard as a figure of influence and notoriety recognizes our merit.

The window of my counselling room looks out over part of the playground and an area of grass. It is also where the youngsters pass by when going home from school. During one afternoon, I noticed a rushing of pupils that suggested a fight was about to take place. Although I could still remember what I was like as a youngster and how I would run in the direction of the crowd to watch a fight, I asked one child, Rob, why it was that people want to watch a fight and appear to have a 'lust for blood'.

'I think,' he said, 'it's because they want to see some action and they're glad it's not them that's getting hurt.' His friend disagreed: 'No, it's not that, it's just that they want to see who wins.' This led to a fuller discussion the next morning with my group of peer counselling pupils. One spoke of an event that took place in a local square, where a pupil everybody hated in school battered somebody who was quite popular. The person who got battered was not a fighter, and since he was recognized by everyone as being a nice person I was puzzled that no one was prepared to stand up for him.

'Why didn't somebody protect him?' I asked the group. They replied variously along the lines of 'When somebody's being battered, and it's not one of your mates, everybody sides with the person who is tough because it's best to be on their side than be against them and have the fear of being battered yourself.'

This left me with an uncomfortable feeling that the quality of personal relationships was being influenced by perspectives of power and domination, and by a cowardly sense of self-preservation. It is commonly observed that many pupils will form pseudo-friendships with those they perceive might offer them support should they become threatened (Luxmoore 2000) and that this regularly occurs in the early part of secondary school (Lines 2006a, 2007). In the two final years, however, where there is more indifference than hostility shown to individuals who are not part of the in-crowd, friendships and popularity are not so much determined by power and control but by common interests and a higher quality of friendship. It is quite common, therefore, to conclude that some bullying behaviour, particularly amongst groups – that should rightly be

Photo 4.2 Bystanders will befriend the tough and often watch people being beaten up by them, feeling relieved not to be in the victim's position

called 'bullying' – stems from a motive of real or perceived popularity or approval from peers of a character who displays an aggressive persona.

Let us now look at a range of aggressive responses that are often termed 'bullying' by parents and teachers, but which under different definitions of the term might be regarded as defensive reactions or responses to perceived threat.

Impulsive 'bullying'

Some children and young people, particularly younger children, will strike out uncharacteristically against another for annoying them. It is as though they have acquired a limited repertoire of responses for dealing with tension other than physical ones (Goleman 2006). Their behaviour is impulsive, in the sense that they act without thinking, as though it is a learnt behaviour. Putting aside all other factors of causation, such as physical or learning disability, a lack of emotional warmth received when a toddler, dysfunctional teaching on how to manage stress, or poor parental management of strife between siblings, it may be that aggressive adult modelling is highly significant. Is impulsive and largely spontaneous behaviour essentially 'bullying'? Is the child suffering a tantrum who hits out at another weaker playmate a bully *per se*? This behaviour is not pre-planned, it is not systematic, and it could hardly be understood as arising from a motive to dominate another weaker human being – these youngsters will often hit out at one who is tougher than them, even adults where the power differential would serve as a disadvantage.

Reactive 'bullying'

Reactive bullying is similar in that it is reflexive and has no preconceived outcome other than one which is primarily defensive. Young children and teen-agers may have to endure considerable torment from those they perceive are more powerful than them, and it is as though they have reached their tolerance threshold and react violently out of pent-up frustration. The spring has been depressed to its limit and must recoil and discharge energy once an opportunity is afforded. It is essential to understand the meaning of highly reactive behaviour, since the peer group may not always be helpful. Volatile young people are prone easily to be wound up, and tormenting peers recognize their own potential to manipulate them. On occasion these perpetrators are left to feel superior, or to feel relieved that they are not in the victim's position of becoming angry through embarrassment (Luxmoore 2006).

And so with children, when stress reaches its peak the individual has a choice of either rolling over submissively, or reacting (often by overreacting) as a defensive response. The adult manager may only notice the consequential behaviour, be unaware of its antecedent pressures and may judge the behaviour as bullying on the basis that the meted-out aggression was disproportionate to the (assumed) cause. Mistakenly, the adult draws the conclusion that this child is a bully for an inappropriate 'abuse of power', quite unaware that he or she may have suffered prolonged aggravation. If we were fully aware of antecedent factors of the reaction, even though there is a power differential, it is surely not reasonable to call this bullying or to regard such a youngster as a bully.

Provocative goading by 'victims'

Anatol Pikas (1989) distinguished between 'classic' or ordinary victims and others he described as 'provocative victims', and although many of these pupils may suffer with communication-behavioural disorders like ADHD or cognitive disorders on the autistic spectrum which leads them to display behaviour that inadvertently invites bullying, there are others who appear to bring on the bullying themselves by their poor interpersonal communications.

One such case was Jack, a 15-year-old pupil referred for counselling after a fight, which was untypical of his behaviour. He had been repeatedly taunted through the early years until he could stand it no longer, and so lashed out and got into a fight. What is more, he was congratulated by his mother and by some teachers surreptitiously for standing up for himself. If the intimidation had ceased, it could be argued that all was well – he had become assertive and the tormentors had got the message! This was not the case, however, and in fact the taunting grew worse.

I asked Jack to log the teasing and tormenting over the week, and his record was pitiful, illustrating that he had suffered low-level physical assault and intimidation three to four times a day. Ideas about the motives for teasing were discussed, but there were blind-spots of social awareness that is common for youngsters with autism – though he was not officially diagnosed as such. I felt that he was not grasping the point but showing only a blind willingness to try out suggestions by rote. I kept the trial period to only one day and his log the next day confirmed my suspicions. When wished 'Good morning' by a peer, he wrote: 'I didn't reply because he always treats me badly.' When James asked if he could work with him in science, he wrote: 'My reply was, "Go away".' In French, when the teacher left the room, the class started to bully him and call him 'sheep-shagger', and he wrote: 'Laura said I should take it easy, but I don't take any notice of her because she's a slacker who does not want to get on in life.' These responses indicated that Jack was unable to be less intense, unable to differentiate between friendliness and spitefulness, and found it difficult to display any comradeship and warmth when socially relating – he was on a social spiral downwards towards becoming isolated and lonely.

When we covered past events in session with a view to learning how he might have responded differently, he looked blank and promptly insisted on writing everything down to retain the idea. I felt uneasy, in that he was not genuinely seeing what was going on, not grasping what needed to change, but was prepared to act under mechanical instruction rather than by intuition. Jack was wholly unskilled in adolescent conversing, and was not in tune with youthful thinking and play. The counselling role was altered to encourage Jack to engage in socializing within protective groups – school clubs and societies, Church groups, small local youth clubs – and this was the recommendation put to his parents (Lines 2006a).

Photo 4.3 There are some pupils who appear to draw aggression from peers through provocative behaviour and others who have poor communication skills and who have equally volatile peers as friends

I have known many examples where some pupils in school whom I term 'provocative victims' find new resources within themselves to make an assertive stand in defending themselves, quite appropriately, then go on to deploy this new-found confidence in bullying others they judge are weaker than them. They are unaware, or choose to be unaware, that their victim is in a position which they once held. Having suffered, they seem unable to empathize with those who similarly suffer. This particular type of individual might appropriately be termed a bully, perhaps more so, because they should above all others 'know' what it feels like to be dominated by the powerful.

But then, according to Goleman (2006), youngsters are 'unable' to empathize or soothe others if they have not experienced the same when being brought up. Although a legal judgement would view all alike, our general morally attuned sensitivity leads us to criticize more severely those who 'should know better', but perhaps many 'provocative victims' do not know better and do indeed require much support to acquire age-appropriate social skills (see the cases of Alexander below and Alan on p.139).

Labelling bullies

The wide range of bullying behaviours and motivations shows how any attempt to label a youngster as 'a bully' upon a limited observation of their social behaviour can be problematic. Whilst some may take a sordid pleasure in beating defenceless children or adults, others engaged in the same behaviour feel bad about what they do. Bullying cannot wholly be determined by aggressive behaviour, nor can it be reduced to singular causal factors underlying the behaviour. I close this chapter by presenting the case of a pupil named Philip who was physically maltreated by his step-father, Alexander, an ex-pupil of the school I knew well as a bullied youngster and one I viewed as likely to have been 'provocative victim'.

Alexander's own father was very violent and aggressively inclined and had limited strategies of managing his son other than to resort to punching and beating. Alexander suffered from capricious treatment of care and discipline which was meted out more according to mood than insight and guidance. Two incidents involved child protection procedures being instigated, a situation that was confirmed by an anonymous letter written to social services by a neighbour who had become upset after what he had witnessed in the park. When he was 15, Alexander had been severely reprimanded at the park gate by his father who punched him so hard that he reeled backwards and was taken home with a torrent of verbal abuse.

It could be reasoned from this family background that Alexander had been nurtured under an ethic that 'might is right' and that such deplorable role-modelling would inevitably lead to him being a violent bully of children under his care, the stylized cycle of abusive deprivation.

When in school Alexander had a violent temper and one common feature of his behaviour was to storm out of the classroom if his teacher challenged him for arriving late or for 'winding up' other pupils. I had witnessed one occasion myself as Alexander slammed the classroom door, shouting and swearing as he strode up the corridor, only being brought to a calm state after I had invited him into my room to settle. I was surprised to find that the cause of his rage was over something that appeared so trivial – his teacher joked with him for missing an open goal in football. From his over-reactive response, it might be judged, quite fittingly, that we should understand Alexander's behaviour as stemming from an impulsive over-reaction from low self-esteem.

Whatever support was offered Alexander at the time, we could not prevent him from being bullied and teachers often remarked along the lines of 'He's his own worst enemy!' His peers tended to isolate him and avoid sitting next to him in class for fear of getting into trouble themselves. 'He likes battering the weaker kids, but he can't take the battering himself,' they would say.

Alexander could be seen as a 'provocative victim' suffering from inadequate social and befriending skills. Indeed, if Alexander were to be at school today, he might be diagnosed as having autism, ADHD or some other communication or behavioural disorder.

I had lost contact with Alexander until his step-son, Philip, came for counselling and began to talk to me about his step-father and about his violent assaults against himself and his mother. This was a particularly upsetting experience for young Philip. He had seen it many times and felt totally frustrated that his mother always 'had him back' after coming out of prison for beating her up. He said that he was as angry with his mother as with Alexander for putting up with him. There is a fascinating piece of research, which we will review more fully later, which suggests that young boys in general identify with their fathers in cases of mild domestic violence, but this turns if the violence passes an acceptable point, in which case a young boy's sympathies turn towards his mother (Winstok, Eisikovits and Karnieli-Miller 2004).

Philip was beginning to get into more trouble with over-reactive behaviour when being criticized for minor misdemeanours and bullying. He came for more sessions of counselling and began to tell me of other reasons for Alexander's violence in the family. Philip's mother rang me at school to say why Philip was particularly vulnerable at the time. She told me that she had kicked Alexander out again for taking heroin – being a 'bag-head'. She said that she could no longer put up with his addictive behaviour, a behaviour which had occurred before they first met when Alexander was 15.

It struck me that the causal factor for the park incident may have had something to do with drugs, that Alexander's own father had 'cause' to remonstrate with him owing to the company he was keeping, through his association with gangs who were heavily into drugs.

On one occasion Philip's mother was beaten so badly she was forced to disclose the assault and underwent treatment in intensive care. The police brought charges against Alexander and he served a three-year prison sentence. After his sentence had been served, Philip was convinced his mother would no longer have him back, but he was wrong. After a month had passed, she relented and took him in again. How was it that this behaviour of severe bullying appeared incapable of change? 'What was the role of the probationary service?' I thought. Whose responsibility is the rehabilitation of violent individuals? Alexander's behaviour towards Philip's mother occurred within a particular family context. There was no evidence I was aware of that suggested that Alexander bullied anyone else other than Philip and his mother. Added to which, Philip spoke in despairing terms at times about his mother, saying, 'Mum's as bad as him sometimes. She punches him when he's done nothing – she sets him off and then it goes too far. At other times she teases him and takes the piss out of him.'

Could it be possible, without passing judgement, that bullying behaviour has contextual relevance that is extremely significant, that Philip's mother exhibits reciprocal behaviour that prompts the bullying and domestic violence? It cannot justify bullying but it seems to facilitate it. There is a whole range of factors already touched upon which could be argued to have influenced Alexander's 'bullying' behaviour in adulthood:

- a deprived nurturing home of emotional warmth (insecure attachment)

- aggressive role-modelling

- internalized ethics of 'might is right'

- miscalculated reactions from low self-esteem

- autism or a communication or behaviour disorder

- having poor social skills in which to relate

- being severely bullied by adults and peers and subconsciously seeking to turn the tables and exercise control of his weaker subordinates

- misuse of drugs

- reciprocal relationships that prompt violence

- or a complex combination of any or all of the above.

However, there is no way to pin down a definitive set of influences – under any definition of bullying, the causal factors for behaviour may be complicated and variable.

Conclusion

Bullying behaviours range from psychopathic aggression involving a voyeuristic intention to hurt and maim another individual to common teasing behaviour. There is a need to separate the two notions of young people fighting and bullying, and whilst bullying behaviour may involve violence in some instances, behaving aggressively towards another person of similar power may not constitute bullying behaviour. Motives and context must be understood before we can regard someone as being a bully or an incident as being bullying.

Although attention has primarily addressed bullying behaviour in school, these principles also apply in a workplace setting – perhaps more so, given that the behaviour of adults is more likely to be mature and controlled. The example of Alexander shows the danger of being too prescriptive in labelling behaviour and individuals from insufficient or nebulous information. The origins of bullying behaviour can be difficult to establish and complex.

Chapter 5

Interpreting Bullying Behaviour

The process of making sense of bullying behaviour involves observation and interpretation. Previous chapters have shown how bullying cannot be treated in 'black and white' terms – that it can be much more subtle and insidious, and can encompass a range of motivations not apparent to the casual observer. Eye-witness accounts are not always reliable, and where several people have observed one act of bullying, individuals' assessments of behaviour can vary substantially. Can we always believe the evidence of our own eyes? And even if we can and are gifted with good skills of observation and recollection, our means and method of making sense of what is observed is coloured by mental processing, which encompasses our belief systems, outlook, prejudices and our previous experiences. Our perception of what we see and hear is not taken in as neutral information, but is shaped and moulded by an elaborate filtering mechanism that has to make sense of incoming data. The material below looks at how we interpret behaviour and draws insights from psychotherapeutic theory and practice.

Making sense of observed behaviour

It is quite common for books on psychology to begin with perception. Most of us have been intrigued by illusions in which shapes and figures are not what they first seem. A common example is a line drawing of two vases which may appear as two faces depending upon whether the eye is drawn to the shape at the sides or at the centre. In art there is a well-known illustration of an ascending staircase produced by Escher – make sense of the print in Figure 5.1 if you will.

Figure 5.1 M.C. Escher's 'Relativity' © *2007 The M.C. Escher Company-Holland. All rights reserved. www.mcescher.com*

Attitudes towards violence and aggression are largely shared across the world, with a general consensus that such behaviour is socially destructive. When we observe bullying and dominant behaviour, however, there is rarely universal agreement, either in relation to what is observed or in values perspectives of how 'bullying' is interpreted, as the example on the opposite page shows.

Now let us examine this discourse and young Simon's plight. Is Simon a bully or a defender of a value system – which could be regarded as commendable? It may not be the wisest course, but then he is only a youngster and this is the way young people are in their day-to-day social relationships. It can be argued that what prompted his response was primarily a gross dislike of Jonathan, and that it was convenient for him to take the moral high ground and

Little Simon came to see me because he was very upset. Something had happened during the morning break which left him worried that he might be excluded.

'I need to see you. I've just thumped Jonathan,' he said. I first met Simon three months earlier when his sister had asked me to support him when being bullied in school. During that time we looked at various strategies he could use to become self-assertive with three boys in his form, and I organized a peer counsellor to help him translate these skills for the many situations that occur during a school day. Since he found this successful he knew he could come to me in confidence and discuss a new difficulty. I asked him to say a little more.

'Jonathan's a prick,' he said. 'Oh! Sorry! I mean, nobody likes him. He thinks he's hard and can push everyone about. There's this girl who fancies me and I've been going out with her for a week, but he keeps butting in. He follows us around because she used to go out with him. But now she doesn't like him. Anyway, that's got nothing to do with it. There's this other girl called, do you know Jessica? Oh well. She's new to the school. Hardly anybody knows her. Jonathan just goes up to her and punched her in the back. So I go up to him and punched him in the face. Then this teacher came along on duty. He'd just come round the corner, saw me hit him and him cry and asked him what had happened. He said, "Simon's just punched me." "I did," I said, "and I'd do it again." The teacher went mad. He wouldn't listen to me. He took me to the isolation room and rang my mum and now I'm going to get excluded.'

'How is it that you're not with him now, Simon?'

'I just went off, it's not fair.'

'What made you hit him instead of reporting it to the teacher? Or better still, take Jessica to the teacher and support her in reporting what had happened?'

'It's the way I am; the way I've been brought up. Everyone from where I come from knows that you don't hit girls. And if I see someone beating a girl I'll thump them.'

'I see that, but then you get done, Simon.'

'Yeah, I suppose I do, but it's the way I am.'

take justice into his own hands; alternatively, he might be defending a weaker person quite justifiably. The question is: should Simon's behaviour be described as bullying? This was what was written on his exclusion letter. At this point I am not interested in whether this judgement was right or wrong, or whether indeed a senior teacher should have investigated the matter more thoroughly before passing judgement. I am interested in how we interpret what we observe.

Observation and emotions

I remember once watching a very disturbing attack from my counselling room window. An assault had taken place by a particularly aggressive youth. He approached his victim and thumped him time and again whilst his friends 'appeared' to hold him against the metal railings. He was hit hard, and in order to apply maximum force from a downward punch his attacker first jumped from the ground. I was so upset by what I saw I began to feel sick. Whilst watching this drama unfold, I attempted to summon senior staff support by phone, temporarily glancing away from the scene, but the line was continually engaged. I became increasingly agitated by the minute. When I eventually got through, something else had happened. Although my view was partially obscured by the crowd, I saw what I thought to be the same youth walking up the hill and thump his victim a second time. 'Is there no end to this?' I thought.

Eventually when the police became involved, I was asked to say what I saw, and in making my statement I dictated to the constable the events as I remembered them and he recorded my account in my presence. After this I had occasion to speak with the victim's girlfriend and she gave me a very different version of events. She told me that her boyfriend ran away across the road to a friend's house after the first assault. She in effect could not confirm what 'I saw', which effectively meant that what I had observed could not be factually correct – it turned out to be someone else only 'miming to another boy how the assaulted lad had been hit'. This reminded me of a sad occasion years ago when a young boy was killed when crossing the road near my home.

One quiet Sunday morning, James was hit into the air by a car. He was admitted to hospital, and after 19 days in a coma he breathed his last. His friend Simon, who was standing beside him at the moment of impact, was, quite naturally, very shaken up. What struck me as bewildering was how contradictory the eyewitness accounts were at the inquest. There was so much discrepancy that the eyewitnesses recorded 'facts' that were wholly contradictory: the two boys were 'seen' crossing the road in different directions; one witness described a red car, the other said it was silver; one said it was raining, the other said it was dry; one 'remembered' a screech of brakes, and the other said there was no braking at all, and so on. When this young boy was knocked over and tragically killed, it must have been a very disturbing occasion; the sight of seeing him hurled into the air and falling onto the windscreen, the blood and his unconscious state, the hysteria as people ran towards the scene. It seems as though when the emotions are stirred so heavily when seeing something so upsetting, the accuracy of perception is affected. I understand that this is a well-recognized phenomenon in the law courts.

The point here is that witnessing emotionally charged events such as aggressive behaviour – whether a fight when one party is losing or getting hurt, or gang humiliation of a defenceless individual, or mockery of an unkempt child for being dirty, having head lice or not dressing fashionably – often stirs deep feelings of protection in us adult managers and mature young people to the degree that we may misinterpret a still frame of what 'we see' because our sense of injustice and feeling upset over innocent suffering overrides. In such cases, negatively labelled pupils can often be unfairly treated through snap-decisions of prejudice and not seeing the whole picture.

Bullying and relational behaviour – Theoretical models for interpretation

In the previous chapter, we explained the influence of attachment theory, but attachment theory serves only to help us understand why particular individuals may have difficulties in their relationships and why past experiences of separation anxiety tend to be repeated in new attachments that are formed: it rests upon largely unknown or irretrievable information; it does not fully account for what is taking place in the present; and offers little scope for explaining the dynamics of dominating and bullying behaviour.

Other theories point more forcibly to relational behaviour – the inter-relationship of behaviours that take place, often unconsciously, between people living in close relationships. Much relational behaviour hinges on control. A growing child can be viewed as being on a journey to get control and become powerful from a position of helplessness and dependence. A newly formed relationship between two lovers may also exhibit two people vying for control in that relationship at an unconscious level. I do not mean to be pejorative by using the term 'control', as though such behaviour is of necessity a bad thing. The desire for control can be seen as a primal drive, evident in the fight for life throughout evolution: mastery of the environment. Control and domination are commonly seen as 'masculine' properties, though the traditionally 'feminine' properties of cooperation and collaboration can also exhibit forms of subtle control.

The two key perspectives of behaviour formation in relationships are:

- individual perspective – behaviour reinforcement

- systemic perspective – inter-reactionary reinforcement.

Individual perspective – Behaviour reinforcement
BEHAVIOURISM

Behaviour theory is rooted in the belief that human behaviour is directed towards bringing personal benefit or meeting a desired long-term goal – Freud's 'pleasure principle' (Freud 1964).

A number of theorists, largely Americans, laid the building blocks of learning theory from the 1920s onwards, which have now become mainstream psychology for those attempting to modify unwanted or self-destructive behaviour (McLeod 2003). The principles of this theory gave insight into why particular people behave the way they do; for our present purposes, why people bully others or allow themselves to be bullied by more powerful individuals.

They proved that particular behaviours – negative and positive – would often be repeated if they brought some benefit to the individual concerned, or conversely might cease if they led to detrimental effects. In other words, reinforced behaviours became habitual through incentives and payoffs or negative consequences and punishment. In a sense, this was a behaviourist manifestation in humans of the 'cost and benefit' instinct that served as the driving goal in the evolution of life for most living creatures.

This principle was known as 'operant conditioning', and has been documented in the studies of Skinner and Watson (Skinner 1953; Watson 1919). Prior to this research, a Russian psychologist by the name of Pavlov had described a different form of conditioning known as 'classical conditioning' (Pavlov 1927) in which fear or pleasure can be experienced in reaction to a particular signal which, in itself, carries no obvious threat or delight but does carry an association with a past fearful or pleasant experience. While Skinner and Watson worked on rats and pigeons, Pavlov demonstrated his principle with salivating dogs, which formed a connection between an expectation of food and a ringing bell.

Classical conditioning is not merely a mental process, it is shown through physiological reactions and symptoms: a fear of being bullied or assaulted may cause diarrhoea, nausea, insomnia or panic attacks.

Both forms of conditioning involve a payoff for the individual concerned, and this also has great relevance when looking at bullying behaviour. Whether school bully or repressive manager, the question is: For what particular benefit or payoff might an individual seek to bully, dominate or control another? With regard to a victim, it is appropriate to ask the very same question, ludicrous as it may initially sound: What benefit or, perhaps more appropriately, what psychological advantage is there to being the victim of bullying behaviour? The person may have an unconscious desire to be controlled, dominated or even hurt by a peer, partner or boss in a close-knit community setting.

One other development of conditioned behaviour which has relevance to repeated victimology is the phenomenon known as 'learned helplessness' (Seligman 1975), which is where an individual has become so submissive to provocation that they figuratively 'roll over' and allow themselves to be violated, hurt or penalized unjustly. Early studies showed how caged animals when given electric shocks would develop a characteristic posture of submission and helplessness even when allowed to escape, and similar behaviours have been observed with children and young people who are perpetually tormented and bullied in situations where they have no power to defend themselves. This may sound controversial, but when closely examining the pattern of a victim's repeated behaviour in low-level relational abuse there are indications that the phenomenon of learned helplessness may have formed, which, at an unconscious level, may serve as a psychological payoff for the victim – rendering them for an audience as being 'worthy of concern' and as being 'exonerated from blame' (Holstein and Miller 1990). Holstein and Miller (1990) show how ascribing the label of 'victim' may be an *interactive, public performance* designed to deflect responsibility, to achieve status in addressing a social or political problem, to link hurt with uncontrollable causes, or to achieve a desired outcome by invoking sentiment through victimization through the use and misuse of presented 'facts'.

COGNITIVE INFLUENCE ON BEHAVIOUR

With the arrival of the 'cognitive revolution' in the 1960s, an extra strand was added to learning theory and social conditioning: the power of thinking and unconscious thought processes. Two theorists in particular, Aaron Beck and Albert Ellis, laid the foundations for two influential models of therapy: cognitive therapy (Beck 1976) and rational emotive therapy or RET (Ellis 1962). These are now used internationally for the treatment of depression, obsessive-compulsive disorders and many other psychological problems. The insight that these approaches brought was a growing awareness that problems in and of themselves only become 'a problem' if they do so in the mind of the individual concerned. It is not problems themselves that create difficulties, but the thinking that underlies them. In terms of bullying behaviour, if I begin to think that a person close to me has intentions to do me harm because of a stare, then not only will I experience fear but I may also over-react in a manner that does not result in an outcome I desire – I may run away from someone who was wanting to make friendly eye contact with me.

We shall see in the following narratives that some young people draw the wrong conclusions from gestures and looks owing to presumptions and constructs – such as 'nobody likes me', 'I'm no good' – on the flimsiest of evidence. Their outlook, or 'social construct', has been formed from bad past experiences, and negative, automatic assumptions often take a lot of work to shift, modify and reframe to bring about better social outcomes. As pointed out in the previous chapter, inappropriate over-reactive impulses often stem from insecure attachments, but cognitive therapy can address what an individual has to do to make things better.

ROLE-MODELLING

One final element of learning theory, which has been touched on previously and which naturally stems from social reinforcement theory, is the powerful effect of *role-modelling behaviour* by significant persons in the individual's social world, particularly the family and the peer group. Bandura (1976) was convinced that the acquisition of particular behaviours, and I am thinking particularly about aggression and violence for our present purposes, results from conscious and unconscious modelling of what was observed in the immediate environment.

According to this theory, aggressive and dominant behaviour, commonly perceived as an instinctive, automatic response for the individual concerned (as a lion attacking an antelope), can be an imitation of behaviour witnessed in family or community contexts.

Systemic perspective – Inter-reactionary reinforcement

This perspective is rooted in the idea that human behaviour is not merely self-directed; it is regulated by the interaction of others, just as the behaviour of others is affected by the individual. Within relationships, behaviour is not only *reactionary*, it is *inter-reactionary*.

All too often, problems to do with bullying in school, victimization in the workplace and domestic violence are dealt with at the individual level. That is to say that professionals, colleagues or friends will advocate for one party in a situation that has a relational context. In school, attention is paid, quite rightly, to the victim in the interests of protection and justice, and alternatively to the bully by personnel whose responsibility it is to avert aggressive or intimidating behaviour by working alongside them as counsellor. Similarly, in the workplace there are unions and associations committed to defending and preserving the rights of their individual members. In cases of domestic violence, lawyers and support groups will work with victims, whilst probation officers may work alongside those who have been convicted for family violence. In all these cases, the focus is upon individual alignment and advocacy, while in fact the problems largely stem from the relationship between *two* parties. It is to the quality of that relationship and its shortcomings that I take particular interest.

Whilst this book records the rationale of perpetrators of bullying behaviour, the reason why I wish to listen to the voices of all those involved is because I am interested primarily in the *relationship* between the two and what is required to make amends so that all parties may move on in the direction that is required.

SYSTEMS THEORY

There are a range of models applied in family therapy which all have in common a view that a family is a 'system' of inter-related parts that give meaning to the whole. Examining the behaviour of one family member is considered to be irrelevant without looking at its effects and context within the family as a unit. This has great significance for bullying behaviour, since whether we are thinking of an individual in class, or a parent in a family, or a worker amongst colleagues, the meaning for a given behaviour has significance within the group context; and without an understanding of the group dynamics, interpreting individual behaviour is rendered meaningless.

There are three basic family therapy models – structural family therapy (Minuchin 1974), strategic family therapy (Haley 1976) and the Milan group of family therapy (Palazzoli *et al.* 1978). Each places a particular emphasis on aspects of family inter-relating (Burnham 1986). All the models subscribe to the view that breakdowns within families arise from poor communications, and each has been developed, albeit separately, along the principles of *cybernetic theory*. Cybernetics was originally applied to mathematics, physics and engineering. It is the notion that

> [d]ifferent phenomena (both biological and non-biological) share the attributes of a system – that is, a unified whole that consists of interrelated parts, such that the whole can be identified from the sum of its parts and any change in one part affects the rest of the system. (McLeod 2003, p.191)

Psychologists have applied this principle to human systems, such as teams, organizations and families (Street 1994). A functioning system, whether it is an internal combustion engine or a family, will tend to operate integrally as a homogeneous unit. When it is 'up and running' all parts work together for the system to reach a 'stable state'; everything is in balance. If an ignition coil in an engine becomes faulty the engine will run erratically, and other parts of the system, such as the transmission, will labour and become less effective.

In a normal family every member has a role and a function within that system. If the mother, who has a clearly identified 'role' and 'function', becomes ill and incapacitated and she is unable to do what is 'expected of her', and what 'she expects of herself' as a 'good mother', the whole family suffers. If there is a disabled child in the family it may be necessary for the father to give up work to help provide the necessary care, and thereby the whole family suffers as a result of reduced income.

In the narratives that follow in Chapters 6–9, there is evidence to show that bullying has a 'systemic role' within the class, family or workplace and that, by altering that role, the balance may be adversely affected temporarily until new changes take place in order to reach balance again with a restructured stability.

When we define a problem within the family, the class or schoolyard, or the workplace, systems theory holds that there is no such thing as 'an individual problem'; there is only a problem within the system, or group, or family, or whatever. All relationships, therefore, are complementary and all behaviours are reciprocal, so that a difficulty, or a symptom, or a dysfunctional behaviour, has a *meaning* within the social group that operates unconsciously according to a script and that understanding the difficulty, symptom or behaviour, outside of what meaning it has for the rest of the group, is considered to be misleading.

Applying this insight to relational conflict and bullying, we might say that when a father or step-father becomes violent and aggressive, or exercises a controlling manner over his family, we may have to consider this not in isolation from the reciprocal nature of behaviours of other family members. The example of Robert (see box) illustrates a case where the systems theory approach could be applied for a broader understanding.

Half-way through his history lesson, Robert picks up his schoolbag, throws it at Marcus and storms out of the classroom shouting, 'Fuck off, you twat!', whereupon Marcus follows him and punches him in the back so that he stumbles over a desk, prompting laughter from some of the class. 'Don't tell me to fuck off!' he yells back to Robert. As his teacher rushes to Robert's aid ordering Marcus to sit down, Robert yells out to her, in temper, 'And you can fuck off as well!' In the corner of the room, behind where Robert was sitting, two girls were to be seen giggling and hurriedly hiding notes under their desks. The teacher was content only to maintain control amongst the rest as Robert had stormed off down along the corridor.

After the lesson she noticed the notes torn up on the floor, and being curious she assembled them to read their content. What the girls had done was to insinuate that Robert was gay and that he had had a sexual relationship with Marcus. Robert's reaction was not to remonstrate with the girls, as powerful as they were in passing notes around the class and bullying through a covert means of circulating insulting messages, but to take out his anger on Marcus and demonstrate through provocative action that he had no fond feelings for him. Whilst Marcus, in return, feels compelled to demonstrate publicly that he is in no way gay, nor is he in love with Robert, since why else would he thump him in the back? Untangling such peer-group conflicts as this occupies many teachers much of their time and illustrates the inter-relationship factors of covert and overt bullying behaviour within groups.

Another important factor to bear in mind is that a social system – whether a class, a family, or the workforce – is not a static entity, because systems in a human context have the properties more of an organism than a machine; they are developing and growing as separate beings. As inter-related members of the group inter-react, the whole system alters in nature and character, following a given direction dictated by the most dominant figures and forces. Systemic behaviour is in flux but gravitates towards equilibrium.

A newly formed relationship between two partners undergoes growth and development; it is a growing process, constantly changing as each asserts control, but unconsciously seeking communion, balance and harmony as the behaviour of each supplements, or conflicts, with the other. There is the paradox of challenge and compliance as new levels are found and as the maturing relationship grows through trial towards a stable state. Inevitably, all relationships go through periods of tension, particularly during significant life stages.

In a similar way, young people in secondary school are growing and developing, and as such demonstrate prepubescent behaviour before passing through adolescence towards adulthood. Tasks adolescents attempt to achieve have implications for self-identity, identity formation and role-crisis as they journey from dependence towards autonomy (Erikson 1968), but these inner drives and impulses occur within the system's group context of family and peer group.

ADOLESCENT DEVELOPMENT

Young people are not solitary, encapsulated entities acting wholly in an autonomous manner, independent of the views, feelings, beliefs and expectations of two groups standing as potential or actual rivals. They transfer their obligations, interests and loyalties from parents to peers – next to achieving intimacy with a partner, that is their chief task. As youngsters pass through adolescence they go through puberty, and the rising levels of hormones in their bodies not only put their emotions in disarray and confusion, they prompt sexual desires to become engaged in relationships (Lines 2006a). It is a time of testing and challenging as loyalties change and as the need to depend more on the peer group replaces outgrown dependence on the parent or carer. Sexual attraction becomes powerful and youngsters feel the need to experiment and to find new confidence for intimacy and relating skills that will equip them to find a mate for life, or for part of their life, so as to satisfy their natural sex drives.

It is common for adolescents, especially boys, to become particularly testing as they try to harness the new-found strength and power that they experience rippling through their bodies. A felt need for companionship, which was once experienced within the safe boundary of the family, needs to be had with a different person, and physical attraction and falling in love produces tensions and trials that lead to the possibility that dominating and aggressive behaviour may spill over to unintended and intentional bullying. Much bullying amongst boys, therefore, can be likened to red deer stags vying for dominance and high social rank for mating with females during the rutting season. Showing off and flirting accompanies romance trials, and both boys and girls (particularly girls) discover the luring power of their own body form and sexuality, sometimes with destructive results, and may prompt a range of bullying encounters.

POWER GAMES IN RELATIONSHIPS

Power games are played between adolescent young people, just as in adult relationships, and in the workplace within employer–employee relations. It is with this aspect that I wish to close this chapter by looking at the powerful effects of the *payoff* that can result from the games people play in relational battles. In *Games People Play*, Eric Berne (1968) hit on a theory that, although voiced in the 1960s, may still unlock some of the mysteries of reciprocal relationships.

It is a mystery why some partners remain in or walk back into a violent relationship after escaping, or 'find' a similarly abusive person to replace the one who made life hell. Similar confusion surrounds a condition of unusual attachment that became known as 'Stockholm syndrome' following a widely publicized episode in Stockholm in August 1973 where bank employees taken hostage in a botched bank robbery began to identify with their captors. *Webster's New World Medical Dictionary* (2003) gives the definition for Stockholm syndrome as: 'an extraordinary phenomenon in which a hostage begins to identify with and grow sympathetic to their captor'. Unfortunately, questions surround the accuracy of the original reports (one captive was reported to have had mental health problems), and there are good reasons for victims in such life-threatening situations to apply survival techniques like feigning support and loyalty in order to escape harm. Nevertheless, the condition has been linked with other reported captivity stories and has been presented as a 'psychology of victimhood' to help account for situations where victims form a bond with and become emotionally attached to their captives whilst under siege. But as critics of the syndrome point out, when applied to related questions such as why battered wives continue to put up with and sometimes defend their abusers, there is the likelihood that what such victims are defending is not their abusive partner, but *themselves* over the choice they originally made for someone as brutal as they turned out to be as a partner and father to her children in the first place, and that confessing such a mistake is much too painful to have to acknowledge (Wright and Cummings 2005). As pointed out earlier, attachment theory may also explain some people's poor selection of a partner; but for Berne, troublesome relationships occur because of a series of games people play:

> A game is an ongoing series of complementary ulterior transactions progressing to a well-defined, predictable outcome. Descriptively, it is a recurring set of transactions, often repetitious, superficially plausible, with a concealed motivation; or, more colloquially, a series of moves with a snare, or 'gimmick'. (Berne 1968, p.44)

And according to Sills (2007), game theory 'has various ways of understanding the repetitive and self-limiting patterns that people get into – the symbiotic dance where stale meanings are created and re-created unconsciously in present relating' (p.17).

A game is a series of interactions – words, body language, facial expressions and the like – between two or more people that follow a predictable pattern. The interactions ultimately progress to an outcome in which each individual obtains a payoff or goal. In most cases, participants are unaware that they are playing the game.

Let us examine those games that 'may' relate to dominating, bullying and over-control in violent relationships. One game Berne identifies is 'If It Weren't for You'. He gives an example of Mrs White who complains that her husband severely restricts her social activities, so that she never learns to dance. His over-controlling behaviour has a payoff for both parties. For him it fulfils his power in the relationship, and for her it avoids discovering that an embarrassing exposure might occur on the dance floor. Why does she select this domineering man for her partner? It is because she has a 'need to complain about lost opportunities' which may expose her unadventurous spirit. Out of her many possibilities, says Berne, she had picked a domineering man for a husband. She was then in a position to complain that she could do all sorts of things *if it weren't for you*.

Many of her women friends have domineering husbands too, and when they meet for morning coffee they spend a good deal of time playing 'If It Weren't for You'. As it turns out, contrary to her complaints, her husband was performing a service by forbidding her to do something she was afraid of, and by preventing her from even 'becoming aware' of her neurotic fears of being placed in phobic situations. Her participation in the game begins when she had unconsciously 'selected' a controlling partner to meet needs she could, paradoxically, complain about to fellow game players.

In the life game 'Please Don't Kick Me', the injured party in a stormy relationship has an opportunity to cry piteously, 'Why does this always happen to me?' What is the payoff for each party? It is possibly a case for both to compete on the victimization scale, which stems from inverse pride: 'My misfortunes are better than yours.' Do some relationships become competitive at times where each feels they are giving too much and becoming too self-sacrificial for no personal advantage? 'Now I've Got You, You Son of a Bitch' is a game that Berne says can be seen in classic form in poker games where one party is more interested in the fact that his opponent is completely at his mercy than that he is a good poker player or is effective in making money. Commercial transactions (haggling over prices) and partner relations (pride in being 'proved' right in family disputes) can be drawn unconsciously into this game. The 'injured party' has the payoff from victimization through the 'Why Does This Always Happen to Me?' game, and the 'victor' recalls that ever since early childhood he had looked for similar injustices and had received them with delight and had exploited them with the same vigour. In many cases he had forgotten the actual provocation, but remembered in great detail the course of the ensuing battle. These games may be regularly and unconsciously played out in the workplace.

The relationship games of 'If It Weren't for You', 'Why Does This Always Happen to Me?' and others all imply that one party in a relationship is dominant and the other subservient. Whether this is understood as 'bullying' is another question; it suggests control and domination, but can it be classed as bullying if the recipient may receive a *payoff* which is naturally of 'benefit', albeit unconscious? If there were a game called 'Why Do I Always Get Battered and Knocked Around', a clear indication of bullying, then the payoff for the perpetrator might be the felt need to be powerful in the relationship, for whatever reason. But for the victim, what would be the payoff? Might it possibly be a felt need to draw sympathy from an audience, similar to that spoken of above? Could it be a justification for not being more venturesome in socializing and getting out of the house and away from a partner's control? Could it possibly be a deeply felt unconscious wish to feel sufficiently valued as to be held in check and owned?

The controversial side to viewing bullying through a lens of the games people play – whereby the 'injustice' a victim has to suffer is reframed to be of benefit to him or her within a close-knit relationship – will appear ridiculous to those who have campaigned long and hard to change patriarchal attitudes and the appalling social conditions for victims of violence and abuse, particularly women and children in cases of domestic violence. Indeed, Berne's work has been criticized for paying too scant attention to the social conditions that bring about such behaviour. In defence, I present the theoretical insight of the games people play as a possible lens through which bullying behaviour may be viewed, not as the only possible perspective.

Conclusion

The chart shown in Figure 5.2 may help as a shorthand reminder of different theoretical constructs that can make sense of bullying behaviour, and throughout the rest of this book the chart may serve as a quick reference to consult when reflecting on child, adolescent and adult bullying and dominant control of weaker individuals.

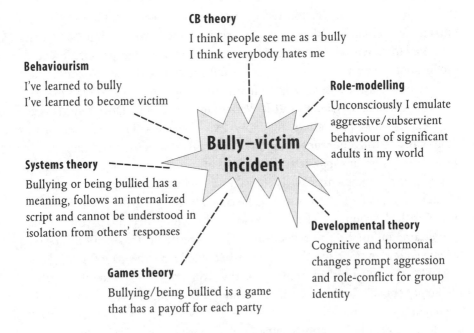

Figure 5.2 Various theoretical constructs for interpreting bullying behaviour

In summarizing the theoretical frameworks that can be used to interpret bullying behaviour, I am aware that at times the points raised and the intimations for interpreting power games will be challenging, even offensive, particularly in *Games People Play*. In defence, I have endeavoured to take a neutral and non-judgemental position and present these frameworks not as matters of fact, but as tools for understanding and reflection.

Whatever sense is made of *Games People Play* in relational battles, bullying and dominance is reciprocal behaviour where a payoff for each party is likely to be found if partners 'choose' to stay together. 'Staying' in abusive relationships through economics or fear of further harm to oneself or one's children by parting is the normal interpretation, but is the evidence for this compelling or is such reasoning a defence which is another game being played? In one sense both are acting in the drama of life, and that reducing the status for one reduces the status for the other. Whilst retaining the perspective of not painting the same picture of every bully, the following theoretical understandings are offered as presenting an account, not the explanation, of much controlling and systematic bullying behaviour.

- We learn that 'observing' bullying behaviour may not be clear-cut, particularly when what is seen may be distorted by strong feelings about a witnessed injustice.

- Learning theory shows that aggressive and controlling behaviour may not be innate but taught, that 'nature red in tooth and claw' in the struggle for social survival offers only a partial explanation of social aggression.

- From behaviourism it is learned that through conditioning behaviour is aimed for personal gain or to meet long-term goals, and in respect to interpreting bullying in relationships it may be informative to examine the potential social and psychological payoffs for each individual involved.

- Cognitive theory shows how behaviour is shaped by beliefs and cognitive constructs, and that an individual's views on the motives of others' behaviour towards them may be fantasies with no empirical basis.

- One powerful factor of learning theory is the notion that behaviour – such as aggression and domination – is imitated at an early age through role-modelling principles.

- Systemic interpretations of behaviour view it through cybernetics, which is the concept that no individual relating can be understood in any other way than how she or he relates to the whole – the family, the school, the workplace. It embraces a holistic view and sees each 'problem' as disturbing the harmony of the 'stable state'.

- Systemic theory accounts for the reciprocal and inter-reacting nature of relational battles.

- Adolescent development involves a transferred loyalty and dependence from adult (parent and teacher) to the peer group, a need to identify and belong with a group, and bullying, isolating and dominance may foster that process.

- Finally, there is the possibility that relational behaviours – including aggression, control and domination – are forms of conscious or unconscious 'games' and that all inter-relating involves a payoff for all parties.

In the following chapters, I will not draw the connection of each presented case and discourse with an explanation or an account, as though confirming any one or a group of the above theoretical interpretations. Instead, I offer an invitation to reflect on significant comments of rationalization as interviewees tell their stories. One salient feature, however, stood out for me when examining the various extracts of protagonists engaged in what was considered bullying behaviour; it was the discernible payoff for each individual involved in relational conflict, and I put this forward as a hypothesis for making sense of bullying behaviour. What is common to all theoretic insights presented above – behaviourism, cognitive theory, role-modelling, developmental tasks, systemic functioning and games people play – is that all behaviour, whether individual or relational, involves a conscious or unconscious reward or benefit, whether social or psychological.

You may be predisposed to 'look for' causes emanating from early childhood experiences (psychoanalytic theory), loss experience (attachment theory), internalized, irrational belief-systems (cognitive theory), or social conditions (social construction paradigms), but the aim of what follows is for the reader to take a step back from their own preconceptions and listen hard to the voices of the protagonists.

Chapter 6

Bullying in School

Chapters 6–9 form the heart of this book featuring the discourses of those that bully others, consciously or otherwise. Each is divided into three main sections. We consider first the general nature of the bullying context, then how it is treated by theorists and society at large, and finally we examine the discourse.

Throughout these chapters, I make such a narrow distinction between controlling, dominating and bullying that they can be considered as behaviours stemming from the same primal drive – a distinction is made in cases where a physical assault has taken place. There is a considerable difference between malicious name-calling on the one hand and murder (not manslaughter) on the other, but these may be regarded as the opposite poles of the same activity – the tormenting and humiliation of another person in order to subjugate them.

The overall emphasis in this chapter is on school bullying, where considerable research has been carried out. Over the last 20 years there have been numerous books and articles written in learned journals on the nature and characteristics of school bullying in Britain, the USA, Australia and nearly every European country, both in terms of whole-school policies to reduce bullying and in terms of listening to the voices of victims. We shall not cover the same ground in this book other than to endorse the general conclusion that in most schools one in five pupils have suffered from a broad range of bullying, and that one in ten confess in anonymous questionnaires to have actively bullied others.

Schools offer the ideal setting for bullying to occur. They are hierarchal institutions, both in terms of staffing and in pupil status, and there are power dynamics operating. Arguably, pupils recognize the power games that occur amongst staff in school and to some extent embody them, or at least reflect them, in their own interpersonal behaviour.

What commonly happens in school?

As a new intake of first-year pupils arrives at secondary school, it is possible to see almost immediately the power dynamics beginning to emerge. I ask student teachers to watch unmonitored pupil activity from a classroom window that overlooks the playground and observe the dinner queue, the jostling for position and the active demonstration of force and power. Those who have observed chickens pecking one another, and have seen how they jump and flap frantically about, how one chases a weakling into a corner, how another will persistently intimidate a youngster even when she is in retreat with blood drawn, are likely to notice similar behaviour in children approaching adolescence.

Many power games of self-assertion do not result in show-downs and fighting but are psychological battles – *see who backs down first* – to establish pre-eminence and domination. Establishing tough-hierarchies within a new social mix, where 'the hard' of one primary school meets 'the knock' of another, is part of the hidden curriculum. A few pupils relish in violence, some view it as a necessary part of their survival toolkit to avoid being 'walked over' and others despise it and view scrapping as the behaviour of morons. Much unsavoury aggression occurs in secret, in the 'no-go' areas away from adult supervision, yet other forms of violence may be open and public.

As a classroom teacher for a number of years, I experienced that unsettling feeling of dreading the 'challenging class' that is almost out of control, where name-calling has become rife and where a fight seems always on the verge of breaking out – that stressful experience of not being in control. What I noticed in that early period was the frequency in which name-calling became the pre-cursor to much violent and aggressive behaviour if not checked. But I noticed also that in some situations name-calling appeared as an acceptable form of communication and banter, not only amongst pupils with each other but between adults and between teachers and pupils, and vice versa. Curiously, in many harmless cases, it appears to serve as a means of social bonding.

There is a fine line to be drawn between the antics of youngsters teasing one another through name-calling and venomous verbal assault, a line which is easily crossed, particularly where the pupil who is teased becomes aware of being laughed at by 'everyone'. Prepubescent and adolescent youngsters are acutely self-conscious, since puberty and associated hormonal activity creates in each a sense of self that is fragile and quite insecure, an internal consciousness which leads to obsession about personal appearance and a dread of humiliation (Lines 2006a).

Some children enjoy poking fun and having a laugh at someone else's expense, but cannot take it when the tables are turned and they become the object of amusement. Their peers are very keen to point this out and see it as a matter of grave injustice if a teacher misunderstands this pattern of behaviour. Young people have a keen sense of what is reasonable, generally speaking, and know when something is fair and part of a game or a case of bullying. Another sense of resentment occurs when some children suffer at the hand of one bully and seek a senior teacher to report the matter but then are discovered to be bullying others who are weaker than them. Jordan, a 15-year-old boy that I considered to be a 'provocative victim', complained regularly of being bullied in school:

Dennis: Can you think of a specific occasion of bullying in school?

Jordan: Yes, Scott and Jacob. There was a supply teacher and they started calling me names so I started calling them back. They started pushing me around, whacking my head and punching me in the head with their sovereign rings. The teacher went into another classroom and they came back. Then I did a runner downstairs. They robbed my coat off me but I did nothing. They said that if I go to the Head of Year I'd get battered even more.

Dennis: And now that you're in Year 10 do you still have the same sort of problems?

Jordan: Nowhere near as much; I don't get bullied now.

Dennis: What has changed?

Jordan: I tend to talk to them more.

Half-way through the year a pupil of 11 years complained of Jordan bullying him, and it is not difficult to see a slight inconsistency in Jordan's account:

Dennis: Tell me about the occasion when Sebastian, the young Year 7 boy, had accused you of bullying him.

Jordan: He told his sister that I pinned him up the wall and strangled him. Apparently I came outside and saw Sebastian and threatened him that I was going to get his sister beaten up by my girlfriend, and then she and all her friends came over and grabbed me, strangled me by my tie, pushed me down the stairs, and then this girl sorted them out, and I think she's in Year 7 or 8. She's only having a go at me because I used to wag with him and she thinks I used to get him to wag it from school, but he used to ask me to wag it with him. He's told his sister in the past that I used to make him wag, and I've got witnesses that can prove that he's asked me to wag with him.

Jordan was a little immature, had poor social skills, was bossy with much younger boys and was resented by his year-group for 'whingeing at the slightest thing'.

Although research estimates differ marginally from country to country, the general results suggest that bullying occurs in all schools to the degree of one in ten youngsters being a 'bully' and two in ten feeling 'bullied'. Research suggests that 'schools do make a difference', that bullying is reduced if the profile of its importance is kept high, but that figures and thresholds of bullying depend on definitions and how it is understood. It never ceases to amaze me how gossip rapidly spreads around the school, particularly with identified or targeted individuals – 'everyone' knows who is tough, who is weak, who has just got beaten up, who has just hit whom!

Apart from aggressive bullying, subtle forms can occur in some apparently rigidly controlled environments, such as in class with a strict teacher where one individual can with the slightest hand gesture or facial grimace give coded signals to others across the classroom that they may get beaten up after school, and it takes a very astute and informed teacher to pick up the signs and stem the problem at source. Technology has provided a less direct and more insidious means of bullying in and out of school through the use of mobile phones and the internet. Let us now look at how bullying is made sense of by professionals and researchers, and by pupils, teachers and parents.

Making sense of school bullying

There is now considerable insight into bullying behaviour, ranging from the early work of Dan Olweus in Scandinavia to the comprehensive writings of Ken Rigby (see e.g. Rigby 2002), together with an imaginative means of dealing with the issue in school – for an up-to-date treatment see Evelyn Field's (2007) work on Bully Blocking. I have summarized research carried out nationally and internationally elsewhere (Lines 1996, 1999, 2006a).

Cussing and name-calling

A cohort of 241 first-year secondary pupils completed an anonymous questionnaire, one section of which asked them to recall abusive terms they had been called throughout the year and record them on a grid. The frequency of each term of abuse was represented on a bar chart (Figure 6.1).

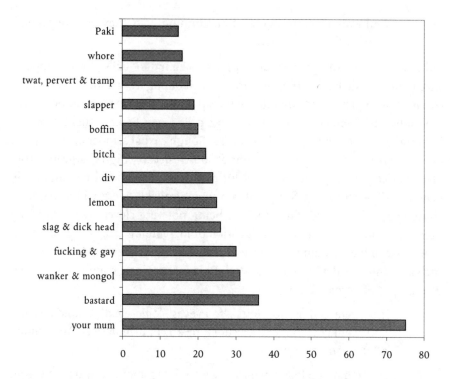

Figure 6.1 Chart showing how many pupils of a year group (241) had been called the most common terms of abuse (each term represented as a percentage of the cohort)

Some terms – such as anything to do with 'mother' or family members – appeared to have had a universal degree of insult, and this characteristic compares with other studies. In the UK, in areas where a high number of children live in single parent (usually mothers) households, there is a tendency to insult, or to have fun at the expense of, peers by denigrating the loved adult on whom the child is dependent, such as 'Your mum's a whore', or 'Your dad's a pervert'. But so sophisticated have young people become in secondary school that the comment of 'Your mum' has become a commonly recognized short-hand form of abuse that is registered by all the group – the hearer, for whom the insult is intended, must fill in the rest from a destructive imagination or known gossip:

> *Amanda*: I know people who have bullied me. I know people who have bullied my friends, my family and I hate it when people criticize your family because your family aren't even there to defend themselves.

> And even though they've done nothing, like, they go 'Your mum',
> which I think is terrible.

Other terms were idiosyncratic and applied to an individual's physical appearance (being small, having big ears), to dialect (coming from another part of the country) or to publicized community gossip (father known to be in prison for molesting children). Boys loathed being called gay or equivalent terms of homosexual stereotyping, and it seems as though sexual slander at the time of puberty is really insulting. Racial terms of abuse can carry high charge in particular districts, although it had very little effect in my school community in general. What terms did fire pupils up uncontrollably were verbal terms of abuse which denigrated individuals as being not very clever – such as being 'thick', 'stupid' or a mongol (a designation of low intelligence) – together with terms that suggest a family was of low income for not dressing fashionably – such as being called a 'tramp' or a 'stig'. Below I provide a couple of examples of this type of verbal abuse:

> *Glen*: They were saying 'frog-eyes', 'four-eyes', 'ogle-eyed', 'stupid bastard' and 'wanker'. 'Your dad's a cunt'; 'he's a child-molester'. 'Your mum's a bitch' and everything.
>
> *Dennis*: How did you feel when they were talking about your dad and your mum that way?
>
> *Glen*: Erm, I was upset, I was crying. So I went into the school toilets, washed my face, came out and they started hitting me.
>
> *Nick*: In maths mainly these kids started calling me 'fox' [*from having a long, pointed nose*], and I didn't like it. So I started like getting upset and then doing silly things [*intake of breath*].

There are cases where teachers and parents over-react to incidents of name-calling and light-touch bullying when the motives are merely fun-loving. Naturally, some pupils use this as an excuse to justify unnecessary and over-reactive physical abuse.

Reporting bullying

Analysing the discourse of a few pupils suggested that their strategies of coping with verbal onslaught, or their decision to report physical abuse to a teacher or parent or friend, appeared to have been based on previous primary school experience. It seemed that if a pupil had disclosed he or she was being bullied or severely attacked and it achieved a favourable outcome, then the young person had confidence to report further bullying to someone in authority. If this was not the pupil's experience, there was little confidence that reporting would bring a favourable outcome. Here is an example of an 11-year-old 'provocative victim' who was suffering continual torment but who felt from his experience that reporting was pointless:

> *Gordon*: I used to get pushed away, pushed around in junior school and when people used to have a go at me, like, in a classroom when I told someone to leave me alone, the teacher used to tell me off for it...sent me out the classroom. I turned around and this one kid I hit in class was sent to the headmaster and the headmaster had a go at me and said, 'What did you do it for?' I said, 'Because he kept getting on my nerves and wouldn't leave me alone.' So the teacher said, 'You've got a letter going home saying the next time you hit someone you'll get excluded. You won't be coming back to this school.' From then I just kept bottling it up and just let people hit me.

Photo 6.1 Reporting to teachers for having been bullied is a risky business

Many prepubescent and adolescent pupils find reporting bullying highly problematic. Even those pupils who might not be referred to as 'provocative victims' will fear, and often experience, reprisals for having done so. As pupils mature and pass through the school there is an unwritten expectation that they should handle teasing and low-level mockery themselves and not report matters to their teachers and parents. 'Why did you grass me up?' they often say – through words, gestures or 'digs' (a thump in the arm or back, tripping up, etc.) in unmonitored locations. Some streetwise bullies capitalize on this fear and deliver further threats or get someone else unknown to the victim to execute vengeance for having broken peer-group codes.

Provocative victims

When listening to the voices of a small but not insignificant subgroup of pupils who were persistently called names and bullied physically, it appeared as though they were so poor at relating and making friends that, whatever they did, matters grew worse. Anatol Pikas (1989) referred to such people as 'provocative victims'. Putting aside young people with communication and cognitive disorders, there are some who irritate both adults and peers alike for a reaction. They seem difficult to satisfy, become drawn into endless squabbles and expect adult managers always to side with them when disagreements arise. They are so regularly moody that they become unattractive to be with. In consequence, they 'force their friendship' onto unwilling parties, fail to pick up social cues and appear unable to read rejection, or at least become so immune to it that their behaviour remains unaffected despite being pushed away – it is a defence, of course. They are hurt but have not the faintest idea of how to become wanted and likeable. They appear to have a 'death wish', sometimes buy their friendships, or have masochistic tendencies to appear tougher than they actually are. They normally befriend younger children whose maturity level matches their own, becoming gang leaders of much younger and equally isolated individuals as themselves.

I am not saying they are wholly to blame, but I am acknowledging that provocative victims are a regular management problem for teachers in school. Some enjoy being chased and will often call names and tease others who are bigger and more powerful than they are and run away – 'having a leg', as they say. Adolescence is a fun-loving period and playing tricks is part of a young person's jovial spirit and gamesmanship, but for these victims testing behaviour often backfires. It is claimed 'they deserve to be bullied' and tougher characters will single them out when they are found bullying their subordinates. Provocative victims abuse their power with the powerless yet consistently get beaten up themselves. When we listen to their sad stories, it seems as though they have very little self-awareness of what part they are playing that exacerbates their difficulties or makes them so unpopular.

Aggressive bullying

There are pupils who 'appear' predisposed to violence, and this suggests that aggression is endorsed or successfully modelled in the home or in the community (see Chapter 5). When it comes to physical bullying, we must first distinguish between fights and physical assault, the former being an aggressive activity involving two individuals where there is no power differential and 'consenting' combat. When youngsters are physically assaulted in school, there is no option but to take the matter very seriously and have very clear sanctions for the school to indicate that such behaviour is clearly wrong and unacceptable. There is little point in elaborating further on this point.

A few parents bring up their children to *look after themselves* through physically aggressive means if they live in a volatile and threatening neighbourhood (Lines 2007). They are encouraged to sort matters out themselves, not through teachers. There then occurs a clash in cultures because the school does not advocate aggressive stances, either as a defence or merely as a means of showing power. It is in cases like these that parents have to engage in dialogue with the school as much as with their offspring. Some youngsters will be in denial of the extent of damage they can inflict on others, and often parents will support their reasoning, but it is essential for the school to understand its role within the community as setting higher moral standards than those which exist on the street or in some dysfunctional and deprived homes. Educationalists cannot shirk from teaching how youngsters might live more harmonious lifestyles with those they may not like or get on with (Goleman 2006).

Some boys, particularly, enjoy rough-play, and through the guise of 'having a laugh' are really attempting to show off their power and humiliate a more reserved and weaker individual. But there are also cases where an observing teacher is too quick to form a judgement that bullying has taken place, when this is neither the motive of the so-called bully nor what is understood by the so-called victim. Those teachers and senior staff who are skilled at looking at the full picture can readily form an accurate judgement.

Photo 6.2 Distinguishing between bullying and horseplay is not always easy, and errors of discretion can arise when teachers fail to see the full picture or if they make snap judgements without consulting all involved parties

Subtle bullying through technology

In these days of advanced technology, pupils spend considerable time speaking with each other on mobile phones and conversing with their friends through internet chat-lines. Bullying, too, has become a much more sophisticated affair. Even cyber-bullying of teachers and created images of them in compromised and indecent situations of humiliation have been posted on some unmonitored sites. It is amazing what power can be wielded through a text and image message.

There are many examples of things beginning as fun-loving ending up as serious torment even though it was never intended to go so far. This occurs quite frequently when youngsters pass on confidential sensitive material through text messaging and chat-lines, only to find that somebody else has passed it on with the intention of humiliating them through making it public. Embarrassing photo images, for example, can be passed around on mobile phones against the wishes of the subject for no other reason than to have a laugh. In recent times some youngsters have enjoyed a perverted and voyeuristic pleasure in recording bullying incidents on mobile phones, such as 'happy-slapping', and recording occasions where innocent victims have been severely beaten up.

Photo 6.3 Bullying on the internet and through use of modern technology has become a sophisticated affair

Victim becomes bully

Below is the voice of one 15-year-old victim who later was accused of being a bully.

Dennis: Am I right in thinking you have been bullied?

Joanne: Yeah. It was like a setup because I was accused of saying something that I didn't say because I wasn't even there. This girl called Annie who used to be a friend of mine apparently wanted to fight me.

Dennis: And what happened to make you think that Annie wanted a fight?

Joanne: My step-mum went up to her dad's and something happened between her son and Annie's brother, Jason. So my step-mum went round to Annie's house and had it out with Annie's mum. And apparently my step-mum said to Annie's mum, 'Well, it's alright because Joanne's going to batter Annie anyway.' And this story that I was supposed to bang Annie went all around our area. But it had nothing to do with me. I said nothing.

Dennis: What was the point of her saying that, Joanne?

Joanne: That was the problem, there was no point.

Dennis: It doesn't sound very helpful, because Annie would have picked up a message from her mum that you were out to batter her.

Joanne: Mm.

Dennis: It's hard to see what your step-mum was trying to do.

Joanne: The problem was that my step-brother tends to pick on Jason, and Jason had a go back at him and beat him up. But then my step-mum rings me up when I was in town and asked me what she should do. I didn't know what to say because I was in town. I just said, 'Why don't you go round and talk to Jason's mum?' And that's what she did, but she made matters worse by getting me involved.

Dennis: So in supporting her son, she went to Annie's house and her way of dealing with the problem was to say that her step-daughter, Joanne, was going to fight Annie.

Joanne: Yeah, that was it. Then Annie comes into school thinking I'm out to bang her. Annie gets a whole crowd together and meets me in the playground and said, 'Do you want to fight?' And I said, 'No. I've got nothing against you.' And then she said, 'That's what your mum said.' I said, 'That's not my mum, and I didn't say that,' because I know I hadn't. I told my Head of Year about it and he said that the best thing you can do is to stay away from each other. So I stayed with my form tutor during the lunch break and they knew that I had stayed with her because it was all around the school, and there was a whole group of them.

Dennis: How many were there?

Joanne: About twenty of them.

Dennis: And they were hunting you?

Joanne: Yeah, and in between lessons they caught up with me. I ran into a classroom that was open and got away from them that day. But then the next day I looked behind me along the corridor and I heard lots of people running. Then someone grabbed my arm and they all surrounded me and were stopping me. And Annie said, 'Don't ever give me that backchat or say anything about me again.' And then I got battered. And when I looked again she'd gone.

Dennis: And how are things between you now?

Joanne: We're not friends, but we're OK now.

There is no need for commentary on this transcript – the poor judgement of an adult exasperates a youngster's peer relations in a different, unmonitored place. What is of interest is how Joanne later becomes accused of being a bully.

Voices of school bullies

Here is Annie's version of the above incident and her rationalization:

Annie: I was in my house and my mum said to me, 'Do you know Joanne Lewis?' I said, 'She goes to my school, why?' She says, 'You know her granddad up the road, apparently she's going to batter you, he told me.' This was because, apparently, he'd said something to Jason and Jason had thrown a water balloon at him. So they came down to mine and spoke to my step-dad about something. In the end it all ended up with arguing and he went home and mum just said, 'She's out to get you.'

Dennis: Was the arguing at the doorstep when you weren't there?

Annie: I wasn't there. I just got dragged into it because of what he said.

Dennis: So as far as you know, was it her mum or granddad that was at your house?

Annie: It was just her granddad, because he lives up the road from me.

Dennis: Do you know of him?

Annie: Yeah, he's OK. I get on with him.

Dennis: So what sort of message did you understand was coming from him?

Annie: That Joanne was, apparently, going to batter me.

Dennis: How did it move on from there?

Annie: I went to school the next day, and I saw Joanne and I was asking her about it. She said to me 'What are you on about?' and all this stuff. That's what she's like. She goes, like, sarcastically, and cheekily, 'I don't know what you're on about.'

Dennis: Could you unpack that for me? What do you mean exactly?

Annie: Like she's saying, as if, like, she's got an attitude to it, like she's got an attitude in everything she's saying, like, as if she's got an attitude.

Dennis: But how would she be saying that? How would it come over?

Annie: I don't know. 'What are you asking me for?' [*expressed sarcastically*] Like that; bitchy and stuff. So anyway, I tried speaking to her the next day and all she done was ran, she ran into classrooms.

Dennis: OK, I understand that.

Annie: So I said, 'Joanne, why do you keep running away from me? Come out of the classroom. All I want to do is talk. I don't want to start anything. I just want to talk to you.' Then – I think it was the next day – I was talking to her and she said something to me and she was down by the Lower School corridor, and she said something to me and I just hit her. I don't know why. I didn't think. I just hit her, innit?

Dennis: Mm, were you on your own or with a group?

Annie: She was with Charlotte, and I was with Lorna.

Dennis: Were there any other kids stirring trouble?

Annie: There was a bunch of other kids who kept running but that was afterwards. But I said, 'Just go back, just go back.' I didn't want trouble. Forget it.

Dennis: Mm, did you hit her a couple of times?

Annie: No, just once. Then she reported it to a senior teacher and I was excluded.

Dennis: How is the situation between you and her now?

Annie: Yeah, it's fine now.

Dennis: One final thing. How do you think Joanne is viewed by most of the kids in her year group?

Annie: Bitchy, she's got an attitude problem. Thinks she's good, and all that. She's not really all that bad when you get to know her, and all that stuff.

Dennis: But what is this bitchiness like when it's at its worst?

Annie: Like starting arguments, and all that, like, immature, say, if she don't get her own way. Say she wanted to go somewhere with her friend, and her friend didn't want to go, she would expect her to go, in a bossy sense. She's a bossy person. If someone didn't want to do what she wanted to do, she'd gossip about them, run them down.

Dennis: Are there lots of kids who seriously dislike her?

Annie: Not so much now, I think we've all grown up now that we are in Year 10. But before she could be a bully, and she used to get Nikki in the alley, and all that when no one was around. Then she'd deny it.

Dennis: Would you see her as a bully or a victim?

Annie: Neither really, a bit of both really, I don't know.

Comparing the narratives of Annie and Joanne over the same incident reveals some interesting points. A number of discrepancies occur and in resolving these disputes in the school senior teachers are often confronted with deciding whose version of events should be believed. Since neither Annie nor Joanne was present during the initiating home visit, neither version could be verified without further investigation. Was it Joanne's step-mother who visited Annie's home or her grandfather, or both? Was the original trigger something that happened against Joanne's step-mother's son or her father? When Joanne was finally assaulted were there just four people present or a large crowd? Was Joanne only hit once or several times? Was Annie's genuine motive one of merely talking with Joanne or was she driven to uphold her – 'so you want to batter me' – self-image by a larger group? Was she acting as an ambassador of the year group against the demonized and unpopular person who was 'cheeky' with 'attitude' and who bullies others? Was Nikki really bullied in the alley according to neighbourhood gossip? These kinds of entangled questions illustrate the complexity of making sense of events which culminate in school bullying.

But there are other issues when interviewing characters like Joanne and Annie, as Michael Toolan (1988) highlights, which centre upon how respondents wish to be viewed by 'significant persons' and how they give supposed 'correct' answers to questions. For example, how is each respondent's discourse fashioned to elicit my approval, as the counsellor-interviewer? Note, for example, how Annie saw good in Joanne towards the end of the discourse. Note, also, how she seemed to interpret her own behaviour as wrong – 'I don't know why. I didn't think. I just hit her.' When I invited her to amplify Joanne's bitchiness she complied but qualified her sentiments, and could not decide whether her adversary should be labelled as a 'victim' or a 'bully', or both, or neither.

Caught out by technology

Let us now return to Joanne's narrative.

Dennis: The tables seem to have turned because now you're being accused of being a bully, is that right?

Joanne: Yeah.

Dennis: How did that come about?

Joanne: Half-way through Year 7, me and Nikki had a big fall-out. When somebody falls out with someone else sometimes a big group will back up the one who they think is having a hard time and support them.

Dennis: So did they see Nikki as a victim?

Joanne: Yeah. I wanted to be her friend, but she's always the one that causes the upset – she goes moody. You see, she's the one that kept sending me messages and going on MSN and saying that I have hit her and all that, and this ended up with fighting. And she said, 'Now you've got everybody involved haven't you?' But that wasn't true, it was just me and Nikki that had a disagreement, but they think because I'm bigger than Nikki they should support her.

Dennis: So that's led to a fight between you and Nikki?

Joanne: Yeah, there's been several.

Dennis: How many about?

Joanne: About ten.

Dennis: Ten!

Joanne: Yeah, literally.

Dennis: And when you say a fight do you mean nasty things like pulling hair and kicking?

Joanne: Yeah.

Dennis: In school or out of school?

Joanne: There's been about four in school. The worst one was in the changing room when Carol [*a pupil who was tough but later excluded*] was in school and Nikki got her to have a go at me. I walked into the changing rooms and she said, 'You can't touch me now, can you?' She came up to me and kicked me, so I turned around and pushed her against a wall and I thought we were the only two in there. But as I pushed her she fell against the bench, then she got up and started kicking me and the teacher walked in and stopped us and she said, 'Who started this?' And then some girls said it was me, when that wasn't true. It was Nikki.

Dennis: Do you feel that because she has the back-up of Carol that she can take advantage by kicking you?

Joanne: Yeah, and she thinks she can take advantage because her brother is a teacher in the school.

Dennis: You're saying that she feels that she is special because her brother works in the school?

Joanne: Yeah. After the fight we was in the Head of Year's office and my mum noticed that he was on the side of this other teacher who's Nikki's brother. When I was excluded for three days, Nikki's brother was in the meeting with my Head of Year and my mum, and he said that I should learn to control my temper. But he also said that some action will have to be taken against Nikki. But then the next day he told me there was nothing to be done about Nikki. He said he'd have a word with her to ease off and that's all that happened. Me and my mum don't think it was fair because she started it. Because my mum says, at the end of the day it takes two to tango not just one.

Dennis: I'm interested in why the group always sides with Nikki.

Joanne: It's because she's small.

Dennis: Is it all about size then?

Joanne: Some people put it down to that, yet they always think that I start it. You see, Nikki is very good on the computer. She writes all these messages against me and draws me into writing things about her, but she has a way of deleting what she first says and then posts it off to other people and they all think it's me who is the bad one, when that's not true. It's just that she's better on MSN than I am and I don't know how to edit things out. I don't know how to do it. She can go up to anybody and say I've said something about them when it isn't true and some of these kids will just believe Nikki.

Dennis: That's quite manipulative in a way, isn't it?

Joanne: Yeah.

Dennis: And that sets the group against you?

Joanne: Yeah.

Dennis: But why is she so against you anyway?

This extract shows what a powerful tool of communication (miscommunication) computer chat-lines and phone text messaging has become in recent years, and many youngsters utilize the technology for abusive treatment to powerful effect. Joanne's plight is pretty hopeless since all the cards are stacked against her – Nikki, her adversary, is small and can invoke group sympathy, her brother is a teacher at the same school, a menacing character backs her case and she has a better mastery of technology than Joanne. This transcript begs a further tantalizing question however – Why is the group so against her? – which might account for Annie's summoning of the troops for gang bullying.

Threat of the group

Let us now look at a transcript of a group of youngsters identified by school senior staff as 'bullies', and who as individuals have been excluded several times for fighting and bullying. To help gain insight into their relational world, we first examine an incident of group bullying behaviour.

Jack: Remember the time when we all battered Lester and got excluded, put him on the floor, and he got his big sister to come up the school?

Larry: Oh yeah, I remember.

Nicole: Oh, yeah. The one with purple hair. But Lester went crying. It was all a play-fight at first, wasn't it?

Jack: We were all play-fighting yeah, and then Jez came running down to just mess about and then he – I don't think he really done anything to his head. I think he kicked him.

Dennis: So why did his sister come to sort you out, Jack?

Jack: Because I was the main one, but we were just play-fighting.

Dennis: But wasn't Jez the one who kicked him?

Nicole: Yeah, you were just play-fighting though, but then it turned into a real fight.

Jack: No, not a real fight. We were just play-fighting. Then after that he just went off crying.

Dennis: Did he see it as the group being against him?

Jack: He knew we were joking, though. He just wanted something done about it…

Dennis: Have there been other times when you in a group have bullied an individual?

Nicole: What about you, Sharon, with Alison?

Sharon: But I didn't get excluded, I just had to go into isolation.

Nicole: We're on about when you come up to the school to batter Alison and everyone followed and…

Sharon: No.

Dennis: What would she have thought if you came with a group?

Sharon: But I didn't come to batter Alison. She was giving cheek to Natalie, and Alison was going to have a fight on her and we all got on the bus, but she wasn't on the bus and we were all going up to town and we stopped by that shop, didn't we, and we all jumped off at the bus stop because she was there. But she wouldn't come out the bus stop because Natalie was going to batter her. And there was this little girl at the bus stop who was scared because Alison just stood by her, so she got dragged out and battered because the little girl was scared…

Nicole: And you got arrested.

Jack: Did she press charges?

Sharon: Yeah.

Jack: So when do you have to go to court?

Sharon: I don't know, because I was waiting in the back of the police van to see whether she would say 'yes' or 'no', but she wouldn't say anything. She chats shit, because she said she wasn't going to press charges.

Pupils 'giving cheek' or 'chatting shit' appears to enflame some to become violent, whilst others seek justification by minimizing 'play-fighting', which occasionally spills over into violence and retribution when a competitor 'becomes victim' through humiliation and ridicule, and family members can often make matters worse as we have seen. Individuals within large groups have also been known to bully teachers.

Bullied teachers

Dennis: Have any of you been excluded at any time and felt it was unfair?

Nicole: Yes, when me, Rachael and Linda bullied Mr Gutteridge.

Dennis: Would you share that with us?

Jack: Yeah, I remember that.

Nicole: Do you remember that, when he took Rachael's phone off her and basically the whole school set against him?

Jack: Yeah, when you pushed me into him, Larry [*laughing*].

Larry: No [*look of guilt*].

Nicole: When we wouldn't let him into school.

Dennis: You mean he confiscated somebody's mobile phone?

Nicole: Yeah, her brother was in hospital and her mother needed to get in touch with her. And then he took it off her and then the whole school wouldn't let him into the building. The school run in front of him and wouldn't let him through the doors. And he got bullied and terrorized and things were taken out of his pockets.

Dennis: Did her brother have a motorcycle accident?

Jack: Yeah. Ryan was her brother.

Nicole: He was in hospital. It was Ryan Jackson.

Dennis: Why were you accused of bullying, Jack? You weren't excluded for that were you?

Jack: No.

Nicole: No, it was me, Linda and Rachael.

Dennis: So what did you do, just challenge him for the mobile phone?

Nicole: The whole school got involved. Well, obviously not the whole school. They all joined in; wouldn't let him come into the school because there were so many people around him and we were taking things out of his pockets and he didn't realize it.

Dennis: What was the real problem? That he wasn't listening to Rachael?

Nicole: It was the break time and you're allowed to have your phones out at break.

Dennis: So he took her phone from her during break and there was a sense of injustice felt?

Nicole: Yeah, mm.

Dennis: Well, how did you get away with that, Jack, if you were pushed into Mr Gutteridge?

Jack: It was Larry who pushed me – about four times it was.

Larry: Oh yeah, I remember that.

Jack: I wasn't excluded, because there was this girl and she said, 'No, he was pushed into Mr Gutteridge', and then they just believed me.

Pupils will turn on teachers they perceive as being unfair or inflexible over school rules, whereas teachers often aim for 'consistency' (a woolly term – see Lines 2003) in their management of pupils. In this case, the teacher was seriously harassed and assaulted when he felt he was conscientiously 'enforcing the school rule'. The wild marauding group have a different design – *get the phone back by any means* – since they operate (or justify their attack) from a 'humane' motive of a mother's need to contact her daughter about a serious motorcycle accident out of school.

Fighting or bullying?

Dennis: Why do you think your fight was viewed as bullying?

Jack: It's because when I fight I don't want to get hurt and I've been taught to wade in hard – get the punches in fast before they know what's happening. I go straight for the face. The trouble is that when the fight is over teachers always blame the one who comes off best. I didn't start the fight and didn't even want it. Sam came to me and went for it, but because he gets battered with blood all over his face I get done. I get excluded for 'bullying' and nothing happens to him.

Bullying or not bullying, was Jack predisposed to fight his way out of trouble from highly influential family members? Goleman (2006) makes a point, which I have often witnessed in boys like Jack, that there is a perceptual flaw with many children who turn out to be bullies, in that they imagine their peers to be more hostile towards them than they actually are.

This leads them to misperceive neutral acts as threatening ones – an innocent bump is seen as a vendetta – and to attack in return. That, of course, leads other children to shun them, isolating them further. Such angry, isolated children are highly sensitive to injustices and being treated unfairly. They typically see themselves as victims and can recite a list of instances when, say, teachers blamed them for doing something when in fact they were innocent. Another trait of such children is that once they are in the heat of anger they can think of only one way to react: by lashing out. (Goleman 2006, p.235)

I observed Jack in a fight once, which was stirred by Nicole, and it was not a pleasant sight, but what interests me in the narratives related above is that the same names keep cropping up in my counselling work with pupils in school – teachers as well as pupil-victims. I have lost count of the number of occasions that Sam crops up as 'a victim' whom so many want to batter, and that goes for Alison and Joanne cited above. When asked why this is, the reply is often *because they're cheeky*. As mentioned earlier, these young people are known as 'provocative victims' who are so devoid of social skills that they 'appear' to relish masochistic behaviour and operate in a self-destructive mode in a reciprocal dance of bully–victim pathology.

Why are 'provocative victims' bullied?

I counselled Sam once on developing more pro-social behaviour when he kept asking peers to punch him as hard as they could in the stomach as he braced himself to prove his masculinity. He listened and reflected on the question of why it was always him that suffered abuse. An established teacher told me that his dad was the same when he taught him. On leaving my room he called out to three unknown sixth-formers, 'You wankers', for no obvious reason but for a reaction and 'to be legged' (chased along the corridor). Alison and Joanne have developed similar reputations around the school for being 'gobby' and 'giving it shit' and for spreading gossip indiscriminately. This came up in the group interview.

Dennis: Do you think there are some characters that 'invite' others to bully them?

Nicole: Yeah, Joanne Lewis.

Jack: Yeah, I do – Sam Brotherton. You know what – this was just recently – because obviously he's weaker than me.

Larry: Oh just listen to him [*mocking*].

Jack: I said, 'Pass us that pencil.' And he said, 'No, I can't.' I said, 'Why not? They're right by you.' He said, 'Get it yourself.' And you know what? You know when you start getting that buzz, like, trying to fight everyone and that.

Larry: Mm.

Jack: Then I thought, 'No way man.' I just got up and threw him against the wall and kneed him in the privates and all that and he just…

Dennis: But Sam found some confidence when he started going around with Liam.

Larry: Yeah, yeah, that's it, Liam McCartney. He thinks he's the top boy as well. He thinks he's the top boy, he does.

Dennis: Do you think Sam became cocky because Liam would back him up?

Jack: No, no. This is what it was like, because I heard him say it, 'I'm not going to back your case, you just got to learn to stick up for yourself.'

Larry: And he interpreted it the wrong way.

Jack: Yeah, yeah, he thought he had to start doing it right away.

Larry: Yeah, he started trying it, and he knocked out Colin.

Jack: And just after he'd knocked out Colin he thought he was hard, but then what's Colin really?

In Jordan's case (cited earlier), being bullied ceased because he tended to 'talk to them more. I talk to Jacob, Kyle, when he's here, Jack; everybody who used to bully me':

Dennis: So there's no hostility with them now?

Jordan: No.

Dennis: So you get on better with those ex-bullies because you talk with them and you don't need the teacher to sort things out any more?

There is little doubt that peer conflicts in class are further manifestations of sibling rivalries of home, and that some testing behaviour for teachers may be an indicator of unresolved parenting anxieties (Luxmoore 2006). Clearly, Jordan was smart enough to see links with his behaviour in school with those which had been honed in the family:

Dennis: Over the period I've known you you've had mixed feelings about home, haven't you? At times you've felt supported at home and sometimes you've got into scrapes with your older brother and...

Jordan: That's because I wind him up. Because I wind him up, and because I used to wind up people in this school and got used to it. I used to wind him up. Like my little brother, but he doesn't stand it no more. I used to wind him up.

Dennis: So there's a pattern there – you wind up pupils in school and you wind up your brothers.

Jordan: And my sister.

Dennis: And your sister? Can you get them wound up easily?

Jordan: Yeah.

Dennis: What sort of things can you do to your brothers and sister that you know will irritate them?

Jordan: I don't do this, but I got into my big brother's bedroom – he doesn't like anybody in his bedroom. My big brother is twenty, I think, and he doesn't like me going into his bedroom. My little brother, I mess with his PC stuff, and he doesn't like me messing with his PC stuff, and my sister doesn't like me messing with anything of hers. It's all because I get fed up with my stuff because it's all boring. Because I have used them and then get fed up with them so I chuck them.

Dennis: Do you not think that is unreasonable on your part?

Jordan: Yeah, because they don't mess with my stuff.

Dennis: Do you feel they have better stuff than yours?

Jordan: No, not better stuff, it's just that I mess up my stuff easily. Like my shoes. I've had four pairs since September [*four months ago*].

Dennis: Why is that?

Jordan: Because in September I had PE and then lost them and then mum got me some more. I wrecked them and then I had some for my birthday and I wrecked them. Then my last school shoes, my football went on top of the shed and I climbed up and jumped down and wrecked them – the soles fell off.

Dennis: If I were talking to your mother now, what do you think she would say?

Jordan: Probably the same. With my brothers and sisters I wind them up so much that my mum has to come into the middle of it. I don't give it as much now because I am never in the house.

It seems that 'any attention' is preferable to 'no attention at all', and whilst weak social skills may account for Jordan's victimization, there may be other more developmental factors underlying the targeting of abuse. 'Provocative victims' may unconsciously present themselves as 'sacrificial' gifts to abusers in a vain attempt to win their approval or reprieve, or may consciously emulate the behaviour of the dominant characters of the group in a futile wish to raise their own status in the eyes of significant characters. But it could also indicate that they had suffered physical abuse when young and the unconscious purpose for continually putting themselves in similar situations that enact the same drama is to hope to bring about a different sequel, to reconfigure their worldview and self-construct of being always the one everyone batters (James 2003).

Beliefs about aggression and bullying

I was attempting to draw from the group the beliefs by which they made sense of their relational world to try and assess how they had been brought up to view aggression, and apart from cultural 'norms' like *boys shouldn't hit girls* and *don't let the bastards walk all over you*, some interesting perspectives came to light.

Dennis: What do you believe about the need to fight?

Nicole: I believe that if you're big enough to give that attitude and cheek people you must be big enough to get it back.

Jack: I just know that I am going to get banged one day.

Nicole: People all say to me, as well, you're going to get battered one day because you're always giving it cheek. And one day you're going to give it to the wrong person. My mum always says it as well. I'll get battered one day.

Dennis: And you don't mind?

Nicole: Obviously I do mind that but...

Jack: You don't think like that at the time when you're bullying them.

Nicole: When you're bullying them you go blank, yet you don't realize what you're doing.

Jack: And then if you think about it, yeah, if it was to happen to you, you don't realize it but you wouldn't like it. You would hate it.

Nicole: Obviously you'd stick up for yourself. That's what I don't understand about people that get bullied.

Sharon: They're scared?

Nicole: Yeah, but they don't like being bullied, but they go around acting hard but don't like being bullied, if you get what I mean.

Larry: They bully others, say...

Nicole: It's like a chain.

Larry: Like, if I was to bully you now, yeah [*Larry looks at me*], and you feel, like, inferior. You're not big enough, you're not strong enough, and then you go and bully someone else who is weaker than you.

Dennis: Would you though?

Larry: I would, yeah.

It was interesting that Nicole was self-aware of being cheeky, an attitude she deplored in others and over which she justified her bullying behaviour. Jack similarly believed some fearful retribution awaited him, and the following discourse intimates the human equivalent in hierarchical human behaviour of chicken pecking-orders, but then something different was hinted at.

Dennis: So for you to deal with bullying and feel better you'd have to intimidate somebody else?

Larry: Yes that's what Sam Brotherton does, innit? He's scared of Jack, so he obviously isn't going to bully Jack because, obviously, he can't beat Jack. He'll bully another person... If we're all friends, like, and we were all ganging up against Jack and he is starting to think, 'I don't want to be here.'

Dennis: But would that make Jack go and find Colin and give him a beating?

Jack: No, I wouldn't find Colin because I know how weak he is…

Larry: Say if I was to bully Sam Brotherton now, then he couldn't do anything about it but he would go on to batter Joshua Holsley.

Nicole: Joshua Holsley! [*mocking*]

Larry: Because he couldn't do it to no one harder than him because he knows he would get knocked out.

There is a suggestion here (confirmed after the interview) that if a victim is intimidated and laughed at, in order to discharge anger he will take it out on someone weaker *but not much weaker* than himself. He must select one who is not a wimp, because there is no 'street-credibility' in beating a defenceless victim as there would in taking on one who in the eyes of the group is high (perhaps, higher than him) on the scale of being tough. I challenged this view in session, which met Nicole's agreement, but on reflection I wonder whether the power dynamics had something to do with group acknowledgement of an 'acceptable reaction' in the event of shame and ridicule.

Dennis: You're almost saying that there is a law in human nature that says if someone takes it out of you, you have to take it out on somebody else.

Larry: Not always, but generally that's what happens.

Dennis: But people take it out on themselves, surely, when they're angry, or somebody close to them – punch a wall or kick a door, or have a go at their mother?

Jack: That's if there's no one there, and they just can't fight back.

Nicole: That's what I do. If somebody has a go at me and I get into the car I take it out on my mum, which is not fair because she wasn't there, and I'd take it out on Barry, but I don't care about Barry. One day I will stab him because he tries to be my dad, but you take it out on someone to stop you getting all stressed up.

Concluding comment

In making a concluding comment, I am not wishing to override the genuine voices of school bullies themselves, but to point out some observations having become immersed in the various interview material. One important question is: Why are some individuals universally viewed by the school as more popular than others? It seems that at the lower end of secondary school popularity and being dominant (Darwinian principle?) are subtly connected – personality and attractiveness are not the sole determinants, as may be the case with older adolescents and adults.

There is no consistency in the accounts of bullies over justifying their actions through reasoning that the victim was 'being cheeky', since the bullies themselves acknowledge that they are cheeky also. The bullies at times illustrated a sense of empathy for their victims, which whilst it did not check their behaviour towards them it left them bewildered as to why their victims might go on to bully weaker pupils than them – as though victims should empathize but bullies do not have to. Maturity and having strong egos undoubtedly affects popularity, but are they the only characteristics?

Being humiliated and laughed at was clearly upsetting for prepubescent youngsters and adolescents, since puberty is a very sensitive period of development. Role-modelling behaviour of aggressive individuals appears only to be in check if the school has a more powerful management regime of control and order. Yet, even so, in examining the behaviour of 'provocative victims', and other characters who are tough and who become humiliated by the dominant group through teasing (say, by being beaten up by someone weak), there is a hint that the humiliated figure must discharge tension amidst the group by taking it out on another who is not a weakling but rather is quite tough, so as to raise their status and show they are not unnerved but are prepared to restore lost dignity.

This may also explain why some victims of bullying become bullies themselves in the eyes of other more neutral pupils. The worrying effect of bullying weaker pupils by the strong, particularly those with weak social skills, is whether their inability to 'fight back' may cause them to suppress their pent-up anger and discharge it later on in domestic situations. When such bullied young people move into adulthood and have families of their own, with obvious weaker characters – partners and children – who can be brought under their dominant control, through being within a 'trapped family context', there is the possibility that their over-controlling dominance might be enacted as an automatic unconscious response through latent role-modelling influences from years ago.

The bullies had a harrowing fear that one day their behaviour would turn against them and that they would be punished by being on the receiving end of physical aggression, even when some 'bullying' (as judged by adult managers) was viewed by them as only 'play-fighting'. It was curious that during this interview, power dynamics were occurring amongst two of the boys who occupied positions in the year group as being the most fearsome individuals of the school even though they had never fought each other to prove who was pre-eminent. Through an illustration, Larry took up a position of dominance over Jack, and Jack felt uncomfortable amongst the girls and me:

Dennis: Have any of you had a fight but then wrongly been accused of bullying?

Jack: Loads, it's happened to me loads of times.

Larry: Oh yeah, when I battered Jack and then I was accused of bullying him [*wry smile*].

Nicole: [*laughing*] Oh listen to Larry.

Dennis: Were you excluded for that? [*I'm taken in*]

Nicole: You are lying aren't you?

Larry: He went home crying and all that.

Jack: [*startled*] Who?

Nicole: He's on about you [*she points to Jack*].

Larry: You can't remember? You went home crying – you can't remember?

Jack: No! [*emphatic*]

Larry: I swear down. You ask Colin.

Jack: Ask Colin? No you're lying now. Why would Colin know?

Larry: Because he was there. And who told us off? Mr Davis.

Jack: I can't even remember, truthfully [*Jack colours up and looks embarrassed*]. I can look you in the face right now and say, 'I can't remember that.'

Larry: [*laughing*] Seriously.

Jack: I swear down. It must have been a seriously hard punch, because I can't remember.

Larry: You punched me and I punched you.

Jack: You're lying now.

Although there was an atmosphere of fun during the interview (where the individuals wanted to continue the exercise beyond the allotted time), power games were operating even in this relaxed setting. We may have to conclude, therefore, that power and prestige are highly significant during adolescent development, whether in fun, rivalry or competition (behaviour more noticeable in boys than in girls) and that avoiding being shown up amongst friends may underlie much bullying or over-reactive coercion. The payoffs for many of the bullying cases presented above centre on 'self-image amongst a powerful peer-group', and to avoid 'at all costs' the possibility of 'losing face or prestige in public' when the fragile sense of self is under threat. Could there also be evidence that some victims may unconsciously seek a payoff by setting up situations where they become humiliated or beaten up in order to invoke the sympathy of others from a repressed psychological need to be valued?

For girls, their dominance in some ways models that of boys, as we saw in both examples above. These occasions are not uncommon where gossip is concerned, and it requires little imagination to see that when individuals encounter a large group they will feel considerably under threat. Even though the bullies rationalize their behaviour as just wanting to 'talk to her' or to 'check what she's said', it seems as though the presence of a large group implies action to follow, as occurred when Annie caught Joanne in the corridor, and Sharon trapped Alison in the bus stop.

Chapter 7

Domestic Violence and Bullying Partners

We need somehow to peer through the keyhole to see what happens in stormy relationships in an attempt to examine the nature of domestic violence, and to understand the dynamics of these conflicts from the perspectives of those accused of physical assault. As a school counsellor, I have had occasion to listen to many young people telling me about their having had to witness physical assaults within the family – one boy, for example, had seen his father stab his mother. I rarely had occasion to speak with the perpetrators themselves. My perspective, therefore, was shaped largely from how a conflict was viewed through the eyes of victims or from views of those who had sided with victims – the perspective of so many practitioners, I suspect.

This study presented a challenge in trying to find individuals I would rarely have had occasion to speak with. In selecting such candidates as my primary source of qualitative research, I am not dismissing personal responsibility or accountability of violent people, nor advocating a thorough change in the way we assess the harm done through domestic violence. Nor am I campaigning for the cause of the convicted. I am merely wishing to hear the voice of the accused. I am seeking to understand the mindset of those bullying partners caught up in relational battles without passing judgement.

In this chapter, I draw attention to current crime statistics relevant to domestic violence. Although problems of drugs and alcohol have not been a factor of study, they do feature in rising rates of offending and are an issue in the case material presented. The chapter closes with an account which has little comprehensive interpretation on my part apart from further questions of analysis, and I invite the reader to evaluate what theories the material supports from those outlined in Chapter 5.

What happens in violent relationships?

Over the years I have had occasion to counsel a number of young people who have suffered stress from living in families where domestic violence has been prevalent. Often it is not the young person that had been abused, rather they had witnessed one of their parents being physically assaulted. We cannot minimize the effects of having to live within a family where domestic violence is rife.

Police 'indifference' to domestic violence

One case I recall most vividly involved a boy called Ricardo I had supported over his turbulent relationship with his father (then separated from his mother), a man who was regularly inebriated and known to the police as an alcoholic.

Ricardo's mother invited me to their family home on the top floor of a block of flats. As I stepped from the lift and began to walk along the balcony, I was met by Ricardo's father blocking my path. He was drunk yet was sufficiently articulate to ask me why I was coming to visit Ricardo's mother. I replied that I was responding to an invitation. At the end of the balcony I could see Ricardo with his mother standing at the door and shouting at her ex-partner, saying, 'John, leave him alone, he's come to see me about Ricardo.' I was a little apprehensive to continue walking towards him, since I knew he could be violent, but being able to secure his confidence that I only had Ricardo's interests at heart he allowed me to pass, but then followed me and entered unbidden into the flat.

I spent six months supporting Ricardo, and heard of countless tales of a lack of support from the police for both him and his mother when John was smashing up the home. I was dismayed to hear that the police appeared to be cavalier in responding to their emergency calls.

On one occasion, I was left feeling angry when Ricardo's mother related an incident that left me feeling that the police were inexcusably negligent, so much so that I contacted the superintendent and filed a complaint on her behalf. Ricardo's father had seriously assaulted his mother and had smashed up the home again. He had run down the steps and gone into the house of his current girlfriend, a house that was viewable from the balcony – the location was pointed out to me. When John became violent, Ricardo had rushed out of the house and rung the police. When the police arrived Ricardo's mother pointed to where he could be found. But Ricardo and his mother watched the police drive towards the house and sit in the police car for about ten minutes and then drive off without even knocking at the door, let alone making an arrest. The reply I received from the superintendent was that the officers were 'probably responding to a more urgent call', an explanation I felt seemed pretty lame for those injured parties.

The sequel, sadly, was that Ricardo took his life by hanging himself from the balcony 12 months after leaving school, when all contact I had had with him had ceased. I never got to know the full facts; I only heard of the tragedy.

Escaping from domestic violence

A 14-year-old pupil named Naomi recently moved to the school from Yorkshire because she had witnessed her mother being severely knocked about by her step-dad. It was a gruesome scene that left the mother hospitalized and led the family into a refuge for domestic violence. The fear for her was that although they were rebuilding their lives in a new area, they could not be sure that the mother's ex-partner would not seek her out and eventually trace her whereabouts. Customarily, the school withheld any personal information asked for by an unknown party without first contacting Naomi's mother.

Last year Lisa and her two brothers were on the run from Leeds because their mother had become embroiled in a drugs network and had been severely beaten up and hospitalized for a month by a drugs baron. Not only had the children witnessed their mother on heroin, they had to suffer the ignominy of having addicts and pushers regularly coming to the house for supplies of drugs from the mother's partner. When Lisa's mother was awakened to the damage being done to her children, she told the police about her partner's activities. In consequence they had to escape under police protection. Threats were made to her life and the whole drug cartel was hunting for her location to carry out a reprisal.

Paradoxical messages and an 'unclear policing role'

In looking at what happens in more commonplace violent relationships, I present the case of 16-year-old Elliot, since this illustrates some of the difficulties which the police have to confront where there are often paradoxical messages and unclear requests from some members of the family over the behaviour and future involvement of the abusing party.

Elliot's mother had four children of three different partners. Elliot's biological father had left his mother when Elliot was quite small. He lived in Scotland, and Elliot would often visit him for long periods over the school holidays. Being in his final year he was coming to the close of his statutory schooling. Although relatively small in stature for his year group, in many ways Elliot was quite mature, owing to periods in his mother's life when he had had to support her emotionally over her fractious relationships.

Elliot said that his mother was not currently in a relationship with Leroy, but there were occasions when they would meet and have violent arguments over their son, Elliot's step-brother. Although not his son, Elliot had spent many years in company with Leroy and was fond of him, not least because he suffered from mild epilepsy, which was a worry to Elliot. One conflict occurred during a group holiday when Elliot was nearly killed in a car driven by Leroy.

They had decided to take a late holiday break and drive to the south of England in two vehicles. They travelled overnight, since this was the best way to keep the younger ones less bored and more likely to drop off to sleep. But Leroy was overtired through working long hours. Elliot was alone with him in one of the cars and he said that Leroy appeared to keep nodding off on the motorway. When they arrived at the caravan site all were hungry, so Leroy said he would go and get them all a meal at the local fish and chip shop. Elliot's mother said that he should not go because he looked very tired, and Elliot agreed that this was unwise. Nevertheless, Leroy overruled them and taking Elliot with him drove off to get food.

This became a long journey, however, since nowhere was open. Still looking very tired, Leroy took a side turning which led to a motorway where he thought he could stop at a service station. Elliot kept nudging him after observing his drowsy condition at the wheel, and insisted that he should pull over on the hard shoulder for a break, yet Leroy ignored him and continued to drive. But then it happened. Leroy's head dropped forward and Elliot had to grab the wheel and push his shoulders to one side. The car veered off the motorway, smashed through a barrier and ended up on its roof alongside a stream. The emergency services were called and Leroy was admitted to hospital whilst the police took Elliot to his mother. After the commotion, Elliot's mum was livid with Leroy and insisted that he should get a train home and that they would continue their holiday without him. She was angered that Elliot could have lost his life through Leroy being so stubborn.

After the holiday, Leroy was banished from the home, but he kept pestering and continued to encroach upon the family. This aggravation would not stop since Elliot encouraged contact and regretted that Leroy was no longer part of the family – he secretly rang him on his mobile because he felt sorry for him and feared he was not taking his medication to keep him calm and under control. Indeed, he wanted him back. Then one day when Elliot was at school he had a call from his mum on his mobile that he should come home immediately after school because Leroy had seriously assaulted her. When Elliot arrived home, the police were at the house and after all the statements were taken a warrant was issued for Leroy's arrest. Elliot could see scratches across his mother's cheeks but there were no visible bruises, though his mother complained about pain in her back where she alleged Leroy had kept thumping her after threatening her life at knife-point. Because of the warrant, Elliot was pressured to promise his mother that he would not contact Leroy, but he ignored this instruction and sent text messages to him on his mobile.

Leroy was on the run for a while, and still Elliot felt sorry for him, keeping secret rendezvous without his mother's knowledge. His mother insisted that she wanted Leroy completely out of her life, and after three weeks had passed she had arranged a tenancy transfer to a new area where Leroy could not trace her, having received support from a domestic violence liaison officer. Elliot agreed to meet Leroy in a park and was lent Leroy's mobile since his had broken. Tracking through Leroy's mobile when in his bedroom, Elliot noticed some saved text messages, which were current and which indicated that Leroy and his mother had kept in regular contact – in spite of what she had told Elliot. This confused Elliot completely, because his mother was insistent in saying that she wanted Leroy completely out of her life. What frightened Elliot, and what brought him to counselling, was a growing fear instilled in him by his mother that Leroy had been into the house again and had taken a sharp kitchen knife and threatened to stab his mother. She told him that the phone line had been cut from the outside, and that the anti-intrusion device and the direct line to the police station had been damaged purposely by Leroy. Apart from confusion on 'whose version of events' Elliot should believe, he was now left scared for his mother's life and thoroughly confused by the paradoxical messages that were coming from her.

This particular case is complex in the sense that it is not always clear what role the police should have in such disputes. They have a public duty to protect the public and maintain peaceful community relations, which inevitably involves arresting members of the public who are disturbing the peace and committing physical assaults. But this is not always straightforward in cases of domestic violence. During the heat of the storm, when tempers are raised, and when the most volatile become excessively violent, there is a need to calm the situation and mediate between quarrelling parties.

But there are occasions when members of the public have called out the police for an assault and when officers have arrived at the scene and made an arrest the 'injured' party has ended up physically abusing an officer. This is because although they wanted the aggressor to cease being violent, they certainly did not want that person, who may be close to them, arrested for committing a crime. This leaves the police having to make some difficult decisions in cases of domestic violence where the abuser and abused are known to each other. Such decisions are far less clear-cut than in cases of physical assault to an injured party by an unknown person.

Making sense of partner violence
Research on gender and cultural difference

Women are more likely than men to experience domestic violence at some point in their lives, more likely to experience repeated victimization and more likely to seek medical help and to experience frightening threats. In spite of this common tendency, one report recognizes that this is by no means the only situation:

> Agencies should however continue to recognise that some domestic violence does occur where the person experiencing violence is a man, and the perpetrator is a woman. In addition they should also be aware of the prevalence of domestic violence within same sex relationships. (Home Office 2000, para.1.17)

The number of women killed by their male partner or ex-partner in the UK in 2002 was 116, which compares with 32 men killed by their female partner; this represents a gender ratio of 3.6:1 (CWASU 2007). We must reckon, therefore, that contrary to popular opinion victims of domestic violence are not always women suffering at the hands of violent or aggressive men, but will also include men suffering at the hands of dominant women.

In terms of sexual orientation as a predisposition for partner violence, it is generally underreported that physical assaults occur in gay and lesbian relationships as well as in heterosexual ones. One study surveyed gay, lesbian and bisexual people over the age of 16 who had been sexually active over the last year and who were resident in the UK. Through anonymous questionnaires and booklets administered by health promoters, the team analysed 1391 male and 1911 female returns and found that same-sex domestic violence was prevalent in 22 per cent of lesbian and bisexual female and 29 per cent of gay and bisexual male relationships (Sigma Research 2000).

Some ethnic groups, such as Aboriginal, Asian and Jamaican, have higher rates of victims of domestic violence compared with indigenous white communities. In general, however, the question is not so much ethnic bias but why some groups are more prone than others to follow traditional patterns of patriarchal in-family domination and partner abuse. Internationally, the possibility of a rape occurring is greater in the USA than in other parts of the world, according to figures provided by the National Victim Center in 1992 (reported in Rigby 2002). The rate is 13 times higher than in Britain and 20 times higher than in Japan.

Changing family norms

The latest social trends survey by the Office of National Statistics (ONS 2007) records that nearly one quarter of children in Britain are now living in lone-parent families, which is three times the number there were in 1972. Nearly 10 per cent of families are now step-families, with less than 300,000 marriages taking place annually (the lowest recorded) compared with half a million in 1972, while the divorce rate remains historically high at about 160,000 a year.

In 1980, 12 per cent of children were born outside of marriage, but now it is 43 per cent (one of the highest in Europe); in Cyprus it is just 3 per cent, in Wales 52 per cent, and in the north east of England 55 per cent. Clearly, many social norms are breaking down. In London, where a higher number of ethnic minorities exist (where more traditional norms break down more slowly), the number of children born outside of marriage is 38 per cent.

Three million lived on their own in 1971, which was about 18 per cent of all households. Today the figure is 7 million, more than double, where 29 per cent of all households are of single occupation, with most of these not occupied by pensioners. Figures collated in 2001 showed that Lambeth in London had the largest proportion of single-person occupancy in the UK, accounting for 48 per cent of families with dependent children of lone parents, nearly double the UK average of 26 per cent (ONS 2001).

This leads to a more atomized, more fragmented society, with more isolation and less trust, which collectively leads to higher risks of social disputes. The implications of these figures are that with the cost of housing rising, with more single accommodation being required, there is likely to be more fluid partnerships in more crowded households and therefore a higher potential for family and neighbourly unrest.

Social costs of partner violence

In the UK, domestic abuse costs £23 billion per annum through services, which include criminal and civil justice, health, social care, housing, education and lost economic output, but out of this sum only £3.1 billion is directed to services for domestic violence support and reduction (Walby 2004). Every minute in the UK the police receive a call from the public for assistance over domestic violence, yet a Woman's Aid survey conducted in 2002 found that 76 per cent of women who had separated from their abusive partner continued to experience post-separation violence (Humphreys and Thiara 2003).

If we wish to live in a civilized society where physical violence and aggression is not tolerated, then society has to clamp down on violent behaviour, rightly so. But the facts are alarming in that over 80 per cent of first-time offenders find their way back into prison within a very short period of time.

According to a recent Home Office statistical bulletin (Home Office 2007), there was a discrepancy between surveyed public perceptions and police reported crime, where the former showed no significant change compared with the previous period and the latter illustrated a significant fall, but even in spite of this difference, high prisoner numbers and constant media attention to violence against the person creates a belief that violent crime is higher than what is reported.

Crime figures in England and Wales are based on two measures: the British Crime Survey (BCS) and police reported crime (PRC) (Walker *et al.* 2007). The BCS records people interviewed in their homes about crime they have suffered, and is regarded by some as a more reliable measure than the alternative of recorded crime, which can be heavily influenced by the prioritizing of police resources as well as by people's fears that certain crimes will not be pursued and are therefore not worth reporting to the police. In light of media portrayals, it may appear surprising for many that both sets of figures record no significant percentage rise for violent crime compared to last year's statistics – see Figure 7.1.

It is not clear what sense can be made of the contrasting PRC statistic that shows a 19 per cent decrease in 'more serious violence' during July to September in 2005/06 compared with the same quarter a year earlier. Public

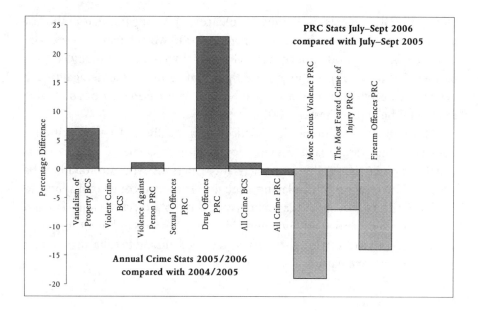

Figure 7.1 Graph showing ambivalent figures for violent crime alongside other antisocial offences reported in BCS and PRC statistics 2005/06 compared with those recorded in 2004/05

confidence may also be undermined when it is learned that BCS figures do not take account of crime among under 16s and that they may suffer from sampling errors, says BBC News Home Editor Mark Easton (Easton 2007). According to the PRC figures of comparison with the same quarter last year, the 'most feared crime' – that causes injury – was down by 7 per cent and firearms offences were down by 14 per cent, and almost one in ten women (7 per cent of men) told the BCS they had suffered from stalking over the past year.

Politically, there is much encouragement in this general trend since the BCS figures compare favourably with those taken in 1995 where the risk of becoming a victim of crime was 17 per cent higher. Yet these trends do not match public perceptions. Domestic violence crime may be masked in the general 'violence against the person' reduction rates through underreporting and underrecording. It is known that domestic violence still accounts for almost a fifth of all recorded violent crime and nearly half of all female murder victims are killed by a partner or former partner. Social commentators have reflected on these figures and have said that many people might find it hard to believe the BCS figures for 'intimate violence', which suggest that in the last year only 60,000 women had been raped, 660,000 women had been sexually assaulted and 120,000 women had been partially choked or strangled by a partner (Easton 2007). Although the figures of serious violence against the person had declined, over 90 per cent of victims who suffered serious hurt were known to the abuser (Easton 2007).

Issues to do with domestic violence are normally understood within a framework that views males as being dominant over females. One question is whether or not the 'guilty' are solely those persons who are found to be wielding the weapon or displaying brutality. These are complex disputes to resolve. Officers arriving at the home have a duty to protect the innocent and the undefended, particularly where children are concerned, but all too often when tempers have been lost there is a need to mediate and to calm anger rather than arrest any one party.

The wider picture

Most societies today have a range of women's groups and organizations dedicated to offsetting the prevalence of domestic violence. Research has shown how damaging battles between parents and step-parents can be for child development (Goleman 2006), and all too often there are cases where women, and men in some cases, want their partners to be permanently removed from the house but are afraid to say so. Family refuge centres exist to protect families where perpetrators of domestic violence simply will not leave. Tensions within families have arisen in modern times owing to the changing nature of male and female roles. In societies like our own, where hierarchical attitudes are less acceptable, where feminism has had an influence on female self-satisfaction and life-fulfilment, many men holding traditional beliefs about marriage, or about partner relationships, have to find ways of expressing their masculinity other than through domination and power. In today's multicultural society, we can no longer assume that societal changes and modernist trends affect all alike, since the power of religion and cultural norms of ethnic minorities are keeping the more progressive views of marriage and family relationships under tight control.

Authors Lorraine Radford and Marianne Hester (2006) have said that the abused have to operate amongst conflicting legislation, such that they seem to be living life on three planets. Life on Planet A is occupied by women's aid groups, refuge staff and criminal and civil law officials who are engaged in *sup-*

porting women through 'domestic violence' and who become highly judgemental of aggressive (usually) male partners. Life on Planet B is occupied by those who have to *secure the welfare of children* by implementing 'child protection' procedures, where the father may be abusive and where the mother may fail to protect her children. But life on Planet C is occupied by family law court officials who have a responsibility to insist on 'supervised contact' to maintain the *father's legal right* to see his children, where the needs of children take precedence over a mother's wishes. In spite of this inevitable confusion of client loyalty, I cannot go along fully with the summaries of some of these studies, which state, for example, 'If there is one main conclusion we would like you to draw from this book, it should be this: to understand the context of domestic violence, you need to explore this from the victim's and from the child's perspective' (Radford and Hester 2006, p.161). While this is understandably important, I think the perspectives of *all* parties are essential, particularly since perspectives do not remain fixed in such cases but often change in short periods of time and rapidly altering circumstances.

Domestic violence organizations can risk having an inbuilt bias, often against men, which, in my judgement, can cloud clear thinking. I took this up with Kate, a teacher assigned to the Prison Education Service. During our discussion, we were talking about the plight of many young men who were serving sentences for violence; we both felt that the pendulum often swings too far in the direction of *men are evil* and *women need protection*:

Kate: The lads I teach generally respect their mums. Generally, if they have got babies they respect their baby's mother, girlfriends as well, but the baby's mother is highly regarded... So, what you were saying about women's views on domestic violence, I think it goes too far one way. Whether male adults are more involved in hitting their kids, I don't know because I'm involved with 18- to 21-year-olds, and, of course, because of their age their children aren't very old. So they're very much at the point where they are saying, 'Oh Miss, I'm missing my baby's birthday.' Or they will say, 'I'm not going to do this for the rest of my life because I will miss my kids growing up.' I think, a lot of Jamaican lads are scared of their mothers. I had one lad, and we were all in hysterics about this, because he was arrested and when the police came round to the house he was at his aunt's next door. So his mum sent them round for her son, and she went out and trashed the police car. It was because she hated the police. She had had a lot to do with them over the years, apparently.

In courses on domestic abuse I have attended, I have seen instances in which speakers *demonize men* and *pathologize women* as helpless victims. Whilst I would in no way excuse violence, issues to do with domestic violence are often not so clear-cut as to regard men as 'the problem' and women as the 'innocent party', and whilst the research is indisputable that witnessed domestic violence is injurious to children and young people (James 2003), the answer is not just to get rid of the father or the male partner of the family.

Family working with violent men

Relatively little study has been centred upon men as the perpetrators of domestic violence in social work practice. Authors have devised risk assessment tools (Radford, Blacklock and Iwi 2006) and have drawn attention to the possibility of social workers having to encounter violence from men when considering the effects of childcare assessments and interventions. This is imperative in cases where men attempt to frighten workers into disengaging from work, or disempower non-abusing family members to silence disclosures (Littlechild and Bourke 2006).

One Norwegian study drew attention to the tendency of violent men to minimize the degree of their domestic violence, to avoid responsibility and to be in denial by blaming their partner as the guilty party (Råkil 2006). Whilst engaging men on an imaginative programme which challenged these tendencies, this study asked whether such abusive men could exercise 'good enough' fathering if their children had witnessed violence at their hands. The author remained sceptical: 'Children *need* non-violent fathers. Children *deserve* a childhood without the presence of violence' (p.200). As a value maxim this is obviously true, but in many cases authorities become involved when the damage in terms of aggressive male role-modelling has already been done, and I cannot fully share scepticism that later change through insight – for violent partner and witnessing child – from therapy cannot bring improvement of new non-aggressive ways of behaving.

Children are often used as pawns ('emotional capital') in parental games and wrestling matches, as leverages in order to score extra points or to fight battles over money, but family therapists have long recognized that some 'innocent parties' are not always 'innocent' and that some young people can be very powerful in causing splits to occur, when there is one family member they want out, by the public presentation of themselves as 'victims' (Holstein and Miller 1990). If we are to gain a fuller understanding of in-family bullying, perhaps it is long overdue to begin listening to the voices of perpetrators themselves and to realize that: *Relationship problems require relationship solutions.*

Perspective of an abusing partner

Alan had served five periods of time in prison for violence. The first occasion was when he was going through a stage of hanging around with 'big lads' involved in burglary when he was 16. He served as a lookout initially, and then by being pushed through small windows to open doors to avoid the big lads making a forced entry and thereby attracting attention to themselves. His periods of internment ranged from three months to five years. Alan described how he started taking up weight-lifting during late adolescence, and how he wanted to appear as one of the 'big lads'. But then he described an incident of stabbing somebody unknown to him:

> *Alan*: It was Euro 96 and we were sat down in this pub and this guy called me and said, 'You're in my chair.' I said, 'Have that one.' He said, 'No.' I said to the lads, 'Do you know him?' They said, 'Yeah, he's OK; he's alright. He's had a bit to drink but he's alright.' We was having an argument and he drove off in a car. About 15 or 20 minutes later he pulled up on the other side of the road and came over to me with a bat. He came over to give it to me, really. I jumped up, and I had a Swiss Army knife on me... He took a flying kick at me. Wham! I stabbed him in the leg with it.

This incident brought him before the courts. At the age of 31, he was becoming more reflective and recognized that he had a 'short fuse'. He told me that most people from school would not really know him now, and that the people he went around with knew he would fly off the handle if he became trapped or pushed into a corner. 'I would always fight my way out of the situation,' he said. 'People like my partner would often say, "Is that your answer?" But I had got to the stage where fighting was my answer.'

Alan began to tell me about his violence in the home with his partner Tamara, but his motives for being aggressive with her left him puzzled because, as he said to me, 'I don't feel threatened by Tamara, but I have lashed out at her.' I wasn't quite clear what he meant when he elaborated further by saying that he had never served time for domestic violence as such, but felt it was because of his record of criminal violence that he had 'kicked off with the police' when they arrived. It was during those times when they had CS-gassed him for resisting arrest. He said, 'Over the years they have broke my nose, and the like, and so when the police come round my guard goes up.' I present below a fuller account of our discourse.

Alan: And because I got arrested for domestic violence I had to kick her. I kicked her, and because of my record of criminal violence they remanded me straightaway into custody.

Dennis: There's a pattern there, isn't there? Whenever Tamara is threatened by you she will ring the police, but your problem is when the police arrive. Suddenly, everything kicks off.

Alan: Yeah.

Dennis: Do you sense that loyalty has been broken when Tamara rings the police? As if to say, 'Tamara, you know what I'm like. That wasn't the way we should have dealt with this. You know what I'm like when the police come round. You know what will happen.' Is there a sense that you feel angry about that?

Alan: Yeah, definitely. I'll say, 'Why did you do that Tamara, because you know what my reactions will be as soon as the police come.' I will defend myself as much as I can, even against the police. I know they are doing a job, and they are doing a brilliant job, but when they rub me up the wrong way I will just flip, and she knows that. And obviously I've felt let down by her. I will say, 'How could you do that to me?'

Dennis: Is your relationship with Tamara a bit like a brother and sister squabbling?

Alan: She knows what buttons to press. She knows the reaction she's going to get, and I think, 'Do you want this reaction?'

Dennis: She always wants you back?

Alan: That's it, I say, 'Tamara, why are you doing that? You know I will react', that sort of thing. We love each other to death, but she knows which buttons to press... You see, it's different as well when she's had a drink [*forlorn look*].

Dennis: In what way?

Alan: Oh, she's got a video under each arm [seemingly, a thieving analogy] and she can take the world on, like a lot of people, because when you've had a drink you think you're invincible, sort of thing.

Dennis: Yeah, I know what you mean.

Alan: You know, you raise your voice a bit, you know. I don't like it when she drinks. No, I don't like it.

Dennis: You notice a change in her personality?

Alan: Yeah. I can't stand it when she drinks.

Dennis: What is the point that she reaches when she decides to call the police?

Alan: I think it's when she reaches that stage when she thinks she has lost the argument. She may have thought, 'I'm getting nowhere now.' And that's the button she presses – the police – because she isn't going to win.

Dennis: What do you say when you have received your custodial sentence and she comes to visit you for the first time, you know, if she hadn't telephoned the police...?

Alan: Then I wouldn't be here. I'd try to explain it, but then I feel bad myself because I got myself into this situation, and I feel bad, and the kids are not with me and I miss the kids, and I'm on my own – I'm in a cell.

Dennis: And it seems as though there have been two of you that have put you there, because she knows the sequence.

Alan: Mm.

Dennis: Or, perhaps, you never have that conversation? Is it just the gloom that comes over you and you think, 'Well, here I am again'?

Alan: Well, yeah, that's it. The defence mechanisms come in. The big wall is up and you have to defend yourself and keep your face up. I have said this to Tamara, I have said, 'Tamara, why did you do this for?' But then she knows with my violence that that is why she phoned the police to stop me, because she's got to the stage where I'm raving, I'm raging. Maybe that is the only way that will help her.

Dennis: You think she might be scared?

Alan: Yeah. She's got to the stage where she's scared.

Dennis: I suppose the ideal would be for you to get away from the house before that flashpoint?

Alan: We've got to that stage now – that when we get all fired up I just leave. I go to my mum's, my brother's or my sister's and I'll say, 'I'll see you in the morning…' Sometimes I get to the stage that if I walked away she'd think she'd lost, and she wouldn't like me walking away. She wouldn't like me walking away. I don't know how she felt about it but she would say, 'You're leaving us again.' Does she think, maybe, that she's lost a little battle by my walking away?

Dennis: As though it's like a brother and sister thing all over again?

I asked Alan about his family background to help him explore the genesis of his aggressive behaviour. He was quite protective of his parents at first, but then pennies began to drop regarding his behavioural traits.

Alan: My mum's always been a worker; my dad's always been a worker. I used to put my violence down to the fact that I have never spent much time with my family. I used to get up to go to school in the morning. My mum would be at work. My dad would be at work. And I would come home and go out and I don't seem to have many memories of spending very much time with my dad.

I asked him how he thought his parents felt about his friends and the company he was regularly keeping during his youth, but his answer seemed to sidetrack my question:

Alan: My dad was so disciplined. He used to discipline me so much, even if I farted in front of him. If I swore in front of Nan, or in front of my mum, he'd say, 'You don't do that in front of a lady.' He was so disciplined, and I always thought to myself, 'How have I turned out like this?'

Dennis: Would he hit you, though?

Alan: Yeah.

Dennis: I know it was an age when parents hit kids more commonly then, but…

Alan: He used to punch me, yeah, and I remember once I lied, because my brother was older than me by five years, and he wanted some money, and I was only about 13. He wanted a fiver off me, so I said to my dad, 'Dad, I need a pair of handlebars for my bike.' And he gave me this money, and… I used to love fishing, and he took this fishing rod and belted me so hard and said, 'You've pinched those handlebars.'

But I hadn't; I just needed the money for my brother. But he hit me so hard. Maybe that's what caused me to be like this, yeah. That didn't help.

Dennis: Is there a connection there between your dad disciplining you in a certain way and you becoming violent, do you think?

Alan: I used to hate my dad. It wasn't until I was about 31 that I began to respect him. I used to hate him for beating me. I used to hate him. It was like that programme, 'You wait until your father gets home!' My mother used to say, 'You wait till your father gets home!' And I was scared, and I got to the stage where I really hated my dad, yeah.

I asked about his relationship with his mother and he told me that he felt very close to his mum, that being the middle one he felt he was a mummy's boy.

Alan: I would always cry on her shoulder, but my mum would verbally warn me with my dad. I had got to that stage where I thought, 'Oh God, now my dad's coming.' Perhaps it wasn't the right thing to verbally warn me with my dad because I was starting to get scared of my dad then.

It struck me that Alan was initially disinclined – or it had never occurred to him – to form a mental connection between his temperament and his upbringing, as though he was wholly self-punishing with little insight as to why he had become the sort of person he had. I could not help but notice the change in tone when I had given him permission to speak more openly about his father. There was palpable sadness and a regretful countenance coming over him when speaking of his past beatings. He did not feel comfortable to speak in such a way, even as a mature adult. Indeed, parents are very powerful figures, even in adulthood.

In engaging Alan in a form of reflective narrative therapy, which analysed patriarchal attitudes and the harmful effects of his own children witnessing home aggression towards their mother, he began to appreciate the harmful effects of aggressive modelling upon their developmental experiences and the genesis of his own impulsive violence through his childhood experiences. His son, a pupil of 14 years, became noticeably less agitated with teachers and ceased being aggressive amongst peers as we worked together as a family – principally with Alan, but always within the whole family context.

Although this was not a long-term study involving controlled outcome design, Alan's son confirmed after 12 months that matters were very much improved at home, with no further violence and with no more calls to the police for safety. I am indebted to Alan for his story and for having the confidence to expose his vulnerability to a therapist aiming to be neutral and non-judgemental yet with a resolve that violence within a family is no more excusable than violence in school or anywhere else.

Concluding comment

This chapter has considered some of the intricacies that centre round domestic violence between partners in a relationship. We have looked at some of the difficulties for the police when having to be called out to enforce the law and to help resolve disputes that arise between quarrelling partners, and we have also touched on the social costs of domestic violence, many of which may be hidden through the knock-on effects of violence within the home. British surveys of crime statistics and police reported figures tend to give a misleading picture on the nature and scale of violence within partner relationships. We have seen that they may be influenced more by percentage falling rates of previous years rather than by the nature of current social unrest; and changing family norms of cohabiting family groupings and same-sex relationships from the traditional nuclear family present different tensions and challenge general perspectives on domestic violence, particularly in the UK.

But the major interest in this book is in listening to the voices of perpetrators of bullying, and in this chapter domestic bullying, and not only is relatively little money spent on supportive services nationally in the UK, such as family therapy for example, but the wider picture appears to support a partisan obligation to particular members of a family rather than a holistic approach of addressing what the family needs to help prevent discord and secure safety and well-being for each individual. What I am seeking to demonstrate through listening to the voice of the perpetrator of domestic violence is that a resolution of internment cannot be the best way forward, particularly if the injured parties are not wishing this to be the outcome of their various trials in relationship battles.

A developmental psychologist would, I suspect, account for Alan's difficulties as being due to 'absent parents' through over-busy work commitments, a behaviourist would be suspicious of aggressive role-modelling of father, and a psychoanalyst might delve into the 'avoidant attachment' needs and his longed-for relationship bonding, particularly with Dad, to make sense of his behaviour, but it is also possible to detect something through the narrative games that were being played in this family. What significance should we give to Tamara's drinking, the phone call to the police and the macho-style behaviour exhibited, to her pushing significant 'buttons' and to her regret in having Alan remove himself to 'avoid an assault'?

And what about Alan? Is there a trace of 'Poor Little Old Me' in his unconscious responses? He wanted to be tough in youth, as do most young men, but found his 'toughness' destructive in the pub scene and in the family when teased by Tamara. But then he could always depend on Faithful Old Mum to protect him from Tyrant Dad, who could punish hard, and sometimes unjustly – like punishing himself. But then Poor Little Alan could always run home to Mum for safety – like stepping up the violence when the police had arrived (Dad coming home from work) to return to the safety of his prison cell – until such time as it no longer worked, i.e. the payoff becomes unfulfilling and Alan becomes lonely again. Finally, Trusty Tamara will visit him in prison to renew their bond, welcome him home again and all will be well again for a short while.

Chapter 8

Bullying of Children and Young People

The phenomenon of children being physically assaulted by adults, and particularly their parents or guardians, is a serious one for both the victim and the perpetrator. Professionals found guilty of physically abusing youngsters face likely suspension from office, and some convicted inmates who have hurt children require protection during internment. It is well recognized that whatever criminals may have done to warrant the restriction of their freedom, the one offence that is not tolerated amongst inmates of penal institutions is that of physical violence or sexual abuse against children.

Whilst men are generally more powerful than women, and can be authoritative in work and family relations, the disproportionate balance of power between adults and children is generally not open to question. By definition, children are powerless and adults are powerful, and whilst children and young people may have developed quite sophisticated ways of winding up their parents and guardians, no amount of provocation can ever excuse violence and physical assault against minors – we may understand, we may sympathize, but we can never justify violence against children. 'Over-corrective' measures in child management may render a carer culpable under child protection legislation and this could leave them deskilled in bringing up challenging adolescents if they know of no other method of control than physical chastisement.

Apart from the fact that adults bullying children violates moral and legal codes, from a behaviourist perspective becoming physically aggressive towards young people role-models behaviour normally condemned when they show the same towards their peers. Judgements are needed to distinguish between impulsive, non-intentional violence against children and its deliberate use through belief in its effectiveness for behaviour modification. Pupils' assessments of how their teachers manage them in class is coloured by their own experience of being managed in the home – 'normal control' experienced by primary carers becomes the benchmark for challenging inappropriate adult management elsewhere.

In this chapter, I shall present the case of a teacher being accused of assaulting a pupil, but primarily we shall be listening to the voice of a convicted guardian who had been sentenced for physical violence against his step-daughter. Misuse of alcohol or drugs, as we shall see, sadly adds to the possibility of violence against children and young people. I will consider changing trends of corrective child management in the home and school, and how, when errors of judgement occur, reactions will reflect what is acceptable as shaped by society or the family home.

What sometimes happens to children
Early child physical and psychological bullying

Delroy presented himself as a troubled individual in the early years of secondary school, and it was not clear what was disturbing him. He was at first reluctant to speak about his worries. When first escorted to my room for counselling he was not very communicative. He sat looking quite glum and disassociated, and when asked why he felt he had been asked to see me he said it was because he was often fed up, but didn't know why. It took some time to reassure him and raise his confidence to speak, but after a few sessions he began to open up. He was living in a situation with his mother, her partner Elroy and his younger brother. He despised Elroy's bossy manner, lording it over everyone, particularly his mother who he believed was wholly under Elroy's control.

We worked in the early period on building his self-esteem, since he was often found drifting as a solitary figure around the school. He complied with most school rules but was not highly motivated to work. The counselling was light-touch till a 'new symptom' emerged during his second year – he began punching himself in the chest, lower arms and legs, particularly when a teacher raised his or her voice in class. It was as if he could not tolerate shouting, even when it was not directed towards him; he became anxious and demonstrative, with or without an audience of peers. He clearly vented anger in a veiled form about something more in the family than had previously come to light.

During this period he began to share his concerns about his mother.

Dennis: What worries you about mum?

Delroy: It's because I'm not there to protect her from Elroy.

Dennis: But why does mum need protection from Elroy?

Delroy: Because he shouts and it's just like before.

He began to tell me of past incidents that had left him traumatized. I will not go into the therapeutic programme that eventually led him out of this maladaptive behaviour, but will tell his story.

When he was about nine he remembers his mother living with another partner named Malchus. He was particularly hostile towards Delroy being hugged by his mother. He recalled one fight when she was beaten and had to seek refuge with her children in a hostel. Tears began to trickle down his cheeks as he spoke. She was bruised and cut all over her face and bled profusely. Delroy and his brother were petrified. 'Mum was nearly killed,' he cried, shaking as he spoke. 'I hate him and one day I'll kill him!'

He began to tell of other things that had happened which had left their mark on him and which had a more direct bearing on his current behaviour. When Malchus noticed his partner giving attention to Delroy, he shouted at them both and she transferred her attention to him. Delroy began 'punishing' himself by digging sharp plastic objects into his arms and legs until Malchus shouted again and slapped him and ordered him to stop crying, after which he stormed out of the house – which, in consequence, allowed Delroy to be consoled and comforted by his mum.

In this child's early life, there had been evidence of physical and psychological abuse and the emotional scars were still present. Shouting was the prelude to physical maltreatment and maternal separation and had become irrationally generalized in classroom contexts when a teacher's voice was raised.

Changing norms on 'corrective' treatment

In spite of increased child protection legislation in most countries, cases of violence towards children are surprisingly still common. A few years back in my role of designated teacher for child protection, I had to manage a number of cases where parents had physically abused their children. Twenty years ago there was more scope for individual discretion and judgement than is appropriate in the current climate, and I must confess to having exercised more personal judgement then than would be acceptable today.

I recall a pupil by the name of Richard whose family were from overseas and who became disruptive in school. His father came up to the school and suggested that the reason his son misbehaved was that teachers were too soft. 'Where I come from, Mr Lines, we don't put up with this nonsense. This is how you should treat my son,' he said. 'Give him a good slapping!' Upon which, he struck him viciously in the face. 'That's what he's used to; that's what he understands. You have my permission to give him a good crack when he mucks about.' I must admit to feeling very embarrassed about the assault, since Richard had done nothing in my presence to warrant such treatment.

Another case comes to mind that illustrates what was probably commonplace in many families 30 years ago. It involved Gabriel, a 15-year-old who, as his father put it, 'was mixing with a bad lot'. During one altercation, his father completely lost his temper and severely beat him up. Gabriel had come in late after being out with his mates and his father was wild with rage – Gabriel's version was identical with what his father 'proudly' confessed. I relate from memory his rationalization:

> I met him at the door, thumped him on the side of his face and dragged him through the corridor into the kitchen. His mother was in the living room watching television. He begged me to stop, the little bleeder, but I took no notice and belted him in the stomach and kidneys. I pushed him over the kitchen table and threw him to the floor and booted him in his belly till he promised to do as he was told.

Amazingly, his father allowed Gabriel to come to school the next day with a heavily bruised face, and what turned out to be a fractured clavicle. I would not compromise my position, even though his father had given me such a vivid account, and social services were contacted. What surprised me was his candour. He was not embarrassed about the assault, and in no way did he attempt to excuse or minimize his action, or persuade me not to take the matter seriously – in fact he was proud of what he had done, and said that he would do it again if his son had not learned how to behave. We live in a very different age today.

A teacher's use of physical force

I still encounter some teachers who lament the abolition of caning pupils for misconduct and who believe it to be the reason for rising misbehaviour in school. Against research findings (Lines 2006a; Munn, Lloyd and Cullen 2000), the erroneous view of such teachers is that corporal punishment works and that the cane modifies a miscreant's behaviour and serves as a deterrent for the rest. There is no doubt that firm management with rapid consequential action and high detection rates seriously reduces misconduct, but we should not assume that firm management is equivalent to or requires physical correction as a sanction. Not only is such a sanction illegal, there is the likelihood of it creating bitterness and resentment. It fosters an adversarial relationship between teachers and pupils that hardly encourages learning and wholesome relationships.

As mentioned earlier, we have to distinguish between willed and unwilled aggression towards children and not be too-judgemental when adults (guardians or teachers) lose their temper or self-control through impatience or pressure.

There has arisen an unprecedented rise in allegations against teachers 'abusing' children in recent times. Whilst most cases do not end in prosecution, there are a few occasions where teachers may not have always exercised good judgement. One difficulty for senior teachers investigating alleged abuse is verifying what actually happened, with an added problem of managing gossip on incidents that rapidly spreads through the school and becomes part of community folklore. One event was cited by the group of bullying youngsters I presented in Chapter 6. They spoke of Mr Gutteridge who was accused of bullying a pupil.

Dennis: What was the incident with Mr Gutteridge about?

Nicole: I had to go to the police station over that. Did you, Larry?

Larry: No, the police came to my house.

Jack: He was involved in the lot, Larry was.

Nicole: What was that all about? Oh I remember. It was because he threw Lester down the stairs, and Lester went flying down the stairs, boom, boom, boom, he came after him.

Jack: I was in that class. The next thing you know, he flipped, innit?

Dennis: What did you actually see as opposed to what you heard from others?

Jack: It was an assault, wasn't it?

Nicole: Me and Larry saw it all.

Jack: What did you see? Tell us.

Larry: Yeah, I was there. One of the security guards – it was Simeon. Lester was getting beaten up and I tried to help him but Simeon held me back, because Mr Gutteridge was pushing him everywhere.

Nicole: So Larry tried to get involved to help him and Simeon threw him up the wall [*said laughingly*].

Larry: No he didn't [*looking embarrassed*].

Jack: And then the security guard threw him into the wall, innit?

Nicole: He battered Larry [*she laughs*].

Larry: No, but d'you remember when he punched me, when Mark spat at him from the tree? Remember, down there in the lower school, when we climbed up the tree?

Dennis: But what did Mr Gutteridge do to Lester? Larry, you said he was beaten up and that sounds as though it was a full-scale assault.

Nicole: He kicked him.

Larry: No, he didn't kick him.

Nicole: Yeah he did. Stop lying, Larry.

Larry: He didn't kick him. He was just chucking him about – stop making it out worse than it was.

Dennis: So he was pushing him around and you went to try and pull Lester away to try and protect him? Then the security guard thought you were attacking Mr Gutteridge and grabbed you?

Larry: Yeah, yeah. Before that, like, Lester was shouting stuff at him: 'fucking this' and 'fucking that'. Mr Gutteridge got him then, just dashed him then.

Dennis: What does dashing mean?

Larry: Like chucking him, throwing him, like. He left that place and went into the classroom then and separated to see someone, but there was nothing else. But Lester was pushed into him, I think. There was nothing else.

Nicole: But he came into your class, Jack.

Jack: No.

Larry: He did.

Jack: Oh yeah. He came in and got terrored out. Everyone was going mad and shouting and that, and saying 'You shit, you prick, and fucking this and that' because he threw Lester.

Dennis: And then the whole school was against him?

Nicole: Of course, obviously, because of what he'd done. He's a dick-head for doing what he did to Lester…did he still get paid if he was suspended? If he still got paid I'm going to find out where he lives and…

Jack: Because he was in the papers, Lester and his dad had it put in the papers.

Such accounts are often riddled with inconsistencies and contradictions. As discussed in Chapter 5, versions of highly emotive events are notoriously inaccurate, and when we add to such 'witnessed' or 'heard of' controversies a human tendency to glory in gossip voyeuristically, memories of what took place often become embellished with 'spicy' and 'fictitious' details, and the later perspectives of the chief parties involved may not always be accurate or reliable.

Making sense of assaulting children
Research on child and youth physical abuse in the family

A Canadian study of maltreatment by parents and peers canvassed the retrospective experiences of 210 college students through questionnaires to assess the frequency of childhood emotional, physical and sexual abuse; childhood victimization by peers; and current psychological distress. It was found that those who were bullied victims in later adolescence had experienced higher rates of emotional and physical maltreatment by parents and more childhood sexual assaults than those who were not childhood bully victims. The study also found that 11 per cent of participants had been abused physically by their parents compared with 18 per cent psychologically. As one researcher said, the problem was compounded for those who had been abused or bullied in the home and at school, where it might be presumed there would be nowhere to turn to for support and understanding (Duncan 1999).

An interesting research project carried out with 1014 Jewish Israeli young people between the ages of 13 and 18 revealed some very interesting results (Winstok *et al.* 2004). The study focus was on the impact of the father's level of aggression towards the mother. The team of researchers were examining adolescents' perceptions of their parents and of themselves and how these perceptions are inter-related. The evidence indicated that in cases in which there was no father-to-mother aggression, adolescents held a coherent image structure of family members. But where aggression was prevalent, family structure coherence seemed to deteriorate. When mild aggression occurred, youths tended to identify with their fathers; but when aggression intensified towards a 'severe' level, they could not easily identify with their father-as-aggressor. In such cases the young people tended to identify with their mothers, but they also were left unable to form a coherent image of themselves as well as the family. The implications of this study barely need spelling out.

My counselling experience over the last 20 years has confirmed these findings, where I have found many cases where young people who were strongly attached to their fathers felt their bonds had been seriously weakened when they had witnessed him beating their mother beyond what was considered to be acceptable. No matter how such occasions were rationalized, I have found that the young person could not generally agree with their father's comment that 'your mother deserved it', or 'had it coming'.

The Domestic Violence, Crime and Victims Act 2004 (section 5) created the specific criminal offence of 'causing or allowing the death of a child or vulnerable adult'. A parent, or another adult regarded as a family member, will be guilty of the offence if they are aware of potential danger to the child, either from their own actions or those of another in the household, but fail to take reasonable steps to prevent serious harm to the child. This criminal provision was introduced to cover situations where it was unclear who actually inflicted the physical harm, such that it was difficult to mount a successful prosecution.

Cleaver *et al.* (2007) point to a considerable body of research that shows that children are at risk of significant harm if they grow up in families where there is domestic violence and parental drug or alcohol misuse, since children are often witnesses to most aspects of domestic violence. They may be physically injured during such incidents, either by accident or because they attempt to intervene (Humphreys and Stanley 2006).

As a foster carer and school counsellor, I have often been surprised by the level to which injured children go to 'protect' and forgive the parent who has abused them. Constance Briscoe is one of the few black female judges in Britain, but as a child she suffered considerable abuse – beaten and made to sleep on urine-soaked sheets, left alone and un-tended. In her autobiography, *Ugly* (2006), she speaks of a final visit to her mother – 'I was still desperate for her love' – and before going to Newcastle University to study law, she said, 'I loved you once. You were my mummy. What did I ever do to you?' Her mother's reply was stark and telling: 'Fuck off, then.'

Domestic violence coexistent with parental drug and alcohol misuse

Cleaver *et al.* (2007) have drawn attention to the inconsistent service provision for child domestic violence and parental substance misuse. The authors examined 357 case files of six English local authorities in rural and urban settings and compared the documents with what practitioners had recorded in postal questionnaires and qualitative interviews of 17 families of the cohort. The authors reasoned that services were more effective with families affected by either domestic violence or substance misuse than with those where the two problems coexisted.

There is much evidence to show that problem drinking is associated with domestic violence (Coleman and Cassell 1995), to the extent that 80 per cent of domestic violence cases have been found to be alcohol-related (Velleman 1993). Authors looking at the combined complexity of domestic violence and drug misuse point to the chaotic circumstances in which some youngsters have to live their lives.

Parents and guardians who misuse drugs and alcohol have few organizational skills, and by comparison with their stable counterparts are less attentive to their child's needs, since their major preoccupation is on getting and using whatever drugs they are addicted to. Emotionally, such carers remain distant from their children and often suffer severe mood swings which leave their children frightened and feeling uncertain and suffering extreme anxiety from an often fruitless desire to please their carer to offset self-guilt. Inattention to practical necessities of a child's day-to-day existence, home cleanliness and the washing of laundry often leaves youngsters subject to physical neglect and name-calling from peers. In short, such carers are unable to engage fully with their children, cannot achieve secure attachments and can hardly undertake the planning of social activities. They often fail to hold down jobs and leave the family in financial difficulties with spiralling debts. Not only is there further risk from used syringes and other debris left lying around on the floor, alcoholic carers and those with severe drug addiction form unsavoury associations, which brings a further risk in the home when fellow addicts meet for fresh supplies of drugs.

The extended family of such drug-addicted families is often non-existent, since their behaviour has cut them off from more stable relations. Past disputes have left them isolated with little extra support to ensure the safety of their children.

Since the report of the Victoria Climbié Inquiry was published in 2003, there has been a call in Britain for improved inter-agency linking, communicating and working together. The study by Cleaver *et al.* (2007) revealed the following facts.

- Over a quarter of case referrals had occurred from more than one source, such as health visitors, the police, nursery workers and the parents, and all with similar concerns.

- A further quarter of cases of referral came from non-professionals such as the child, parents or neighbours.

- The police were responsible for half of all cases, which is a common procedure that often leaves area offices overwhelmed.

- In spite of government guidance, only 57.2 per cent of practitioners had discussed the matter with parents before making a referral to social services, with practically half being re-referrals.

The study also showed great disparity of procedural practice between different authorities over the expected sequence of initial assessment, core assessment and strategy meetings which should precede a child protection inquiry being undertaken. Study of these files also illustrated that:

- over a quarter of children lived in families where there was evidence of both domestic violence and parental substance misuse

- a further quarter lived in families where parents had poor mental health

- 10 per cent of cases involved parents with physical or learning disabilities.

A further disparity in practice between different authorities was the point at which other voluntary and non-voluntary agencies were brought in to support families suffering from domestic violence and alcohol or drug misuse. Some of these files indicated that managers were sometimes unaware of what agencies actually existed. This was in spite of a government minimum requirement that local authorities should have a service directory providing comprehensive information on local providers, eligibility criteria, geographical location and referral procedures for all relevant workers.

For those families who reported unsatisfactory service (about half in the study) the reasons seemed to centre upon long waiting lists for specialist services, family services ending prematurely, and relevant services not being locally available. As the authors conclude, in cases where domestic violence and parental substance misuse did not coexist, six out of ten parents were satisfied with the outcome.

In those cases where they coexist, parents had compounded difficulties of poor parenting skills with substance misuse, which rendered identification of the tasks complex and demanding of resources, resulting often in children being taken into care. Parents expressed satisfaction with the outcome if they received both practical help and emotional support in managing their difficulties. Practical help included advice about parenting, respite child care, specialist support in controlling alcohol or drug addiction, anger management and rehousing. Emotional support was generally provided by the social workers themselves and included support, empathy, advice and reassurance (Cleaver *et al.* 2007).

'Justifying' youth violence?

Needless to say, in contributing to a book such as this, respondents will be wary of talking about moments in their family life where they acknowledge they have been unduly aggressive towards their children. I say 'unduly aggressive' because to use a term like 'over-dominating' may give an unclear perspective on what this book is trying to examine. Parents of different secular, religious or ethnic groups will view it as appropriate to be in full control of their children, and indeed governments expect this to be the case, which is why the state holds parents accountable for the behaviour of their children. And perhaps it is a narrow distinction between being 'in full control' and being 'over-dominating' within the family context.

Extreme aggressive behaviour towards minors borders on physical assault, and in such cases parents are liable to prosecution and possible imprisonment. In this sense – and this has become a dawning realization for some parents – physically assaulting one's child is no different in real terms than physically assaulting another adult or person unrelated to the abuser.

Physically abusive parent

The case presented below involves the family of a mother, Ruth, daughter, Suzanne, and step-father, Jim, who had lived in the family home for 14 years and was regarded by the daughter as her 'real dad'. The family had been known to social services for a considerable period of time owing to charges of physical abuse arising from misuse of alcohol. The school had managed a child protection investigation when the step-father had been accused of grabbing his step-daughter aggressively by her arms and leaving her bruised. Child protection procedures were not implemented. Twelve months later a further disclosure was managed initially by the police, and this disclosure led to her father receiving a custodial sentence of six months. In the report and the police statement the daughter described being assaulted by her father. He had attempted to strangle her following a minor argument and her mother had to resort to punching him in the face in order to get him to release her. He had no recollection of this event the next morning when he rang his partner from the police station. He wrote to his step-daughter later saying that what had happened was in no way her fault but his.

Dennis: Can I ask you first, Jim, what you can remember of that day?

Jim: What really got on my nerves was Suzanne's friends coming to the door, her mates constantly knocking. She will talk to them for a good half hour, leaving the front door wide open. We have the heating on and we are just wasting money on electricity. Financially, it was affecting me. When I've got upset I'd have a few drinks, and when she came in I had a little moan at her. Basically, I took the mickey out of her at the door and she became abusive to me and I hit her. It was at that point that she shut the door and her friends had gone and she came into the living room and threw abuse at me that I hit her.

Dennis: What was she saying specifically?

Jim: Every single word virtually was a swear word.

Dennis: Was this because she felt you had put her down in front of her friends?

Jim: Yeah, and I suppose they took the mickey out of her, saying, 'Ah listen to your dad shouting at you', type of thing. Then she came in, swore at me. I hit her and threw my mobile phone at her and said, 'If you want to ring the police on me you can.' And she did.

Dennis: Right there and then?

Jim: Right there and then. Then I went to court and they said I shall be sentenced in a fortnight and in that fortnight, although I had seen her I stayed drunk for the whole fortnight, knowing that I was going to go to prison for this. I knew they would sentence me and I knew I would end up in prison.

Dennis: Can I ask you to comment on what has been written in social work reports about the assault? You have said three times that you hit her, yet in the reports it says that you grabbed her round the throat.

Jim: Oh, everybody says that, but no, I did not do that. I clobbered her one. I had her by the throat while I hit her, but no, I didn't do anything serious, not in that respect, but I did class it as actual bodily harm.

Dennis: Does it annoy you what has been written about the incident?

Jim: I can understand it because it has come up again – how I have behaved since coming out of prison. And yes I have gone for her a few times since, although I'm not supposed to have seen her, because she's just abusive towards me now…

It might appear at this point that the relationship is exclusively a hostile one where a dominant man has forced his way back into a family when child protection restrictions and a custodial sentence have ended, but this was far from the case.

Jim: She still calls me dad.

Dennis: It's strange that, isn't it?

Jim: It is strange because when she wants something she's all over me, like, every fortnight I might get my money from the unemployment, as soon as she comes home from school, if her mum is at work, she's all over me and says, 'Dad, can I have some money? Tell mum that you've spent it on something else.' 'Well what's it for?' 'So I can get some fags.' 'Hang on, you're only 15!' And she's never told me what shop she gets them from because I'd probably report them, because, as she knows, it gets me angry. I'm dead against smoking. But Ruth smokes and gives Suzanne a couple.

Dennis: There's something that still puzzles me about the incident. You gave her your phone and invited her to tell the police and I am wondering why she decided to do it. When she came into school the next day she was very uncomfortable having made the disclosure that led to child protection procedures being taken out. It was as though she needed to have reported it but somehow she didn't feel she had wanted to. Once she had reported the matter and set everything in motion there was a great sense of regret expressed.

Jim: I had that in one of my letters that she'd sent me, saying, like, how much she was missing me. She couldn't wait till the time that I would be getting out. She couldn't wait to see me again.

Dennis: Did that make you feel angry, make you feel then why the bloody hell did you do it?

Jim: Yeah, but at the same time I shouldn't have hit her. How can I explain it?

At this point, Jim goes into his past to help clarify his impulsive treatment of his step-daughter.

Jim: When my dad was alive, at a young age when I was on holiday, I walked into the toilet and I didn't realize that he was on the toilet, and when he come out he pulled my pants down and walloped me and a half, sort of thing. I can remember he smacked me six times so that I couldn't sit down for a few hours, and now this has been reported you've got to be careful what you say, what you do. You can't do anything any more, I suppose it's till the age of 16 or 18. I don't know, it's got to be over 16. I don't know.

Dennis: When she actually rang the police what then happened precisely? The report said that Ruth had to hit you to let Suzanne go. Was Ruth there?

Jim: Err yeah, I think she was.

Dennis: The report said, as I recall, Ruth had to punch you to get you off. It presents a very gruesome picture of the incident.

Jim: Yeah, I think Ruth was there and she did pull me off, because I would have hit her several times. I remember, I'm sure I walked out and said 'Carry on', sort of thing, 'If you want to report it, report it.' Then I was arrested and then I was in court.

Dennis: How long was it till the police came round to the house?

Jim: Not very long. I think about 15 minutes.

Dennis: What was the atmosphere like between you and Suzanne?

Jim: We just didn't speak.

Dennis: There was a stony silence, like?

Jim: Yeah. The police kept me in the station overnight. I was kept in all night, then I came out. I don't know why, but they let me out. Obviously, they breathalysed me again. They breathalyse you several times and found me OK, again, so I went straight to my brother's. So that was it for two weeks and I carried on drinking. I still saw Ruth. I saw Suzanne. And she did tell me that she actually regretted it, but I said, 'Look, it's gone to court now. I can't stop it.' It's not worth trying to hide because the police find you. I'm always in trouble with the police. I do cause problems. When I went to court it was only me that went, not Suzanne or Ruth. My brother went with me, sat in the dock, sort of thing, and saw me handcuffed, and all that and then I went to prison. I didn't speak to Ruth for the time I was in prison.

Dennis: Did she visit you?

Jim: No one visited me; that's purely because I was in Liverpool. If I'd have been local she would have visited me. But then she was working full-time and virtually lived at work – it was up to 80 hours a week…

Dennis: Can I ask you about your experience in prison? Did fellow inmates know what you had done? Were they aware of your offence?

Jim: Everybody asks you why you're in prison.

Dennis: But you don't have to tell them do you?

Jim: No. I just told them I had a drink and got into a fight and I was arrested, and they would ask, 'And you're put into prison for that?' I would say, 'Yes, because it was classed as actual bodily harm.'

Dennis: So what's the experience of prison like?

Jim: Everybody I know who's been to prison doesn't seem to mind. A lot of people I've met, and I would say the same, if you haven't got anybody else out there you're better off in prison. If you're a drug person, if you're a drinker, you can get what you need. Obviously you're not allowed mobile phones but if you want them you can get them in prison. And there was this guy in my cell who said, 'You don't mind the smell do you?' I said, 'I can't smell anything at the moment.' Because when I had a fall downstairs I lost my sense of smell. I fell down the stairs and I was in hospital for six weeks because I kept having epilepsy fits. I've damaged part of my brain and even now I lose my memory from one day to the next, like, come tomorrow, I'll get up and I can't remember what I've done today. I'll remember this meeting, type of thing, or if I was stuck in the kitchen for a few hours washing up and, admittedly, I did do a fry-up and everything – yeah I will remember that.

Dennis: You seem to be saying that prison life is quite comfortable.

Jim: You wouldn't believe how comfortable. You have a fry-up every morning ready for you. The doors were opened at eight o'clock in the morning and if you were up your breakfast would be there at nine o'clock. You could do what you like all the way through the day until about 8.30 when you're locked up. You've got your own television. No, you've got everything.

Dennis: So you can understand why there's such a high rate of people returning to prison.

Jim: I can understand it, yeah. You've got spending money – you can make a list of what shopping you want. They bring it in and deliver it for you. You're not allowed anything sharp and stuff like that. You're allowed razors but not anything too sharp.

The discourse to this point reveals certain ambivalence in how Jim made sense of the incident of physical abuse and the resultant conditions. He was not comfortable with the social work report of Suzanne's disclosure in that it paints a more violent, life-threatening bout of aggression than he felt was the case. But there again he admits that it was 'actual bodily harm' and that his period of imprisonment was quite justified. However, accused parties – both those convicted and those who profess their innocence over an allegation that does not come to court – want the authorities off their back. This results in social workers being suspicious of an abuser's expressed regret and promises to change. Since apportioning blame was not my interest in the interview, I was keen to move on to see how this family might function with greater harmony and with less risk of further abuse. In this respect we had to examine the possible tensions that might lead to a further loss in self-control.

Dennis: It must be difficult when her friends are there and you feel the need to control the situation – you're thinking, 'I'm the adult here. What's going on?'

Jim: I mean now that I've come home and I'm allowed to be on the premises and all the social involvement has gone, if I tell her off she just goes berserk at me.

Dennis: Is that difficult for you being the man of the family, and effectively being her father since the age of…?

Jim: Three months old.

Dennis: Three months old. Is that difficult having to take a backward step when before you may have had more control in the family?

Jim: Yeah.

Dennis: How does that feel for you now that the system – the child protection procedures and the aftermath – has pushed you into a changed role?

Jim: I don't know, to be honest. It's nerve-racking.

Dennis: And I suppose that's always going to be a problem because Suzanne will always be Suzanne and she'll still do the sort of things that all parents find challenging – not doing what she's told, not getting up – but then how can you cope with that without getting angry and hitting her?

Jim: I don't know.

Dennis: Let's look at Suzanne's behaviour a little more closely. You said earlier that when you handed her the phone – knowing how you would react in such situations from having lived with you for such a long time – she still chose to do what she did. She knows you are vulnerable, particularly when you've had a drink. Is there a sense, do you think, that she can engineer what might happen?

Jim: Yes, definitely. She did the other day. She asked me to do certain washing for her. She asked me to do a tracksuit top which when she came home from school she could wear. So I just took it that I didn't need to get the washing out straight away, but when she came home she says, 'Where's my jeans that I asked you to wash?' I said, 'They're in the washing machine.' I said, 'I'm waiting for them to dry.' So she says, 'So I've got wet jeans to put on?' So she threw them at me, and I threw them back. She threw them back again and then I said, 'I'll rip them if you want me to.' She said, 'No, don't do that.' I slung them back and she knew then I was going to lose it and I did lift my arm to go and hit her again and I said, 'That's what you want me to do.' I held myself and didn't hit her, and then went off to my brother's, only for about 30 minutes. I got back, again, she got the bass music blasting, which I can't stand and she's got it on full blast. I walked in. She'd got friends there again and they're smoking, and I almost lost it again, but I just turned the music down and then went out again.

Dennis: Would Suzanne behave that way if Ruth had been there?

Jim: No [*said emphatically*].

Dennis: So she's choosing to behave that way with you?

Jim: Most of the time, yeah.

Dennis: So in one sense she has control over you, and can behave differently with you than she can with her mother.

Jim: She gets away with an awful lot, but then again she'll ask her mum for the odd cigarette. Yesterday I was ironing Ruth's uniform and I'd got the cigarettes on me. Because if they're lying there – I could be on the toilet and she would be in the kitchen – she'd secretly nick one. She would say, 'I'll be back in a minute.' And she's in the back garden smoking, and I can smell it on her. Because we've always got the window open for the cats to run in and out to save the front door being open.

Dennis: If you're a non-smoker you notice it, don't you?

Jim: I notice it instantly.

Dennis: So, with that particular situation, like with the jeans, did you share that with Ruth or does Suzanne expect you to keep it from her?

Jim: No, because Suzanne will tell her mum anyway, and her mum will just question me then and ask what went on and I'll explain.

Dennis: But what version of events will she believe?

Jim: She'll try and get her mum on her side.

Dennis: But where's Ruth coming from? Is she wise to Suzanne now?

Jim: Oh yeah. She knows because we've been together so long we can look at each other and know what each other think.

Dennis: Is that sufficient for you though? It sounds like she's testing you out all the time. And that's a very common pattern with adolescents. If there's division young people know how to exploit it. If one parent might react, they know which button to press. They have learnt where they have control. I wonder if as a family there needs to be change collectively. Perhaps that's the area we can work on together, with all parties together as a family, so we don't reach this point of a loss in self-control with the drinking – where you have to escape from the house and go to your brother to save you becoming aggressive with Suzanne and get into further trouble.

Both Jim's parents had died, and at one point in the interview he became upset, particularly over the death of his mother, but then, without prompting, he began describing a pattern of behaviour where the misuse of alcohol was prevalent during childhood.

Jim: When my dad was alive he was very, very, very strict. My mum was a drinker. She used to drink about four Guinness a day, about two pint bottles, sort of thing, and my dad used to drink two Newcastle Brown when he was alive, sort of thing, but when he died, that was it, she hit the drink hard.

Dennis: Would you say you were brought up in a house where alcohol was misused by your mum after your dad had died?

Jim: Yeah, because the local shop would serve me, and I know this might sound strange, it's going back a few years, they would serve to you a pint of sherry so long as you supplied the bottle. Otherwise you would have to pay extra for the bottle.

Dennis: How old would you have been then?

Jim: It started when I was about four.

Dennis: So, at the age of four you could go into a shop and purchase a bottle of sherry for your mum?

Jim: Yeah.

Dennis: How old were you when you lost your dad?

Jim: Twelve.

Dennis: That's quite a sensitive age to lose your father.

Jim: Yeah.

Dennis: You mentioned earlier the incident when you were hit after you burst into the toilet; was that typical of your dad to give out that sort of punishment?

Jim: I don't know really. I had just come in from off the sand and it was only ten steps to where we were stopping. I just walked into the sitting room and everybody was there, all but dad. I just opened the door and there he was sitting there reading the paper. Obviously, I got frightened and hid behind a settee. He was very strict.

Dennis: Was he more strict than physical?

Jim: More strict, but if we did anything wrong you'd know about it. But it worked. He used to get up and on the one occasion he made me mum go up to the local shop and get cornflakes in, because he always had cornflakes ready for him to get up to. He would come downstairs and his cornflakes would be ready, his milk would be warmed up. He would put it into his dish and then go to work. He would come home from work at 5.10 and his dinner would have to be ready for him and then he would just sit down and relax. Again, I would have gone up the shop for four bottles of Guinness and two Newcastle Brown, because although I didn't know what my mum was drinking through the day when he was at work I knew what she had at night. And when my dad died I had three months off school because of how upset I had kept getting, and at the same time it was to do all the running about for my mum.

Dennis: In trying to draw some patterns from your story, would you say that many of the problems seem to stem from alcohol?

Jim: Nine out of ten times, yes.

Dennis: And your father, you say, was quite a disciplinarian and controlling man?

Jim: Yeah.

Dennis: We tend to unconsciously model our own experience of being parented and brought up in the way we parent our children. But in your case, in light of what has happened, the system won't allow you to have that degree of control. And this you find difficult when Suzanne becomes particularly challenging. In fact, she's in trouble at school now through behaving in a way not too dissimilar to what had occurred when you hit her. She had been escorted to a senior teacher for something and was not being cooperative, and when she was escorted to the nurse she became verbally abusive, regularly using the 'F' word. She's not one of the school's most difficult pupils, but she can be challenging, as a lot of teenagers are. If when you were brought up you had a fear of your father, say, in the incident when you hid behind the settee after bursting into the toilet, for example, that is not Suzanne's experience of being parented by you. So how do you exercise authority and control when Suzanne becomes cheeky and breaks the rules? I'm wondering how you cope with that?

Jim: I just go through Ruth now.

Dennis: Your hands are tied behind your back?

Jim: I'll say, 'Look, she's up to this or that, you'll have to speak to her.'

Dennis: So you've had to sidestep. You've had to acknowledge that you can no longer manage her in a way because you are so vulnerable and it may lead to a situation in which we'll all regret. And this is OK if Ruth is around, but how will you manage if she's not?

Jim: That will happen tomorrow when Ruth's at work. Ruth won't get home till seven o'clock, and I have to take her into school for this exclusion meeting. She'll come home from school for about 3.20 and she'll be out of the house with her friends within five minutes.

Professional management and the family script

The links between this family's troubles and the misuse of alcohol were evident throughout: during the incident, subsequent to the abuse with after-management and even during our therapy sessions there were occasions when Jim smelt of alcohol, which made me consider at times whether to foreshorten my engagement. His difficulty in recalling details of events he put down to a different cause from being inebriated: to 'a fall downstairs' and 'having epilepsy fits' after damaging part of his brain, which caused short-term memory loss.

Whatever may be the case, as pointed out earlier, social workers are principally involved with the protection of the child, quite rightly, whereas the family therapist will work with the family as a unit. Whatever interventions the police and social services make are normally short-term, but all professionals realistically know that if this family wishes to go on following the same script, then it will.

Both lay readers and practitioners will, I suspect, notice and be concerned about particular comments in this discourse, depending on one's particular experience or professional background. The social worker from a child protection perspective may be troubled by statements Jim had made in confessing his vulnerability to strike Suzanne again and to have not fully complied with the child protection care plan agreements. Parents of challenging teenagers will recognize in this narrative the tensions that arise in normal parent–adolescent altercations and the familiar tussles when teenagers push the boundaries and become defiant. Psychologists would be interested in the root causes of Jim's aggressive behaviour, and drug and alcohol clinicians might look at how Jim's vulnerabilities could be managed in day-to-day family trials in order to get therapeutic leverage for change.

I consider that few of us would be able to examine such a discourse as this without interpreting the material from preconceived convictions or without having a view on how the matter should be dealt. Regarding the rights and wrongs of permitting this family to live without professional interference, in the absence of legal and mandatory obligations it remains a question of personal conviction, of how our passions have been aroused and how the narrative has affected us.

At a case conference, Suzanne was asked repeatedly whether she wanted her dad back home within the family. I had asked her the same question, and so did pastoral teachers and practitioners at school, and consistently she said yes – as did his partner, Ruth. Here is the dilemma. How can this family function together without risk of further abuse? Was the prison sentence required or wanted by the injured parties? And if it was not, apart from upholding the law, what purpose does it serve to lock up perpetrators of domestic violence, even against their children? We return to this social question in Chapter 10, 'A Better Way Forward'.

Concluding comment

The conventions and attitudes on appropriate child management in challenging circumstances have been examined in this chapter. What may have been acceptable in earlier periods of social history and in other cultural contexts might not be the case today in secular and democratic countries of the Western world. Serious cases of child physical abuse will fall under child protection legislation, as we have seen, and perpetrators, justifiably, can count on receiving a prison sentence if successfully convicted. There is little doubt today that bullying children by adults can have grave consequences for the psychological development and social well-being of young people, both during childhood and into later adulthood. Domestic violence involving the bullying and maltreatment of children and young people within families becomes a much more complicated affair if alcohol and the misuse of drugs are involved, as the research has shown. In this chapter we have seen that excessively corrective measures in formal and close-knit relationships – whatever the pressures or mitigating circumstances may be – are an issue which is not so clear-cut when we ask the pressing question of what the 'injured parties' want from authoritative intervention.

We looked in more detail at a formal example of corrective measures through a teacher's management of a conflict through his pupils' eyes, and found in general that they were unforgiving of him and also critical of how the incident was managed by the authorities. A rising rate of allegations against teachers for using what pupils judge to be undue force to maintain discipline and control has been a particularly controversial issue in UK schools in recent times. Investigating authorities, such as senior teachers, the police and social services, have a delicate role in forming judgements when balancing lawful action with well-intentioned though unskilled management in tense and exacting situations. The problem when examining such cases is getting to the facts, along with the difficulty of separating the issues of fairness and appropriateness from the personalities involved – both in regard to the 'offending' teacher and the pupil or pupils making an allegation.

A case of alleged bullying within a family relationship was then looked at in much closer detail through the eyes of the perpetrator, in this case a step-father against his step-daughter. In listening to the voice of the perpetrator it seems as though he had no malice against his plaintiff, even though her call brought about in the end his internment. The example illustrated that whilst he felt his conviction was justified, and unquestionable in terms of the law, this was not what his step-daughter wanted. With more penetrative questioning it became evident for the perpetrator that his instinctive and impulsive behaviour was not wholly unrelated to his own past of behavioural modelling in which he had been subjected as a child. Our interest was not in questioning the judicial judgement, however, but rather in exploring a way forward that might better suit all parties and that would be more in line with what may be considered to be fitting for this particular family.

As in former chapters, it would be naive and over-simplistic to draw general conclusions from only one narrative of a parent abusing his youngster, and although I deliberately avoid the tendency to relate the discourse directly to theories presented earlier I think there are some general observations that are helpful to highlight. This book is concerned with 'the meaning' of dominant and abusive behaviour amongst close relations. As I reflected on salient comments of this discourse, I wondered what hints of a payoff could be detected for each party.

For Jim, although he felt he could depend on his brother for support at times of crises and regular company when not working – where the hours can be long – his paternal needs and life-meaning needs were met by his immediate family of Ruth and Suzanne. When speaking on 'comfortable' life in prison, he said 'If you haven't got anybody else out there you're better off in prison', which suggested regret, but there again I did not feel he regretted internment in prison as much as his step-daughter regretted making the disclosure that got him there. His whole life-story seemed pitiful to me; he appeared lost and in need of parenting and I began to wonder whether he may be drawing his daughter and partner into the game of 'Poor Little Old Me', in unconsciously drawing them to parent him. Berne (1968) parodies the alcoholic's lifestyle and discusses the role of the family in playing the 'Alcoholic's Game'. The payoff, and point of the game, is not the binge-drinking (which is merely the prelude) but the hangover, for it is within the stage of hangover that players take up their respective roles – *Feel sorry for me, 'Parent' me, I am sick 'child'* (Lines 2006a).

A payoff for Suzanne may be found in one innocuous but significant comment through her step-father's narrative. Jim had no doubts about Ruth being the boss and at times she had pacts with Suzanne 'against him' and, whilst smoking was a greater issue for him than for his partner, Suzanne still felt she could rely on her Daddy's Little Girl relationship, reverse the pact and manipulate him for money: 'Dad, can I have some money? Tell mum that you've spent it on something else.' 'Well what's it for?' 'So I can get some fags.'

Some caution should be exercised in seeking a payoff for Ruth because so little is said of her part in the relationships. However, there is a hint in the narrative of a payoff for mum to serve as Authority and Judge – a very powerful position. Obviously, she has some say as to whether Jim continues to be in 'the family', she benefits from his domiciliary responsibilities while she earns the money, but, more particularly, she 'sits as Judge' in the various battles that ensue between father and step-daughter: 'Suzanne will tell her mum anyway, and *her mum will just question me* then and ask what went on and *I'll explain.*'

Chapter 9

Bullying in the Workplace

Workplace bullying has been under-researched in comparison to school bullying. Some media figures appear so proud of a 'bossy' management style that it has become for them a token of celebrity status to be rude and provocative for television appeal – the Scottish chef, Gordon Ramsay, comes to mind. Managers of all organizations are under pressure to meet targets – whether these are financial or reduced client waiting lists – and no doubt the pressures placed upon them will inevitably cascade to other tiers of the workforce. Employee rights and workforce legislation are designed to see that fair play and a sense of reasonableness occurs in industrial disputes. Inevitably, there will be tension between managerial targets and employee regulations whether or not unions and associations are employed to restore an imbalance of power. Whereas employee injustices and tribunal decisions of unfair dismissal become public, it is quite rare to listen to the voices of those who sit on the opposite side of the fence.

Instances of unfair treatment in the workplace are commonly discussed amongst friends and acquaintances, but few if any managers are prepared to come forward to present their side of a case when being accused of harassment, bullying or dominating their employees. This may be because they are in denial, of course, and they do not see a ruthless and exacting management style as being 'bullying' as such (clearly, a pejorative term), but it may also be because from their position they have no choice but to present firm leadership and execute forthright judgements over slothful or unproductive personnel within a culture of increased litigation and human rights sensitivity. We cannot be fully sure without listening to their perspectives.

In examining workplace bullying, this chapter is broader in scope than commerce and industry, and covers patterns of dominant management in public institutional settings where there is a clear difference in power. After relating two victim case examples, we consider how bullying might be understood from the limited research carried out amongst public sector employees and officers and inmates in prisons. This choice is significant in that there are striking similarities between schools and prisons in relation to freedom of choice, large numbers of people being managed and power differential. Although the evidence of workplace bullying is limited, there are some interesting features even though the definitions of what constitutes 'bullying' varies so much as to make strict comparisons with schools largely meaningless. Selected narrative of two business executives is presented before a much fuller account is considered of an ex-soldier.

What commonly happens in the workplace

In all competitive workplace environments where margins are tight and personnel resources are expensive there is a challenge for managers to achieve the highest productivity for the least possible cost – the Darwinian principle we reviewed in Chapter 2. This is how profits are made, how bonuses are justified and how funding is secured. This is the *productivity* = *target reached* formula of 'successful' market economies. In public service industries, like education, health and prisons, productivity is not always measured by money, but often instead by other, sometimes arbitrary, targets.

But what happens when the manager feels that employees are not pulling their weight, that they are unproductive, cavalier, or perhaps unpunctual or prone to regular absence; in short, a liability to the company? What can an employer do if she wishes to avoid wading through a tide of protective legislation, such as formal verbal and written warnings, and yet has to be rid of an employee to avoid going bust or putting pressure on others of the team? One human course of action may be to make life so unbearably unpleasant for the employee that he or she is forced to resign. One 'justification' for bullying might therefore be 'to get someone out for a greater good'. Conversely, a manager may have an ulterior motive to bully a subordinate. This was the case with a young trainee electrician.

A bullied young trainee

This first incident of bullying in the workplace involved David, a young man of 18 years of age, serving his apprenticeship as an electrician in a leading company. His training went well for the first two years, but during his third year his personal adviser informed him that his training schedule was behind, that he should have been carrying out more technical work than merely wiring up houses. David's reply was that his team manager was not providing him with this type of work; that he had pointed this out to the foreman but that the team manager had ignored what he had said and still given him mundane electrical work to keep up the monthly targets for the branch. In agreement with David his adviser elected to take up the matter with the team manager and foreman in his absence, whilst he attended block release at college.

Unfortunately, this meeting did not go well and David's team manager took the complaint 'personally' as a slight against him, and when they next met he laid into David, called him into his office and verbally assaulted him in no uncertain terms. He called David 'a fucking waste of space', and said that he had wished he was no longer part of the team and that he would review his situation at the end of the month. David was a sensitive person, and there was clearly a power imbalance. He became dispirited and worried over the next few weeks. From being the 'blue-eyed boy' he was now made to feel like a leper, as 'scum', as he said.

Two weeks later he was called into the team manager's office for an unannounced meeting, and for no other reason, David's workmates surmised, but to get his own back. He had contacted David's adviser to register a 'formal complaint' over David's work, and therefore to give him a black mark. During a factory wiring job, each electrician is expected to write a report about safety checks carried out, and David was criticized with a tirade of verbal abuse for recording an inaccurate meter reading, a trivial mistake that David's foreman said anyone could make. Nevertheless, the team manager claimed, it was an error that cost the company a thousand pounds in order to keep good relations with the customer. No one believed it of course, but how could a young apprentice already intimidated challenge one so powerful?

Although in time the customer gesture proved to be false (David was dating the firm's accountant), it nevertheless had a great effect on David's confidence, and all because some justified criticism was taken personally by a manager – disliked by the workforce generally – who looked for an opportunity to carry out a vendetta. To date, David still works under him, without the normal courtesies and amidst simmering tension: 'The atmosphere is terrible. I have to suck up to him and he treats me like shit! But what can I do till I've finished my apprenticeship?'

A teacher 'bullied' because of falling standards

A friend spoke to me about her plight in a junior school when under pressure to resign her post. She had been the deputy head of a junior school for 20 years and felt she had contributed the major part of her life to the children and the community. She was dedicated, although she regarded herself as 'one of the old school'. Parents and fellow colleagues valued her, and she contemplated finishing her working career as a primary school teacher at the same school since she was approaching retirement age. The post of headteacher became available, and in view of her age she decided not to apply. When the new appointment was made there was a 'clash in personalities', at least from her perspective.

She was told abruptly that her leadership and management style had led to a lowering in standards for the children of the school, that there was no evidence that the quality of teaching had improved for some time and that the children were not reaching their potential. Although it was not said, it was intimated that she was a stumbling block in the way of the school's progress. The headteacher felt this was ratified when the school failed an inspection, and inspectors declared the school to be in special measures owing to poor behaviour, poor standards of teaching and learning, and weak leadership. The headteacher, being only a recent appointment, was not held accountable, and so the fault lay at the door of the deputy head. She took this news very hard and quite personally, and after an extraordinary meeting with the governing body she was asked to attend a meeting with her headteacher. She told me that she sat mute for nearly an hour and had to listen to a barrage of criticism for having allowed the school to be placed into special measures. 'I could not get a word in,' she said. 'I felt thoroughly intimidated, humiliated and bullied. There was a clear agenda to this meeting, which was that I was expected to resign.' She complied and gave in her notice since she considered there was no point working in an atmosphere of being the scapegoat. She felt demoralized and undervalued, and thought that her 'last 20 years of exemplary service', as one teacher told her in her final speech, was to no avail.

Bullying in prisons

Bullying in prisons is not entirely unexpected given the growing and worrying rise in drug culture and the effects of its unregulated practice in hostile and largely unsupervised contained environments. Bullying is perhaps inevitable given that inmates may be serving sentences for violence and physical assault, and particularly within institutions where reporting an injustice is not likely to happen.

It has long been known that cartels of power and domination exist within prisons, and that powerful barons lend money, tobacco, alcohol, cannabis and harder drugs for high rates of repayment, and with physical consequences for non-payment. Exacting rates of tax from novice inmates as well as initiation rites for new entrants has been a common bullying pattern in prisons. Whilst bullying may be anticipated, if not excused, *amongst* inmates, should we expect bullying behaviour *towards* inmates by prison officers? I raised this question with Kate, a teacher in a Young Offender Institution, and she had no misapprehensions about the matter:

Kate: Bullying occurs amongst the prison guards more than amongst prisoners themselves. Occasionally we send a prisoner to the guard at the entrance of the school for a radio and we have to write a note for the prisoner to take to the guard. Without the note the guard will not give him the radio, and we are not supposed to leave the education unit to speak to the guard ourselves. Often, the guards will screw up the note as a gesture of power and indifference. A lot of officers don't think civilians, of any description, should be in a prison, and that prisons should be run by them and that's it. So officers resent the fact that civilians whatsoever go in – CARAT workers, probation staff, health care even and people like that – who actually have contact with the inmates. What on earth do they think that inmates would do if education was not there I don't know, because they'd be banged up 24 hours a day.

Dennis: Are all guards the same, the young and old?

Kate: There is no difference in age. Some of them are getting on a bit and they are quite respected by the inmates, and some are detested, and it's the same with the young ones. So I can't see that it's got anything to do with a certain age. There's good and bad in the whole age range. Generally, officers are not liked at all. In terms of numbers this accounts for about 80 per cent of them. Listening to the lads they chat and time after time they get round to talking about particular officers of their own wings and the same names come up. 'He's a bastard he is', or 'That one is OK. Yeah, he's a good chap.' 'Oh you don't want to have anything to do with her' or 'She's sound or sick' (that means she's OK). And the same names keep cropping up for one reason or another. And then, of course, they come down when they're on duty for education hours in the morning or afternoon, and we have contact with them and that's when you realize what they're really like.

Dennis: Could you not file a complaint?

Kate: You can put a security information report in about an inmate. You can file a major 'nicking', which means that it will go to the governor and could affect an inmate's sentence if it's really serious… Let's say an inmate turns round and says 'Fuck off!' to your face in your class. That shouldn't happen, but occasionally it does. You can actually report that lad and put in a minor nicking or a major one. That could end up with the inmate losing his television for a week, or a fortnight; it's up to the governor. If it is more serious than that, if they are fighting in education, or in that area, obviously that has to be reported and then that can involve that lad going into the segregation area for a period… But complaining about an officer there is no chance, no way. You do not go down that road.

Bullying in the armed services

In the movie *A Few Good Men*, Tom Cruise plays the part of defending counsel for two American marines accused of murdering a recruit who was a whistle-blower and not quite up to scratch. The film wrestles with the moral dilemma of when unquestioning obedience overrules an individual's sense of right – as judged by unjustified bullying that led to murder. A 'Code Red' was a conventional, yet unwritten, military 'punishment' that would be administered to a fellow marine to instil unwavering discipline and a sense of group loyalty. 'Justification' for issuing a Code Red centred on a 'believed proven method' of psychological conditioning for marines in combat to face an enemy without fear of loss of one's own life and risk to one's fellow marines.

The question is whether institutional violence, even if sanctioned at a high level, should be termed 'bullying' by those of us sitting in privileged positions of peacetime contexts. And even if it should, can there ever be a justification for aggressively dominant management styles within recruitment training even within military organizations?

An abuse of power has been the charge levelled recently against Deepcut Barracks, one of Britain's most notorious army training camps, after four recruits had died in mysterious circumstances. A British investigation (BBC *Panorama*) uncovered a climate of fear, where intimidation, beatings and bullying were commonplace. Private Sean Benton was found dead in July 1995 from five bullet wounds with an army rifle at his side. He had told his parents he was sorry that he had failed as a soldier and had let them down. Although the army quickly came to the conclusion of suicide, a number of ex- and current soldiers disputed this and claimed that sexism, bullying and beatings were rife.

Confidential army documents revealed that there were five suicide attempts between June and November 1995, and a particular sergeant was named as being particularly brutal when dealing with new recruits. All were in fear of the consequences of reporting matters to higher or outside authorities. One of Sean Benton's friends at the base, Glynn Boswell, backed up this claim, saying: 'If every bullying incident was reported you'd have something along the lines of the Britannica volume… You can't report it. You could be reporting it to the person who was actually doing it.'

Making sense of workplace bullying

Whilst legislation is in place to help protect itinerant employees, in practice employment rights for refugees and migrant workers have often been abused – they have rates of pay less than the minimum wage and have to endure long and illegal working hours. Following the Morecambe Bay tragedy in England, where 23 Chinese migrant workers were drowned in fast-moving tidal waters when cockle-picking, stricter regulations came into place. The case illustrated that bullying stretches further than intimidation and abuse of power towards *economic abuse* for those whose desperate subsistence levels leads them to become prey to exploitation. The London Hazards Centre issues the following legal advice in a fact sheet:

> There is no specific legislation on bullying. The Health and Safety at Work Act places a general duty on employers to protect the health, safety and welfare of their employees and the Management of Health and Safety at Work Regulations sets out the means of doing so. Anti-discrimination legislation, the Sex Discrimination, Race Relations, and Disability Discrimination Acts, may apply in some instances. The Criminal Justice and Public Order and the Protection from Harassment Acts may afford protection. The Employment Rights Act deals with the right to claim

'unfair constructive dismissal' in the face of an employer's breach of contract which could include a failure to protect health and safety. However, expert advice should be obtained on all of these measures before any reliance is placed upon them.

Research on workplace bullying

Rigby (2002) comments on bullying practice outside of school and education, by first looking at the context and the ambiguity of definitions, then moving on to examine the scant research carried out in this area. I shall briefly summarize his findings. He considers the type of bullying that is commonplace and the type of personnel who become principally involved. It is worth noting in passing that other places where bullying commonly occurs, and where it is con-siderably under-researched, are:

- *in the home* – where child abuse and domestic violence between adults and physical and sexual assault of women tends to cloud the issues of bullying behaviour

- *in prisons* – where a growing amount of evidence suggests that bullying is commonplace

- *in sport* – where bullying becomes confused with rules of the game

- *in politics* – where parliamentary leaders openly abuse one another in the name of open debate

- *in stalking behaviour* – where motives and intentions become confused with mental health issues.

(Rigby 2002)

Definitions of bullying in the workplace are inconsistent in the limited research available, and this factor accounts for considerably varied statistical data. Some definitions centre upon hurtful intent, whilst others register less explicit desig-nations as:

- group ganging up

- negative actions

- less favourable treatment

- behaviour intended to humiliate or denigrate an individual

- failure to acknowledge a colleague's efforts

- standing in the way of promotion or self-advancement

- setting unrealistic goals and deadlines which are unachievable

- denying information or knowledge necessary for undertaking work and yet expecting the work to be completed

- excessive monitoring, supervision, or micro-management.

(Rigby 2002)

A further complexity in comparing statistics arises when some researchers assess bullying behaviour amongst colleagues of equal status whilst others focus on superior–subordinate hierarchies, and for this reason Rigby settles for the simplistic definition of workplace bullying outlined by Smith and Sharp (1994): 'the systematic abuse of power'.

A comprehensive and well-researched report was carried out at the Manchester School of Management (Hoel and Cooper 2000) in which questionnaires from 5288 employees were collated and analysed. This study of workplace bullying sampled a wide range of work organizations, from breweries to National Health Trusts in the UK. The report concluded that in general 10 per cent of workers indicated that they had been bullied over the last six months, and 1.4 per cent reported they were bullied on a daily or weekly basis. These results were less than the general results of bullying rates in schools and those of another study carried out by Charlotte Rayner (1998) of 761 members of UNISON, which represents local government, healthcare, higher education, electricity, gas, water, public transport, police and voluntary employees. This study estimated that 14 per cent of union members were being bullied in any six-month period.

Both these studies reported wide variations between areas of work, but both series of figures still fall below those for bullying in schools, which remain between one in five (Lines 1996) and one in six (Rigby 1997). Given that employees have more choice than children in schools or inmates in prisons, and given also that adults are likely to be more self-assertive than children, it is surprising that figures are not much higher in workplace contexts, unless, of course, there is something endemic in the nature of bullying in some large and 'contained' group settings that does not apply as much in the general workplace.

In terms of who bullies whom, Hoel and Cooper (2000) reported that 74.7 per cent of bullied respondents reported that they had been bullied by managers and supervisors, as against 36.7 per cent by colleagues, 6.7 per cent by subordinates and 7.8 per cent by clients, customers or students. As Rigby notes, adding up these figures indicates that some employees may be bullied by managers and others alike, and again, as we found with children in school, such statistics 'may be' suggestive of particular personalities being prone to become victims of bullying in particular contexts. Weekly bullying rates as reported by employees in prisons, teaching and police services by (inferred) managers are well above the mean of 20 per cent, but bullying in higher education is relatively low (Hoel and Cooper 2000). As Rigby (2002) sums up:

> Explanations for such variations have at this stage been notably absent and one is left to wonder whether the variations are due to working conditions, the kind of people who are employed in given areas, the sensitivity workers may have to being bullied, or what. (pp.81–82)

Research on bullying in prisons

One piece of research (Leddy and O'Connell 2002) found that over a quarter of inmates in Irish prisons became highly stressed after being subjected to bullying – with, surprisingly, women bullying more than men. Research carried out in Holland confirms the prevalence of bullying amongst officers and inmates in prisons. Vartia and Hyyti (2002) found that 20 per cent of employee bullying was due to the poor social climate in Dutch prisons.

In March 2000, a 19-year-old Muslim, Zahid Mubarek, died in Feltham Young Offender Institution after a savage racially motivated beating from his cell-mate. This resulted in an inquiry into the state of eight prisons. Lack of multi-faith sensitivity amongst officers and management has been reported on at Belmarsh Maximum Security Prison in London following inmate bullying in light of the suicide bombings and attempted bombings in the capital in July 2005.

Other studies have highlighted the high correlation of suicide and suicide ideation with in-prison bullying, where suicidal inmates reported that 'correctional officers' and other inmates bullied them in contrast to non-suicidal inmates who identified only the former as their bullies (Blaauw, Winkel and Kerkhof 2001). Governors in British prisons are putting inmate bullying down to overcrowding and misallocated placements that are unsympathetic to family contact.

Unquestioning obedience

Applying excessive authority over subordinates recalls the well-known study of Stanley Milgram in a classic experiment published in 1963 following the trial of Adolf Eichmann. Milgram was interested in the often repeated excuse of Nazi camp guards who claimed that they were 'only obeying orders' when executing their victims. Was the claim in itself justifiable to absolve someone from moral conscience? By claiming 'I was only obeying orders!' did that make the act morally justified and excusable?

Milgram took male volunteers from different backgrounds (ages 20–50, drop-outs to doctors) and invited them to take part in an exercise. He staged a situation in which actors posing as subjects were supposedly administered electric shocks simply because they had got the wrong answers to a range of questions. 'Shocks' were administered by the volunteer participants tripping a range of switches, which released an electric shock from mild to dangerous (45–450 volts), up a scale with each successive wrong answer. Volunteers became uncomfortable as they noticed subjects (actors) appearing to pass out as the switches were tripped towards the danger zone. Many of them refused to go any further, saying 'I can't do this; this is wrong', particularly when they were told that the subject had a heart condition. What was surprising to Milgram, and what may be a disturbing feature of human nature, is that nearly everybody continued to inflict suffering when the experimenter, dressed in a white lab coat, gave cold, objective instructions, such as:

Please continue.

The experiment requires that you continue.

It is absolutely essential that you continue.

You have no other choice, you must go on.

Some gave the full 450-volt shock even when the subject (actor feigning) passed out. It was as though the heartless manner of giving the order gave respondents the permission to override their conscience and inflict violence upon an unknown person. Milgram also noticed that the closer persons were to their victims the less inclined they were to continue towards the danger zone. Proximity and distance, whether spatial or psychological, seems to be important in granting or refusing administering pain to an innocent party, and there is also something about the white lab coat in a particular setting that carries mystical 'authority' – think of the consultant on a ward round in hospital advising a patient to undergo an operation, or the traditional picture of sectioning a member of the public: 'They're coming to take you away!' There are implications here also for soldiers in wartime and for police and prison officers.

A relational perspective of workplace bullying

In Chapter 5, 'Interpreting Bullying Behaviour', we considered an interpretation of bullying behaviour through the games people play. This perspective is drawn from a counselling approach called transactional analysis, a therapeutic style that assists people to see their inner Child and hidden Parent operating in their unconscious and relational encounters. This approach holds that human behaviour within relationships is rarely rational and consistent, that we tend to behave towards some people as though we were a child (sulking, moody, belligerent, playful, etc.) and towards others as though an adult (admonishing, controlling, nurturing, caring, etc.).

One very imaginative presentation of this process is found in Robert de Board's (1998) book, *Counselling for Toads*. It is a tale based on *Wind in the Willows* where Toad of Toad Hall is told to visit Heron for counselling over his depression. Toad is encouraged to reflect on his Child Ego State that is revealed when he becomes passive, obedient and subservient when being bossed about by Badger – who operates unconsciously in his Parent Ego State. When a powerful parent functions, not as Nurturing Parent but Critical Parent, the defenceless child will not experience Fun and Affection but Sadness, Anger and Fear. In order to survive he must become Adapted Child. Put diagrammatically, the child/parental dynamics might look like Figure 9.1.

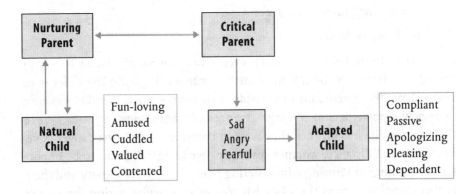

Figure 9.1 The unconscious transition from Natural Child to Adapted Child and the observable mannerisms of adaptation

Translated into professional and workforce relations this means that managers and employers may have a tendency to become Critical Parent – depending on 'their childhood history' – since such responses have been learnt from young, and employees adapt complementary behaviours like Compliant, Apologetic, Pleasing and Subservient – depending on 'their childhood history' – often to the annoyance of their colleagues and themselves. It is a reciprocal relational process.

Downtrodden and bullied employees will displace their anger by 'passing it down' to a subordinate, or – through what psychotherapists call 'projective identification' – by getting another person to feel their angry feelings as if they were their own (Luxmoore 2006). If this is not possible and they cannot fight back, they have no means to discharge the anger other than through maladaptive behaviours like sulking, petulance, delaying, withdrawal and depression (rebelling is much too risky); behaviours all learned from young. Even though a dominated employee may operate in a Child Ego State, he or she may also function thereafter as Critical Parent, but if there is no safe other to be critical of, only self-criticism is left. Self-criticism is much more destructive than reproof from others.

Another feature of power differential in the workplace, again learnt from young, is an unconscious manipulation of the employee considered as 'worthless' in contrast to the boss as 'worthy'. In transactional analysis terms, this is a relationship tendency to make the powerless feel not OK and the powerful feel OK. The most productive relation is 'I'm OK; you're OK', the most destructive is 'I'm not OK; you're not OK', and the most common employee–employer dynamic in bullying situations is 'I'm not OK; you're OK', since the payoff for a bullying or dominating employer or manager is to bolster their pre-eminence in having a workforce afraid because of their position. Represented diagrammatically this appears as shown in Figure 9.2, where the bullied employee is the lower right quadrant.

A favourite game that bullying bosses play is called 'Now I've Got You, You Son of a Bitch', which operates from the quadrant 'I'm not OK; you're OK'. After a mistake, which anyone can make, the boss notices it and calls in the erring subordinate and proceeds to give a dressing down, yelling and remonstrating out of all proportion to the offence committed. Inevitably, the subordinate becomes angry but cannot fight back, and so becomes depressed or fed up. Such bosses

> have the proof that other people are essentially incompetent and unreliable, and second, that it is their duty to chastise and punish them.

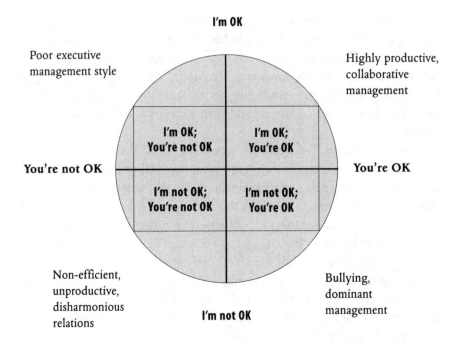

Figure 9.2 Employee–employer relations of worthiness and productivity (employee = I; employer = You)

'Otherwise,' they say, 'they will think they can get away with it'... Unfortunately, this game seems to be on the increase, especially in organisations... It's all too easy for people in authority to act out their phantasy of the punishing parents and train their staff like naughty children. (de Board 1998, p.119)

Some employers, like many teachers, play games like the one called 'Guess the Word in My Head'. It is a game that allows the powerful always to remain as Master over a Subordinate in order to feel superior. Some counsellors play this game in the nature of asking questions and refusing to answer those put to them. The basis of the dominant hierarchy is 'knowledge is power', where the boss believes that 'I haven't got where I am for nothing; I'm in charge on merit'. The employee is made to feel that he or she must sit at the boss's feet as one who must serve and learn from a master.

Both case examples of workplace bullying mentioned above might suitably fit into a transactional analysis interpretation of power and domination games.

The payoff for David's manager in the game 'Now I've Got You, You Son of a Bitch' appears to be self-aggrandisement and control, but what could the payoff possibly be for David, or my teacher friend? Neither David nor she wanted to play the game because they both felt 'I'm not OK' in their respective situations.

Heron asked Toad why he kept getting into situations where he ended up looking stupid and where someone got the upper hand, which made him feel like a poor little child again. Is it just wretched bad luck, or do you in some way collude in the process? Some children unconsciously select behaviours that reinforce an identity of 'Poor Little Old Me'. Child is 'colluding' with the parent. The Badger was in the Parent Ego State, and Toad was thrown into the Child Ego State through collusion. Badger had become Critical Parent and Toad had become Subservient Child.

Could it be that David and my friend unconsciously project behaviour that draws criticism, that they are playing the game 'Poor Little Old Me'? We cannot be dogmatic because the point is not to analyse David or my friend, nor is it to apportion blame. Bullying is wrong and there is no denying that. We are attempting to cast light on bullying and dominating behaviour in the workplace, and to view the dynamics from a broader perspective than the customary bully–victim dichotomy and to consider the pattern as a relational activity, however contentious this may first appear. Let us now hear a few voices of employers and managers.

Rationale for dominant management
Bullying in the workplace is out of date

Ross managed a steel stockist business; I talked with him about the type of pressures that he was under in running his business if he felt one of his employees was not quite coming up to scratch. He had spent time in the armed services and was used to bullying from superior officers, but, as he explained to me, that type of bullying you can't transfer into business today because it simply does not work. I told him about young David's experience and whilst he recognized it as being possible he said that such managers in the business world are quite rare these days. This was not merely because of the legislation that is now in place to protect employees: 'It simply doesn't work in business relations and in productivity. It's best to get your employees working as a team and getting on together.'

Employee not 'pulling his weight'

Stephen ran a family-style hotel catering business in a large stately mansion, a listed building of English Heritage. His central income was in weddings since there was a chapel on the premises. There was much about Stephen that projected a confident and proficient management style, a nice person to work for, I thought, but even so there were times with a few personnel when he has had to be tough and assertive. He employed about a dozen, which could double in the busy season, and these included senior managers and operational managers, front-of-house personnel, waitresses, chefs and others. Stephen valued the personal touch and felt that ensuring his clients had the best day of their lives was his main aim, because with a wedding you are offering them 'a suspension of reality' for just one day. It has to be right. 'We are selling the idea – the young girl will become a princess for the day.' He would say to the young couple, 'I would rather you go somewhere else than stay with us and be unhappy.'

Stephen's key right-hand person had been with him for 19 years, so there was stability in the business, although since weddings have become popular for those having big properties he recognized that the time was coming for him to adapt and perhaps move into hosting conferences. I drew the questioning towards how he might discipline employees he judged were not pulling their weight.

> *Stephen*: If I noticed someone who has arrived late, or that they are dressed scruffily, or their skirt is too short or their tie is not right, I never talk to the member of staff individually because for all I know my manager might already have done so... We have made mistakes in the past in employing the wrong people, but we tend to find out quickly, and they go. To be honest with you, if they aren't up to it they sack themselves. We had to sack one lad once. I think it was his second wedding and it was because we caught him having a towel fight with the washer-up. You see, with a wedding you only get the chance to do it once and everything has to be right. I went mad at him and he came and apologized the next day. He said it would not happen again... I forget what happened in the end. I think he told the head chef to 'Fuck off' or something like that and he went...

> *Dennis*: Have you ever had an employee take you to an industrial tribunal or been accused of unfair dismissal?

> *Stephen*: I belong to an organization that deals with that matter and I would never take action without doing it properly. In a sense I am quite cagey about saying the wrong thing because when my father first

managed the business, and when this legislation first came in, he got into trouble and was fined, I think it was £200, which was a shedload of money then... Usually we find people hand in their notice when we have to administer discipline, and it usually is young chefs, and, I mean, they tend to be volatile and they move often anyway... We once had a lad who was the archetypal bad lot, he looked like a bad lot, but he was cheerful and you can't dismiss him on the iconography alone, and he was a washer-up. Anyway, we had stuff go missing within two days of him starting. I wasn't there, but other members of staff caught him and chased him. One was a girl and she completely got the stuff back from him. I thought, 'Blimey, I don't think I would have done that!' She was completely incensed about him nicking. What he was doing was reaching through a grill and taking a bottle of champagne and then leaving it by the back door, and then taking it home with him when he left. So I rang up my adviser and he told me I've got to write to him and let him know what will happen – tell him he's got to come in for a meeting and what he needs to know is the consequence of what could happen, and so on, but then we never saw him again...

Dennis: Have you at any time felt torn over employing someone who desperately needed the job, but then in a real sense they were not coming up to scratch?

Stephen: No, but I wouldn't find it difficult to dismiss them. I wouldn't hesitate because my real responsibility is toward the client and the successful stewardship of the business. I know what you're saying, but if I am not running this business to the best of my ability, I am letting down everybody else. I don't mean to say that if I don't sack this washer-up the whole business is going to go bust, but once you let that thinking move along those lines where you're not stewarding that business to the best of your ability, given your limitations, you are not upholding your responsibility towards everybody else in the business. It is the cost and the greater good I suppose...

The forthright manner of Stephen's management could hardly be described as 'bullying' – even his other employees in such a family-natured business supported him with the young washer-up who was found stealing. Firm and decisive management is not 'bullying' – 'a systematic abuse of power' – even though in some cases a suspended employee might not view their dismissal that way.

When does decisive action become bullying?

One of the most significant stresses for British teachers in recent times has been to 'perform' as an effective teacher before a school inspector. I personally have witnessed teachers cracking up under 'adversarial style' inspections to improve learning, behaviour and standards. Some have left the profession, and many others have been discharged for making no improvement or for being a poor manager-leader. Arguably, within bullying definitions of 'power differential' and 'hurt to others', school inspectors may be experienced as bullies. But inspectors are safeguarding the potential for youngsters to have a bright future. They are not in place to secure teacher employment; their interests are more for pupils' welfare, not for teachers' job securities.

We saw earlier a case of a bullying management style for a subordinate teacher, but what was critical in that case was the manner in which the meeting with the headteacher was conducted, not the decision that had to be made. Was the meeting 'a systematic abuse of power', designed to hurt and bring a subordinate down? I don't know; I wasn't there. David's put-down was indefensible, but with a tough decision, which affects others who are judged to be clients of a service, the issue is less clear.

School inspectors make no bones about the fact that their responsibility is primarily for pupils and the quality of education they receive. Having had the experience of working in a failed school where a replaced leadership team (with all that that costs) has improved the prospects for pupils, I find myself divided on the matter. I felt angry during that time of seeing the school where I work slipping into decline – through lowering standards, ineffective management and chaos. I was sad that youngsters were not getting what they deserved, but one cost for improvement was for one very popular teacher to have to leave. He was dedicated to pupils and their parents. He ran extra curricular activities after school and went that extra mile, but pupils played him up and there was little effective learning taking place in his classroom. I was one amongst many who initially felt a sense of injustice when the decision was made for him to go. But then an extremely upset pupil came for counselling and put a different slant on things:

> I'm absolutely fed up with that lesson. I need a good grade in science but I know I won't get one. I've learnt nothing this year. The kids all play up and he's got no control. I really hate having to go there. How can I get what I need?

She has a different teacher now and is well on track to reaching her goal, but would not have been in this situation if the school had not failed an inspection and her teacher was still in post.

The power of the uniform

I spoke with a number of police officers, prison guards, security guards and servicemen researching for this book. Although they preferred not to give full interviews, they each in different ways made reference to how different they felt as human beings when wearing a uniform. It made them feel somehow more secure, as though they had a powerful system backing up every decision they made. The policeman said he would not enter even a remotely hostile situation when not on duty without his uniform. 'It's the uniform that gives me a greater sense of strength and authority,' he said. 'People behave differently towards you when they see your uniform.'

The mother of a naval officer told me how significant it was that the jackets of military uniforms tended to be padded out at the shoulders, often with tassels, to broaden out the male physique and to emphasize masculinity and power, and that this could hardly be without significance.

A prison guard told me how nervous he once had felt when walking through town and noticing an ex-prisoner whose eyes had met his. He was unsure whether he should speak and draw his attention or not, but chose to glance to the side and pretend he had not recognized him. Although he could recollect being 'firm' though not 'unkind' towards him whilst in prison, he nevertheless felt nervous without his uniform and outside the framework of the institution:

> I must admit I was scared when I saw Paddy, but I don't know why. We got on OK, as far as I remember, even though I had to 'correct him' a few times when he became aggressive and 'out of order', but I wasn't as bad as the other guys. There in the precinct I felt very exposed, naked almost, as though he had control over me and I was vulnerable. I can't explain it but I was very glad we crossed each other's paths without comment.

Teachers can sometimes feel this way when meeting ex-pupils in the street. Are the characteristics of workplace settings, uniform or dress to mark rank, the involuntary nature of subjection to particular rules administered dispassionately from one in authority, and the back-up of institutional legitimacy, the psychological hallmarks for bullying to take place more easily?

Bullying in the army

Lewis shared three experiences: the first recruitment practice, the second his own role and involvement of 'breaking in' a recruit, and the third a volatile occasion in the field. He was asked what sort of person made an effective trainer of recruits.

Lewis: He was normally an ogre-ish sergeant. I wouldn't say he was unapproachable but you would avoid him if possible. He'd be quick-tempered, aggressive and very free with his hands. Not someone you would sit and have a conversation with. But he would be surrounded by corporals who were softer and far more approachable. The corporals would be given certain duties and responsibilities regarding the welfare of recruits and their training.

Dennis: Would you say the section sergeant's behaviour was bullying in any sense?

Lewis: Yes I would. There are two examples of bullying in the services. There is the sergeant out there on the ranges managing what is called butt-party – which is checking the targets after another lot of lads have fired – and there is the sergeant in charge of recruits. He is in a very responsible position, and he would hit, show up or humiliate the men. These wouldn't always be the most cocky lads, the best soldiers. It would be the type of lads who had decided the army was not for them. They'd put in their papers to leave and they would really get it.

Dennis: Really?

Lewis: Yeah, definitely. If they decided to leave the army it was taken as a failure on their part. They would victimize them and bully them. The army is their world, and if you don't want to be part of their world you are a wimp, you're insufficient. That's when a lot of bullying would take place. Bullying has always been in the army, and rightly so. And you have to bully, in a sense, the recruits for them to follow what to do, to follow orders. You know as a recruit, if you don't follow orders and do what you're supposed to do, that you'd get it. It may be a swift kick, a punch…it could even be more if you had been really slack. You could get a real hard punch in the mouth. I found this out once when I had back-chatted the sergeant and it was during parade and the sergeant told me to 'stand in line, step back', and I said, 'I am!' I gave a smart comment and got a punch in the mouth, and I wouldn't do it again.

Dennis: What would happen if you took him on?

Lewis: He would kick the crap out of me, to be honest. When you get to that level, like he had, you're a physically tough chap. Even recruits who were tough out in Civvy Street were not tough in the army.

Dennis: So he is selected for a special role then?

Lewis: Yeah. There's terminology in the army called 'the world's oldest corporal' and those guys, although they'd have rank, haven't got much higher because they didn't have enough about them to become a good troop sergeant, to be a good NCO. Those are the guys that don't make the grade, but because of their physical presence and toughness they are selected for that particular role, and on the flip side there's normally a fairly decent corporal underneath that sergeant that the lads can go to and say, 'This has happened at home' or 'I'm really finding this difficult to deal with', etc. He's your counsellor, your mentor, the shoulder to cry on, because it's really rough when you leave home to join the army even for tough individuals. It's a really tough experience.

During the interview I asked Lewis whether he had become drawn into bullying a weaker subordinate under the 'Milgram principle'.

Lewis: I have, yes, and I'm divided on this because I'm not particularly proud of what I did – it was essential. I'd been brought into the recruiting team and we were training soldiers for the British Army and part of their training was to get them used to firing weapons and a lot of the exercise we did was with blank rounds, with blank ammunition, but during the training it was required to use live rounds, to get them used to real-life situations and the feel of firing 'live'. We had to get them used to using live rounds, and we had a fairly important range day coming up. And there was a particular individual who had had a negligent discharge before. He was a consistent joker, mostly harmless, but there was the potential there for him to mess a lot of things up. I was instructed by my senior sergeant to make it clear that this lad would not mess around on the range day, and the term that is used is 'beasted'. It's quite an ominous act if you 'beast' someone. It could be a severe bollocking, or it could be three hours on the parade square. But mostly it was a physical 'beasting', which involved me getting him running across the parade square, giving him lots of different physical exercises: squat thrusts, star jumps, short burst running, sprints, and press-ups, and he knew that his behaviour had built this up. We got to this point when I knew he had had enough. He was pretty much up to his chin straps, he was knackered, he couldn't do a great deal more, physically. But you always feel he could go one step up, one more hill, sort of thing, so I continued with the 'beasting'. In fact, I stepped up the 'beasting', and he had to run alongside me and beat me back from wherever I chose for him to run. But there was no way he could beat me back because he had run for three parts of an hour and had done the world's amount of press-ups and sit-ups and he was physically suffering. Plus, as an NCO, I was physically fit anyway; I personally was starting the game. Every time he didn't beat me across the parade square or wherever it was that I had ordered him to run to he would get ten more press-ups, and after every sequence he would get a severe verbal roasting from me. I remember thinking at the time that this was wrong, but for the greater good it had to be done, and the greater good was that if this man messed about on the range as he had proven before he had the capabilities to do just that, it could cost someone their life, so I was backed by the army – this was the way we had always done things, this was the way we dealt with things. I had kind of convinced myself that morally I was doing the right thing because the other alternative was a risk to life.

Dennis: Were you conscious of becoming a different person, like a beast almost?

Lewis: Yeah, the authority that you could wield over someone to the point of exhaustion to follow what you did. And it says such a lot for this chap because now a lot of lads would say, 'I'm not doing it. I'm not going over the trenches – I just won't do it!' Whereas back then, it just wasn't done. You'd get shot for desertion, for disobeying orders... After about two hours he was in fairly bad physical shape, and I felt I had changed. I felt bigger somehow – I had grown in size regarding this individual, because of the way I'd acted over the things I got him to do. I was getting a bit bigger and more aggressive all the time, and then stopping and thinking, 'I've gone too far now.' The guy wasn't bleeding, it was nothing that a good couple of hours of rest wouldn't put right, but he was certainly suffering. The 'beasting' did work. The recruit began to take life a little more serious after that. But I wrestled with myself for a couple of days after that and I wasn't particularly proud of myself, and I thought to myself, 'If I'm asked to do that again I won't do it.' But, unfortunately, I didn't keep to that promise; there was another incident when another guy wasn't toeing the line and needed a physical 'beasting' and I carried out the same again. I never really had the spirit to say to my sergeant, 'I don't want to do it!' You just don't question orders.

I asked Lewis whether he felt it impossible not to carry out such an order, whether he felt that a soldier should never question orders, since to do so might cause the institution to simply implode and break up from the centre. He replied, 'It's true; you can't question hundreds of years of discipline and tradition.' Lewis described an occasion in the field of action that the regiment might draw on to justify its rigorous ('bullying') training methodology. Being posted to central Belfast, his regiment had to patrol the Falls Road, a long road towards the river.

Lewis: I was still a young boy. We had passed the cemetery and opposite there was a large collection of trees, a wood surrounded by a wall. As we passed this area there were some shops on our side and at every opportunity we took cover in these doorways. As we patrolled we heard a shot. Instinctively, we tried to make ourselves as small as possible by ducking into a doorway. What normally happens at this point is that we are given a fire control order after someone had established where the shooting was coming from. When a shot rings out someone will say where they think the fire is coming from and they will give a description of that area. You work off a clock face where they might say, 'It's at one o'clock, by a tree.'

Dennis: I see.

Lewis: But the shooter hadn't been located. When you hear a single shot, although you are 98 per cent sure it's a shot, if you did not hear another one you begin to wonder and think, 'Was it a shot?' You begin to un-clench. But then another shot rang out and then we realized we were under fire. It was not just a one-off, not a car going off in the distance, but that we were under fire.

Dennis: How well protected were you?

Lewis: Not very well, to be honest.

Dennis: So if it were a marksman you'd be vulnerable.

Lewis: Very. The equipment even now doesn't stand up to a great deal of punishment, but then we patrolled in our berets, which were felt. We had helmets but rarely wore them. We also had thick combat jackets on, which would not stop a round [bullet]. We could get Kevlar body armour from stores but at this time they were bulky and restricted your movement. We still didn't know where the shooter was. But what I did notice was that our section sergeant was making a trip from man to man, and I am not afraid to admit that I was really, really scared at this point. I look back now and smile because of how scared I was. I was very scared. Yet after a short conversation with each man – and we were still effectively under fire, even though there were only two shots so far – the section sergeant came up to me and said, 'Are you OK?' I nodded. Then he said, 'When I ask you to move, you will move!' And he pointed towards a corner of this wall – and, thinking back, I could have gone across the line of fire, effectively, and I knew this at the time – and he said to me, 'What I want you to do is this,' there was no ifs or buts, and he said to me, 'On my orders, you will move to that point,' and he showed me where that point was.

Dennis: You alone or did he brief everyone the same?

Lewis: Yeah, everyone, but they had different points, so that we could keep moving and changing positions.

Dennis: I see.

Lewis: And then he stopped and looked me square in the eyes and recited to me the motto of the regiment in Latin, *Celer et Audax*, which translated means 'Swift and Bold'. Swift and Bold! In your mind, there was no doubt what was going to happen. It was as though he'd turned a switch in my head, and although I was still very scared I was more scared of disobeying his orders than being fired upon. It was very, very strange.

Dennis: Is it like the rugby squad losing and the captain psyching them up to continue pressing forward?

Lewis: It was, yeah, just like that. We'd been taught about the history of the regiment, and the motto, and where it came from, and because the lads were not all from academic backgrounds (being infantry) we didn't know Latin, but the translation meant more and it typified who you were. You were, then, Swift and Bold. He could trip that switch and you would feel yourself fill up and I wouldn't say we were invincible, but we felt we could outrun that bullet. We ran as fast as we could, with equipment, with weapons, and we were confident in our-selves because we had been trained by this man, who had confidence in us. We had been through a lot together, and when he gave me an order there was no two ways about it, and when he said, 'You've got to go to that point,' you went to that point. You had faith in him, in his skills as a soldier and a leader.

Dennis: It's mental control in a way isn't it, as though the only way we can function as a unit is through discipline, loyalty and being bonded, which is reinforced by recital of the motto 'Swift and Bold' – you just go. Because what he can't afford presumably is...

Lewis: Hesitation.

Dennis: Hesitation and doubt, the fear of one's life and the risk to the regiment.

Lewis: Yeah. If you look at it statistically, it doesn't always work, but for us then the reason why we were moving there had gone out of my head. When he said 'Move' – you move. It's quite a funny thing because the shooter didn't matter, you had to obey that order; you had to go.

Dennis: It's a strange phenomenon, that unquestioning observance of orders. It reminds me of the First World War when soldiers went over the trenches...

Concluding comment

In looking at bullying in other contexts than the school or the family, and yet continuing to examine it within close-knit relationships, there are striking features which stand out as being different in the workplace. Similarly, there is a power differential between abuser and abused, but then there is a little more choice for the individual to remain subjected to dominant behaviour than is customarily the case within the family or school. The power of the uniform or the office, the organization or the system, etc. seems to serve in some cases as an *authorization* of some aspects of bullying and controlling behaviour.

Two respondents made mention of 'for the greater good' to serve as a justi-fication for their management style, and the last example – that of the soldier in the field fighting for his own life and the lives of his men – seems particularly telling in that a fear-induced, social conditioning demarcation of power serves as a valid rationale that arguably is designed to save life.

Institutional bullying and subtle manipulation is becoming a social concern in Britain and elsewhere in recent times. Many traditional services, such as nursing, the police, prison and the army, are having to review their operational styles of management in light of changing European laws of human rights which have begun to question traditional ways of working, particularly in regard to sexual orientation and race. In schools there was a time when one's office as teacher was sufficient to demand respect from pupils; nowadays respect has to be earned. It seems as though a similar trend of re-evaluation has begun in many public sector and private businesses, and it is not clear where it will end or how such services may have to adapt, or if indeed they can adapt, to relational requirements of the modern world.

It was interesting that a former soldier now a businessman could not translate the type of 'unquestioning carrying out of orders' regime that he was used to in the army within the modern workplace environment. No doubt a sound psychology of teambuilding and collegial approaches in different settings pays dividends in employer–employee relations and productivity. There seems little dispute that effective employment law should be based upon a contract where one party is paying for the labour of another party, who in turn is willing to work for an agreed salary or wage, but even within those parameters it seems that good industrial relations appears to further an objective of meeting mutually agreed targets.

In Lewis's case, whilst recognizing the ambivalence he felt when subjecting his recruit to bullying, I could not help but feel 'there was a point' to over-dominant management styles when lives are at risk, as he so eloquently expressed through his experience in Ireland. I expect games will always be played by both parties in hierarchical situations of boss and worker, guard and prisoner, policeman and criminal, and sergeant and recruit, and each will adopt positional play. Comedy dramas such as *Porridge* and *The Office* have capitalized on the absurdities of real and pretence power in close working, hierarchical environments. Indeed, Lewis said at one point 'I was starting a game basically' when putting his recruit through the mill. It may also be the case that disenchanted recruits may have elected to play the 'Incompetence Game' merely to get thrown out of the army, similar to the young lad who breaks the dishes from an unconscious wish not to be asked to do the washing-up chore again; we cannot be sure. Payoffs for dominant prison officers and recruiting sergeants may centre on a perceived need to maintain the status quo of discipline and orderliness, where each functions in their Critical Parent Ego and where the relational dynamic appears to be 'I'm not OK; you're OK'. If inmates and recruits cannot, or will not, comply and play the game and become Adapted Children they can expect very rough treatment indeed, particularly where surveillance is weak and reporting cultures are not part of the institution's tradition.

In light of little research being carried out in looking at other elements of bullying in the workplace, elements which are more covert and infinitely more subtle than school bullying or domestic violence, such as preventing promotion of a candidate, withholding information to do the job whilst still expecting the target to be met, or excessive and unnecessary over-monitoring, this chapter cannot take the subject very much further forward than to draw general lessons from anecdotal study. The question of how society deals with the severest type of bullying behaviour that leads to sexual harassment and physical assaults takes up our interest in the final chapter.

Chapter 10

A Better Way Forward

In this closing chapter, I pull together a few thoughts and reflections arising from the discourses of those principally involved in bullying and physically assaulting weaker people. Having put aside dogmatic interpretations of bullying behaviour in school, the family and workplace contexts, there are legal, social and psychological implications arising from the narratives of perpetrators who bully others, and in closing this book I raise some that come to mind. First, we examine the common targets of blame.

Who do we blame?

In Ken Rigby's *New Perspectives on Bullying* (2002) a closing chapter is titled 'Beyond Blame'. He cites a popular passage from Aristotle's writings to illustrate that proportionate anger is not in itself a bad thing:

> The man who gets angry at the right things, and with the right people
> and in the right way and at the right time and for the right length of time,
> is to be commended.

His main point, however, is to separate the two behavioural responses of *blame* and *responsibility*:

> Blame looks for a cause so that its source can be condemned. It does so
> with righteous anger. It cries out to high heaven that bullying should not
> be. And it points the finger. (Rigby 2002, p.263)

In general, we deal with bullying by apportioning blame and by administering justice through punishment, in spite of the mounting evidence that punishment rarely works in the long term. And whom do we blame? We blame the bully, the victim, the parents, the school, social services, the government, the system, etc.; in fact, we blame everyone and everything.

We blame bullies

We blame the bully, quite naturally. This has always been the case, and why should we alter this judgement if we wish to live in a humane, caring society? Victims do not deserve to be intimidated and why should they? But our recourse to *demonize* the bully loses sight of a principle once outlined by a Galilean preacher over 2000 years ago: 'Let him who is without sin amongst you cast the first stone.'

Apart from the most serious of cases, there are occasions when nearly all of us bully and are bullied by another person, and so we are talking about questions of degree. The most insidious and damaging forms of bullying are not the extreme cases of physical assault, but the ongoing, low-level undermining of confidence and self-esteem that results from the abuse of power from someone known to the victim and from putting others down for no other reason than the enjoyment of hurting them (Rigby 2002). If we assume, then, that 'a leopard cannot change its spots', we will set up our strategies and systems that reinforce that belief. If we assume that bullying is as much a problem to the bully as to the victim, then the doors begin to open for rehabilitation and change (Lines 2006a).

We blame victims

Then we blame the victims, by claiming either that he or she might bring on the torment through provocative responses, or that they suffer a pathological ailment that renders them unable to relate well to others. After all, much of the research suggests that most children avoid being friends with kids who 'will not stand up for themselves', or who are unpopular, since such rejection reinforces their own normality and popularity (Rigby 2002). Blaming the victim brings a sense of relief, even for those who take a middle course, and after all provocative victims have 'only themselves to blame'. Bullying can lead to depression, and children as well as adults do not like to mix with depressed people.

Provocative victims can appear irritating in that they complain that their cases never get heard, and that after fixing one problem another lies just around the corner – 'the world is against them'. A pupil approached me one morning alleging that he was being accused of pushing around a much younger pupil: 'I'm always getting the blame,' he said. And since I see him almost daily over the same needy complaint about being unpopular, I have to admit to having felt irritated on occasions, even though my professional role demands that I be fair-minded and empathic. Vulnerability appears to be blameworthy, and blaming the victim ensures a sense of security and group cohesion through negative labelling. Canadian research has shown that only one in four bystanders will give support to victims involved in bullying encounters (Pepler and Craig 1995).

We blame parents

But then we blame the family for spawning a child who is so inadequate that he or she becomes a bully or a victim. Schoolteachers and office managers feel impotent at times to support the downtrodden, and will all too easily resort to pathologizing the family. It is argued that youngsters grow up in a culture having few personal resources and limited strategies to deal with conflict because their social relationships are merely a reflection of those of their parents.

Developmental psychologists use terms such as 'dysfunctional families', 'poor role-modelling', 'insecure-ambivalent attachments' (or 'anxious-resistant attachments') in childhood, and a lack of the right kind of love. It is for these reasons that children are blamed for being bullied. Perhaps victims are mollycoddled, overprotected and have had limited opportunities for honing their social and survival skills. Perhaps bullies have witnessed too much violence and aggression within their families or on the street. But there is no research as yet that has correlated being victimized or turning out a bully with certain parenting practices and family dysfunctionality (Rigby 2002).

We blame the school

If we choose not to blame the family, then perhaps it is the school that is to blame and there is certainly lots of anecdotal evidence, backed by research (Lines 1999; Olweus 1991; Whitney and Smith 1993), to prove that how schools are run does make a difference to the amount of bullying that takes place, and that it is not merely the pupils or the social deprivation of the local community.

We blame social services

We might blame social care and health departments for not registering with sufficient gravity that some children are at significant risk while remaining within their family homes. It may be that the children have to put up with their parents misusing alcohol or drugs, that they suffer neglect, or that they become prey to aggressive role-modelling influences that earn them the title of being a bully at school.

One particular family at my school at the moment have had social work input for the last ten years. Routinely, as many as 20 professionals meet every three months to discuss the concerns of this family where no child attends school, where there is mounting debt and where the housing department have threatened a second eviction for damage done to the council property. There is great cynicism and frustration, sometimes voiced, when the social worker with case responsibility counters every suggestion to have the children placed in care. Not only is this because no children's home or foster carer will take all the five children (aged 3 to 16), but also because when it has been tried in the past it has broken down due to the parents sabotaging the care plan, with the children frequently running away to a secret rendezvous before being returned again by the police. The expense of placing all the children unwillingly into care is a consideration also. There is the expense of foster care provision, the demand on ongoing resources to manage supervised family contact and the hidden costs of placing children into care. It is held by all professionals, apart from the social work team, that if the children were taken from the family and placed into care there would be no threat of further abuse and bullying.

We blame the government

And if not the school or social services, perhaps governments are to blame for doing so little to improve social conditions, where 'the haves' and 'the have nots' appear to be growing ever wider apart. Do nations bully other nations? Perhaps 'bully' is the wrong term to use in this context when analysing international conflict, but certainly the same ingredients of an imbalance of power and a desire to hurt seem to operate on a much grander scale. However, we must remember that nations are composed of citizens, and even in democratic countries where the only power is through the ballot box, when one country invades a weaker one, in principle every citizen must take some form of collective responsibility.

We blame 'the system'

Perhaps finally we can blame the system for allowing bullying to occur because all organizations are composed of groups and hierarchies where there is a potential payoff for those who are most dominant. If bullying occurs in school, in the workplace, amongst children and amongst adults, then in light of this ubiquitous behaviour we should not be surprised when bullying occurs so regularly.

Apportioning no blame

It is possible to play games with language and argue that there's no such thing as a bully, there's only bullying. Such reasoning would lead one to say that there's no such thing as an aggressive youth, only aggressive behaviour, no partner-beater or child-batterer, only violent behaviour; thus avoiding making a judgement and apportioning responsibility to those who are responsible. The risks here are obvious in that through semantics we move into denial of a very real and painful experience for some who suffer at the hand of a bully. While apportioning no blame is clearly out of the question, there is a useful debate to be had as to whether punitive measures, such as imprisonment, are an appropriate way to rehabilitate people who engage in bullying behaviour – the extent to which we use 'the carrot' or 'the stick'.

Carrot or stick?

I will use the English legal system as an example to explore the general principles of how best to approach bullying, but it is hoped you will be able to extrapolate the general points I make here if you are living within a different legal system. Imprisonment is one regular option of penalizing an offender, but increasingly conviction rates in the UK and high recidivist rates (70 per cent of prisoners are convicted of another crime within two years of being released from prison) indicate a need for radical rethinking. Is punishment through exclusion and penalizing individuals by incarcerating them the best way of dealing with the problem? It depends on the crime, of course, but with regard to young people and those committed for domestic violence the prison 'stick' may reinforce the same violent behaviour it is intended to deter, at least in the opinion of some of the psychologists we have considered in this book.

Philosopher Jamie Whyte (2006) argues coherently that the point of prison is to reduce 'offending' not 're-offending', by serving as a deterrent for the rest of us, not for those on the inside. In his opinion, prisoners are the people for whom the threat of prison is not a sufficient deterrent to crime. It is very expensive for the taxpayer to keep someone locked up in prison, but, says Whyte, this is money well spent. Although Britain imprisons a higher percentage of its population than any other Western European country, this figure is misleading. Contrary to popular belief, Britain has a low imprisonment rate when compared with the extraordinary criminality of the British public – Britain imprisons 12 people per 1000 crimes, Spain imprisons 48 and Ireland 33. Whyte reasons that high imprisonment rates correlate with low crime rates, pointing out that Spain and Ireland have lower crime rates than Britain. Indeed, when Britain began increasing its prison population 13 years ago, the number of crimes started to decrease, and a similar phenomenon has occurred in the United States.

But 'protecting the public' is not the only aim of a penal system. Punishment is not the principal motivation for behavioural change; it is only one amongst others we might choose to support. Ostensibly, the British penal system, with its educational programmes for the personal advancement of convicted criminals, is still supposedly designed around the notion of rehabilitation. But does this work? I took this up with Kate, the teacher in a Young Offender Institution, where she was sceptical about prison guards supporting education for prisoners, but then I asked her whether there was genuine remorse if someone had been violent against another person, and she said, 'Yes, in a lot of cases.' But then she began speaking of the dispiriting nature of the cycle of violence within some families.

> *Kate:* There are rival gangs on different units taught at different times. And certain characters stand out, having their nicknamed guys, and they'd asked, 'Was he in this morning? Did you teach him?' And they are trying to learn information about each other. They're all very much into their straps, which are their guns. But it's not bravado as such. It's a way of life that they have inherited from dad, and he's inherited from his father. So this rivalry goes back generations, it's not a new thing with these lads. So how do you break that? It's not the way it's done. You shouldn't be using a gun. 'Oh well, my dad gave it me. It was his.' And so you think, 'Oh.' I mean, if my dad walked in now and said 'I've got this for you' and he gave me a gun, how do you cope with that? And that is the way they live. And to them it's not bravado – 'It's the way we operate. This is the life we know.' I have heard a lot of these gang-lads say they want to pull out of it because a lot of them have babies, and they say, 'I don't want my kids growing up like this.' But, I think, 'How on earth are you going to do it? How on earth are you going to get out of that situation?'

Many of the world's religions – particularly Christianity with its central figure of an unconditionally forgiving, itinerant preacher from Nazareth – have highlighted the transformative potential of a forgiving spirit. And the non-retaliatory pacifists like Dr Martin Luther King and Gandhi stand out more in the human psyche than the names of their judges or jailers. As every teacher will tell you, punishing children is only part of the process to improve and raise standards. A far better way, established by progressive educationalists, is to motivate individuals not only with 'cost programmes' that penalize pupils immediately after breaking the rules but also with approaches of praise and encouragement. As behaviourists have shown, re-teaching offenders *how to behave* is much more effective than reinforcing behaviour *how not to behave*. It is such a pity that these principles are not embedded in the British penal system. So, do we follow the reasoning of Whyte or progressive educationalists and behaviourists? And if we see value in both, or various weighted combinations of both, is the weighting too heavy for the 'stick' as opposed to the 'carrot'? I wish to go further and to suggest that the justification for penal systems – as the only means of reforming characters – is based upon certain presuppositions of human free will that are not universally accepted.

Moral education

Questions arise if punitive means are recommended as the only solution to relational bullying, and these centre on what we understand about our 'freedom to act' in a given manner: Is behaviour always and in all circumstances determined through volition, or is it 'programmed by genes' or 'determined by a social situation'? The moral and philosophical issues around personal responsibility for one's behaviour centre on the extent to which free will or biological determinism influence that behaviour (Hick 1990). Augustine raised questions of free will; Hobbes, Locke, Rousseau, Kant, Bentham and John Stuart Mill wrestled with its implications in terms of conscience and society (Howard 2000). If genes contribute substantially to the development of personal characteristics, such as intelligence, personality or a predisposition towards violence and aggression, does this imply that genes effectively determine who we are? Biological determinism is the thesis that genes determine how personality is principally made up, but the majority of geneticists and moral philosophers have largely discarded the notion that biology solely determines human behaviour (Greenfield 2004). Susan Greenfield (2004, pp.251–253) has said that neuroscience research has shown that we cannot assume that 'anything as universal as human nature would simply be wired into our genes'.

There are other influencing factors like styles of parenting and upbringing, internalized mores and religious beliefs that are the product of our culture during early youth – these shape our personality. If all our traits are determined as much by our environment as by our genes in some complex admixture and irreducible formation, what implications arise from this in terms of human volition and free will? Without the premise of human free will any moral accountability is doomed to confusion and injustice, but British, American, Australian and European judicial systems rest largely upon the premise of human free will.

Although psychotherapy embodies a rich diversity of theory and practice, the major schools of thought still hold to the view that childhood experience leaves an indelible mark upon the self-construct and personality. If we should ask how our morality is formed, the overriding view of various schools of psychology still hold the Freudian view that most of us as children learn our moral codes from our most dominant parents or carers (Goleman 2006), who in turn have internalized them imperceptibly from their parents. But later on we adjust them through cultural influences and a desire to win the approval of significant people or a divine being, since children do not remain as children. Indeed, part of the developmental phase through adolescence involves the rebellion against the values and standards of parental upbringing towards those of the peer group (Lines 2006a), a phenomenon that would be meaningless in a culture of genetic determinism. What then are the internal processes by which each 'becoming adult' determines particular courses of action that are 'right' or 'wrong' for him or her in later life?

Philosophy of 'right' and 'wrong'

Within the field of meta-ethics, there are two main schools of thought: 'realists', who hold that ethical principles are intrinsic and intuitive; and 'non-realists', who propose that moral values are acquired through relationships with other individuals and the environment in which an individual develops. The latter belief has particular interest when considering bullying behaviour, as it forces us to ask ourselves 'What are the consequences of my behaviour?' There is a cost for fleeting sexual satisfaction, which is a sense of shame and disgust in viewing myself as an uninhibited amorous being; an appropriate punishment for raping a woman who has not been complicit in the affair; and rejection from friends and family as a result of reprehensible behaviour that shows no empathy and fails to recognize the dignity and free will of another person. I learn, therefore, that such behaviour is inappropriate and that, indeed, it is morally 'wrong'.

If I decide to take my life and the lives of my children during a particularly low period of despair by driving my car recklessly into a river, but am saved by the rescue services, have my children taken from me and have to face the judicial authorities that will determine whether I am any longer fit as a father to rear my children, it is possible that my moral action will be judged as 'wrong' because no matter how depressed I may have been I have no moral 'right' (as defined by society) to take the lives of my children, nor the moral 'right' to behave in such a manner as to leave them permanently damaged by a course of action that causes bitterness and low self-worth. What 'tells' me this is the case? It is the law courts, child protection legislation and the scorn from friends, family and my children in later life – collectively, it is *the voice of condemnation* from my social group.

According to this outlook, the learning and shaping of morality – assessing what is 'right' and what is 'wrong' – is the testing out of appropriate behaviours against their consequences, in a conscious or subliminal aim to invoke admiration from significant people and avoid their condemnation. This is not to say that selfish hedonism might not bring its own 'rewards' (other than the obvious) and appear 'right'. It all depends on how I wish to be viewed as a person by significant people of my world. The point at issue is whether 'punishment' has greater potential for changing behaviour – that in the longer term 'protects' society – or whether desired images of self amongst one's fellows has a far greater impact.

How radical should we be to eliminate bullying?

We have deduced that the social environment has a greater bearing upon personality make-up in terms of aggression and violence than genetic factors. If Kellerman (1999) and James (2003) are correct in reasoning that some young children stand no chance at all of becoming rounded, non-bullying citizens whilst they remain in their impoverished, aggressively inclined households, then the political implications of radical recommendations like 'child removal' seem so extreme that few politicians, if any, in the modern democratic world would risk their reputations by embracing them wholeheartedly.

Removing children from their natural parents entails the risk of them being deprived of their emotional attachments, but if these attachments are largely inadequate – avoidant, anxious, insecure or ambivalent – with deplorable role-modelling behaviour thrown in, then it may be wondered where the greater cost is – maintaining the status quo in leaving young children within families with no realistic hope of improvement; or grasping the nettle by removing them to homes where positive parenting can be guaranteed?

While such considerations are controversial, it is indisputable that psychology has a valuable role in informing policy and practice relating to bullying. It shows us different approaches to influencing and changing behaviour, and it is from this body of knowledge that I think we shall discover a better way than punishment alone when dealing with bullies.

The contribution of psychology

The family therapies collectively have taught us that we cannot fully understand relationship difficulties by an exclusive concentration on individuals. *Relationship problems require relationship solutions,* and to conceive problems systemically gives us greater insight into how we may find a way forward that satisfies all parties. The behavioural and cognitive-behavioural therapies show us that the basis of faulty moral behaviour is faulty moral thinking, and that change comes with the altering of consequential effects of particular courses of action. This is not to say that we are automatons, or that we always behave in mechanical, rational and pragmatic ways, far from it, but it is to recognize that both conscious and unconscious behaviour tends to be directed towards a goal, or payoff, which can be psychological as well as social. I am not suggesting there is no such thing as an injustice, but I am saying that in many relationship difficulties the polar construction of 'bully versus victim' is much too simplistic, and that the punishment of the one involves, paradoxically, the penalizing of the other in many cases, certainly in the long run. Excluded pupils don't just 'disappear', and sentenced perpetrators of domestic violence are eventually released and commonly return to the same family home.

The humanistic strand of psychotherapy offers us an encouraging way forward. At its very heart, person-centred psychology places an undiminished valuation of the human person and inspires a sense of hope for a better humanity (Thorne 2002). Through higher-quality human relating, there spring improved human relationships. Carl Rogers, the pioneer of the person-centred approach to psychotherapy, once said, 'I do not have a Pollyanna view of human nature. I am quite aware that out of defensiveness and inner fear individuals can and do behave in ways which are horribly destructive, immature, regressive, anti-social, hurtful' (Rogers 1995, p.21). But he qualified his defence with, 'Yet one of the most refreshing and invigorating parts of my experience is to work with such individuals and to discover the strongly positive directional tendencies which exist in them, as in all of us, at the deepest levels.' Rogers was stressing the human potential in every person to lead a higher-quality life through the principles of behaving towards another with unconditional positive regard, by not pre-judging them critically and by showing empathy towards all those going through a rough patch – yes, including bullies. I believe that in the limited discourses presented above of bullies' rationalization of their own behaviour there are hinted traces of 'positive directional tendencies' towards healing of damaged relationships through bullying behaviour.

What does life look like embodying these principles? It does not leave much to the imagination to grasp the central point that if human beings in their inter-relations could begin to be a little less judgemental of the faults of others, if they can be a little more accepting of themselves and the differences of others, and if they could show in their day-to-day relationships a little more empathy and understanding for the difficulties others have to face, then this must become a seedbed for a better humanity.

I cannot see that these values can emerge for some bullying youngsters and abusive partners unless they are regularly modelled by professionals in the social care, education and legal systems (Lines 2006b, 2007). Kate, the teacher in a Young Offender Institution mentioned earlier, recalled one inmate who had murdered someone. She said:

> He's turned into the most polite, trustworthy chap. He's actually got a job in the prison. He's come out of his shell; he's got about seven certificates. He's very pleasant, he doesn't brag about what he's done. He will talk about it, individually, and say how remorseful he is and how he didn't mean it to go that far. It's somebody he had known for a long time, and this person, apparently, kept stalking him and he had just had enough one day and murdered him – tragic, absolutely tragic.

Obviously, his victim's family will not have the slightest sympathy that his attached worker will have, yet our interest is not in apportioning blame, but responsibility, and in attempting to set up conditions of reparation where anger and ill-feeling do not go that far.

Applying restorative justice

Restorative justice involves getting offenders to repair what they have damaged, bringing abusers face to face with the abused to hear how their behaviour has affected the injured party, and in some cases getting offenders to write letters of apology. This is not a soft option as many offenders find it difficult to face up to the impact of their crimes. Perpetrators and victims are brought into contact through direct mediation, where victim, offender, facilitator and possibly supporters for each party meet face to face, and through conferencing – where all supporters for both parties and members of the wider community come together and find a way forward, often using the family as a support structure for the offender (this is particularly useful with young offenders).

Great claims are being made in some quarters for the effectiveness of restorative justice for reducing low-level criminality (Liebmann 2007). According to the Home Office (n.d.), pilot studies indicate that restorative justice approaches can reduce post-traumatic stress disorder in victims and, in some cases, motivate offenders to turn away from a life of crime. The Home Office (n.d.) also states:

> Restorative justice approaches can be used for a wide range of incidents, from minor anti-social behaviour like graffiti to serious crimes like assault and robbery. Victim participation is always voluntary, and offenders need to have admitted some responsibility for the harm they have caused.

Restorative justice is a process whereby

- all the parties with a stake in a particular conflict or offence come together to resolve collectively how to deal with the aftermath of the conflict or offence and its implications for the future

- offenders have the opportunity to acknowledge the impact of what they have done and to make reparation and victims have the opportunity to have their harm or loss acknowledged and amends made.

Restorative justice takes place in the criminal justice system, and helps communities to deal with conflict in schools, the workplace, and neighbourhoods. It is a relatively new idea here in the UK (since the 1980s) but it has been practised across the world. Government, the EU and the UN believe in its potential and are starting to legislate or make recommendations for the implementation of practice. Restorative justice has a growing research base from around the world of crime reduction and victim satisfaction (for more information, see www.restorativejustice.org.uk).

Penalizing someone who by nature is aggressive and dominant towards those with whom they are in a relationship can only be justified and make sense if the individual is made aware of the consequences of their behaviour such that it leaves them feeling regretful; and that, whatever their nature and predisposition towards controlling others, such behaviour is judged to be 'wrong', not only in the eyes of society at large – which has a vested interest in protecting the community – but also in their own eyes. In both Alan's and Jim's cases (see pp.139 and 157), custodial sentencing seemed to bring no remedial benefits apart from, arguably, a period of separation for reflection – a psychological effect that did not require months of incarceration.

Refraining from blame is not tantamount to steering clear of responsibility. When one bullies or assaults another and we bypass blaming, this is not to say that restorative justice requires side-stepping an ownership of what has taken place, quite the converse, in fact (Liebmann 2007). When guilty parties have to face their victims it is to take *full responsibility*, a course of mediating action that assailants inevitably never have to face with incarceration or exclusion from school.

There are practical strategies that can be pursued in place of punitive justice. I for one would like to see a greater emphasis on funding for restorative justice programmes, more imaginative educational programmes that address emotional intelligence and bullying, more support for mothers during those vital early years of child development and the use of talking and support for troubled children and young people.

Towards owning and modifying bullying behaviour

In moving forward beyond blame, it is appropriate and more meaningful to separate 'responsibility' from the 'instilling of guilt'. Guilt is a destructive force in human nature and is rarely reparative and never brings healing. I agree with Rigby (2002) that blame cultures draw us towards a behavioural determinism that fixes identities and gives no breathing space for free will and decision making. The most therapeutic way forward is to practise the so-called 'No Blame Approach' of Mains and Robinson (1992). Time and again I have found this the best method of healing discord amongst children and young people, as the following example makes plain.

Yussef, a Year 11 student, approached me quite upset because his art teacher had left the classroom and in her absence two boys approached him, one grabbing him around his shoulders whilst the other thumped him in the shoulder and back. Becoming upset, he walked out of the classroom and made his way to my room. In a report his teacher made she assessed it as being quite trivial, but Yussef said that most of the serious bullying occurred when she was out of the classroom.

Conventionally, I would contact pastoral managers or a senior teacher to follow up the matter in accordance with the school's anti-bullying policy, but since none were available I kept Yussef with me. Having prestige and kudos amongst students, when the culprits had discovered that Yussef was in my room and not in his next lesson, they came to see me a little apprehensive. The first to arrive was Abdulla, the lad who had held Yussef by his arms. He told me that he was 'on his last chance' and that he had regretted what he had done, and I commented that perhaps it would be best if he could tell that to Yussef, not to me. I allowed him to enter a room with Yussef to discuss the matter. The result was that Yussef was satisfied with Abdulla's apology and his willingness to put matters right, although Yussef was still a little teary-eyed. Yussef said that Abdulla was not the main bully.

I advised Abdulla that Yussef may want to file a complaint against him, which was his 'right', which he agreed it was, but that to take matters forward perhaps it would be best if he went to find the other student to see what position he wished to take. Ardeshir came to my room looking troubled, and like Abdulla before him he wanted an opportunity to put things right, if only to avoid getting into trouble himself. Although Yussef was a little less inclined to speak with Ardeshir, they went into the room, albeit begrudgingly, to discuss the matter. After ten minutes they came out and Yussef looked visibly more relieved. I said to Yussef that he was now in a very powerful position, that the tables were turned, that he had control over both the bullies since neither wished to get into further trouble for bullying him in class, and that it might be best if we held over a decision of whether to report the matter to senior staff depending how relationships continued in the next few months.

Needless to say, there were no further occasions of bullying in class or around the school, and Yussef looked visibly relaxed in that a problem that had been going on for months before was now resolved. Had

Abdulla or Ardeshir been excluded, it might be argued that justice would have been done, but how would this have left Yussef feeling with having to come back to the school to sit his final exams, where, quite possibly, there may be no teachers around as he walked to and from the building?

I am not saying that the No-Blame Approach is the best method to apply to suit pragmatics – in that, in this case, it avoids Yussef being beaten up in the long run. Nor do I acknowledge that justice has been meted out. What I am saying is that Yussef feels satisfied with the outcome, that both Abdulla and Ardeshir have had an opportunity to examine behaviour that they formerly minimized as 'just messing about' in order to make changes that will, it is hoped, prove more beneficial in their relationships later on in life after leaving school: *Relationship problems require relationship solutions.*

With regard to domestic violence in the case of Alan, further therapeutic work involves him analysing his behaviour, not apportioning guilt. There is need for him to take responsibility and for me as his therapist to encourage a changed outlook in order that he may express his sentiment 'we love each other to death' in practical obligations. In Jim's case, opening up his awareness of the source of his impatience and aggression and teaching him a firm but more flexible style of managing Suzanne, together with devising escape strategies when tempers have blown, will be the means of healing and restoring better his relations with his step-daughter – let's hope so.

References

Ainsworth, M., Blehar, M., Waters, E. and Wall, S. (1978) *Patterns of Attachment: Assessment in the Strange Situation and at Home.* Hillsdale, NJ: Lawrence Erlbaum.

Bandura, A. (1976) 'New Perspectives on Violence.' In V.C. Vaughan, III and T.B. Brazelton (eds) *The Family.* Chicago: Year Book Medical Publishers.

Beck, A.T. (1976) *Cognitive Therapy and the Emotional Disorders.* Harmondsworth: Penguin.

Berne, E. (1968) *Games People Play: The Psychology of Human Relationships.* London: Penguin.

Besag, V. (1989) *Bullies and Victims in Schools.* Milton Keynes: Open University Press.

Bjorkquist, K., Eckman, K. and Lagerspetz, K. (1982) 'Bullies and victims: Their ego picture, ideal ego picture and normative ego picture.' *Scandinavian Journal of Psychology 23*, 307–313.

Blaauw, E., Winkel, F.W. and Kerkhof, Ad J.F.M. (2001) 'Bullying and suicidal behaviour in jails.' *Criminal Justice and Behavior 28*, 3, 279–299.

Bohman, M. (1996) 'Predisposition to Criminality: Swedish Adoption Studies in Retrospect.' In M. Rutter (ed.) *Genetics of Criminal and Antisocial Behaviour.* Chichester: Wiley.

Bohman, M., Cloninger, C.R., Sigvardsson, S. and von Knorring, A.L. (1982) 'Predisposition to petty criminality in Swedish adoptees.' *Archives of General Psychiatry 39*, 1242–1247.

Bowlby, J. (1969) *Attachment and Loss. Vol. 1, Attachment.* London: Hogarth Press.

Bowlby, J. (1973) *Attachment and Loss. Vol. 2, Separation: Anxiety and Anger.* London: Hogarth Press.

Bowlby, J. (1980) *Attachment and Loss. Vol. 3, Sadness and Depression.* London: Hogarth Press.

Briscoe, C. (2006) *Ugly.* London: Hodder & Stoughton.

Bully OnLine (n.d.) 'Workplace Bullying Definitions.' Accessed 6/9/07 at www.bullyonline.org/workbully/defns.htm

Burnham, J.B. (1986) *Family Therapy.* London: Routledge.

Cadoret, A., Yates, W., Troughton, E., Woodworth, G. and Stewart, M. (1995) 'Genetic-environmental interaction in the genesis of aggressivity and conduct disorders.' *Archives of General Psychiatry 52*, 916.

Chodorow, N. (1978) *The Reproduction of Motherhood.* Berkeley, CA: University of California Press.

Cleaver, H., Nicholson, D., Tarr, S. and Cleaver, D. (2007) *Child Protection, Domestic Violence and Parental Substance Misuse: Family Experiences and Effective Practice.* London: Jessica Kingsley Publishers.

Coleman, R. and Cassell, D. (1995) 'Parents who Misuse Drugs and Alcohol.' In P. Reder and C. Lucey (eds) *Assessment of Parenting: Psychiatric and Psychological Contributions.* London: Routledge.

CWASU (2007) Child and Women Abuse Studies Unit. Accessed 4/10/07 at www.cwasu.org/page_display.asp?pageid=STATS&pagekey=16&itemkey=19.

Dawkins, R. (1976) *The Selfish Gene* (30th anniversary edition, 2006). New York: Oxford University Press.

Dawkins, R. (2006) *The God Delusion.* New York: Oxford University Press.

de Board, R. (1998) *Counselling for Toads: A Psychological Adventure.* Hove: Routledge.

Dubin, N. (2007) *Asperger Syndrome and Bullying: Strategies and Solutions.* London: Jessica Kingsley Publishers.

Duncan, R.D. (1999) 'Maltreatment by parents and peers: The relationship between child abuse, bully victimization and psychological distress.' *Journal of the American Professional Society on the Abuse of Children 4,* 1, 45–55.

Easton, M. (2007) *The Today Programme.* BBC Radio 4, 26 January 2007.

Ellis, A. (1962) *Reason and Emotion in Psychotherapy.* New York: Lyall Stuart.

Erikson, E.H. (1968) *Identity: Youth and Crisis.* New York: Norton.

Farrington, D. (1993) 'Understanding and Preventing Bullying.' In M. Tonry (ed.) *Crime and Justice: A Review of Research,* Vol. 17 (pp.381–459). Chicago: University of Chicago Press.

Field, E.M. (2007) *Bully Blocking: Six Secrets to Help Children Deal with Teasing and Bullying.* London: Jessica Kingsley Publishers.

Freud, S. (1964) *New Introductory Lectures on Psychoanalysis.* London: Penguin.

Gerhardt, S. (2004) *Why Love Matters: How Affection Shapes a Baby's Brain.* Hove: Routledge.

Goleman, D. (2006) *Emotional Intelligence* (10th anniversary edition). Bantam Dell: New York.

Goodhart, C.B. (1995) 'The Heritability of Intelligence.' *Galton Institute Newsletter,* March 1995. Accessed 25/9/07 at www.galtoninstitute.org.uk/index.html.

Greenfield, S. (2004) *Tomorrow's People: How 21st Century Technology is Changing the Way We Think and Feel.* London: Penguin.

Haley, J. (1976) *Problem Solving Therapy.* New York: Harper-Colophon.

Hick, J. (1990) *Philosophy of Religion.* Upper Saddle River, NJ: Prentice Hall.

Hoel, H. and Cooper, C.L. (2000) 'Workplace Bullying in Britain – Results from a Study of 5298 Employees.' In K. Rigby (2002) *New Perspectives on Bullying.* London: Jessica Kingsley Publishers.

Holmes, J. (1993) *John Bowlby and Attachment Theory.* London: Routledge.

Holstein, J.A. and Miller, G. (1990) *Rethinking Victimization: An Interactional Approach to Victimology.* Accessed 25/9/07 at www.lub.lu.se/luft/kurslitt/kriminologi/holstein.pdf.

Home Office (2000) *Domestic Violence: Breaking the Chain: Multi-Agency Guidance for Addressing Domestic Violence.* London: Home Office Publications. Accessed 3/10/07 at www.crimereduction.gov.uk/dv/dv08d.htm#1.

Home Office (2007) *Police Reform e-Bulletin.* Issue 102, May 2007. Accessed 4/10/07 at http://police.homeoffice.gov.uk/news-and-publications/publication/police-reform-e-bulletin/e-bulletin-may-07?view=Binary.

Home Office (n.d.) 'Restorative Justice.' Accessed 29/11/07 at www.homeoffice.gov.uk/crime-victims/victims/restorative-justice.

Horn, M.J., Green, M., Carney, R. and Erickson, M.T. (1975) 'Bias against genetic hypotheses in adoption studies.' *Archives of General Psychiatry 32,* 1365–1367.

Howard, A. (2000) *Philosophy for Counselling and Psychotherapy: Pythagoras to Postmodernism.* London: Macmillan.

Huesman, L.R., Eron, L.D. and Warnicke-Yarmel, P.W. (1987) 'Intellectual functioning and aggression.' *Journal of Personality and Social Psychology 52,* 232–240.

Humphreys, C. and Stanley, N. (eds) (2006) *Domestic Violence and Child Protection: Directions for Good Practice.* London: Jessica Kingsley Publishers.

Humphreys, C. and Thiara, R. (2003) *Post-Separation Violence: Exposing the Issues.* London: Routledge.

Hyun Rhee, S. and Waldman, I. (2002) 'Genetic and the environmental influences on antisocial behaviour: A meta-analysis of twin and adoption studies.' *Psychological Bulletin 128*, 3, 490–529.

James, O. (2003) *They F*** You Up: How to Survive Family Life.* London: Bloomsbury.

Kellerman, J. (1999) *Savage Spawn: Reflections on Violent Children.* New York: Ballantine Publishing Group.

Leddy, J. and O'Connell, M. (2002) 'The prevalence, nature and psychological correlates of bullying in Irish prisons.' *Legal and Criminological Psychology 7*, 2, 131–140.

LeDoux, J.E. (1993) 'Emotional memory systems in the brain.' *Behavioural and Brain Research 58*, 68–79.

Lerner, J.V., Hertzog, C., Hooker, K.A., Hassibi, M. and Thomas, A. (1988) 'A longitudinal study of negative emotional states and adjustment from early childhood through adolescence.' *Child Development 59*, 2, 356–366.

Levenson, R. and Ruef, A. (1992) 'Empathy: A physiological substitute.' *Journal of Personality and Social Psychology 63*, 2, 234–246.

Liebmann, M. (2007) *Restorative Justice: How It Works.* London: Jessica Kingsley Publishers.

Lines, D. (1996) *Early Secondary Pupils' Experiences of Name-calling Behaviour through a Discourse Analysis of Differing Counselling Interviews.* Unpublished dissertation. Westhill College, Selly Oak, Birmingham.

Lines, D. (1999) 'Secondary pupils' experiences of name-calling behaviour.' *Pastoral Care in Education 17*, 1, 23–31.

Lines, D. (2001) 'An approach with name-calling and verbal taunting.' *Pastoral Care in Education 19*, 1, 3–9.

Lines, D. (2003) 'Insights into the management of challenging behaviour in secondary school.' *Pastoral Care in Education 21*, 1, 26–36.

Lines, D. (2006a) *Brief Counselling in School: Working with Young People from 11–18* (2nd edition). London: Sage.

Lines, D. (2006b) 'Aggressive youth.' *Therapy Today 17*, 7, 13–16. Rugby: British Association for Counselling and Psychotherapy.

Lines, D. (2007) 'Violence in school: What can we do?' *Pastoral Care in Education*, June, 14–21.

Littlechild, B. and Bourke, C. (2006) 'Men's Use of Violence and Intimidation against Family Members and Child Protection Workers.' In C. Humphreys and N. Stanley (eds) *Domestic Violence and Child Protection: Directions for Good Practice.* London: Jessica Kingsley Publishers.

Lorenz, K. (1969) *On Aggression.* London: University Paperback, Methuen.

Luxmoore, N. (2000) *Listening to Young People in School, Youth Work and Counselling.* London: Jessica Kingsley Publishers.

Luxmoore, N. (2006) *Working with Anger and Young People.* London: Jessica Kingsley Publishers.

Mains, B. and Robinson, G. (1992) *Michael's Story: The 'No Blame' Approach.* Bristol: Lame Duck Publishing.

McLeod, J. (2003) *An Introduction to Counselling* (3rd edition). Buckingham: Open University Press.

Mealey, L. (1995) 'The sociobiology of sociopathy: An integrated evolutionary model.' *Behavioural and Brain Sciences 18*, 523–599.

Mednick, S.A., Gabrieli, W.F. Jr and Hutchings, B. (1984) 'Genetic influences in criminal convictions: Evidence from an adoption cohort.' *Science 224*, 891–893.

Mellor, A. (1997) *Finding Out About Bullying.* SCRE Spotlight No. 43, Edinburgh: SCRE. This paper can be downloaded (www.scre.ac.uk/spotlight/spotlight43.html) or requested from the Anti-Bullying Network at the University of Edinburgh.

Minuchin, S. (1974) *Families and Family Therapy.* London: Tavistock.

Munn, P., Lloyd, G. and Cullen, M.A. (2000) *Alternatives to Exclusion from School.* London: Paul Chapman Publishing.

Ness, C.D. (2004) 'Why girls fight: Female youth violence in the inner city.' *Annals of the American Academy of Political and Social Science 595*, 1, 32–48.

Oakley, A. (1981) *Subject Women.* Oxford: Martin Robertson.

Olweus, D. (1991) 'Bully/victim problems among school children: Basic facts and effects of a school based intervention.' In D. Pepler and K. Rubin (eds) *The Development and Treatment of Childhood Aggression.* Hillsdale, NJ: Lawrence Erlbaum.

Olweus, D. (1993) *Bullying at School: What We Know and What We Can Do.* Oxford: Blackwell.

ONS (2001) National Statistics Online. Accessed 22/9/07 at www.statistics.gov.uk/cci/nugget.asp?id=1166.

ONS (2007) *Social Trends* (37th edition). Office of National Statistics. London: Palgrave Macmillan.

Palazzoli, M., Boscolo, L., Cecchin, G. and Prata, G. (1978) *Paradox and Counterparadox.* New York: Aronson.

Panskepp, J., Siviy, S.M. and Normansell, L.A. (1985) 'Brain Opioids and Social Emotions.' In M. Reite and T. Field (eds) *The Psychobiology of Attachment and Separation.* Orlando, FL: Academic Press.

Pavlov, I.P. (1927) *Conditioned Reflexes and Psychiatry* (trans. W.H. Gantt). New York: International Publications.

Pepler, D.J. and Craig, W.M. (1995) 'A peek behind the fence: Naturalistic observations of aggressive children with remote audiovisual recording.' *Developmental Psychology 31*, 4, 458–553.

Pikas, A. (1989) 'The Common Concern Method for the Treatment of Mobbing.' In E. Roland and E. Munthe (eds) *Bullying: An International Perspective.* London: David Fulton.

Plomin, R. (1990) *Nature and Nurture – An Introduction to Behavioural Genetics.* Pacific Grove, CA: Brooks/Cole.

Plomin, R. and Daniels, D. (1987) 'Why are children from the same family so different from each other?' *Behaviour and Brain Science 10*, 1–16.

Plomin, R., DeFries, J.C., McClearn, G.E. and Rutter, M. (1997) *Behavioral Genetics* (3rd edition). New York: W.H. Freeman.

Plomin, R., Fulker, D.W., Corley, R. and DeFries, J.C. (1997) 'Nature, nurture and cognitive development from 1 to 16 years: A parent-offspring adoption study.' *Psychological Science 8*, 442–447.

Quinton, D. and Rutter, M. (1988) *Parenting Breakdown.* Aldershot: Avebury.

Radford, L. and Hester, M. (2006) *Mothering through Domestic Violence.* London: Jessica Kingsley Publishers.

Radford, L., Blacklock, N. and Iwi, K. (2006) 'Domestic Abuse Risk Assessment and Safety Planning in Child Protection – Assessing perpetrators.' In C. Humphreys and N. Stanley (eds) *Domestic Violence and Child Protection: Directions for Good Practice.* London: Jessica Kingsley Publishers.

Raine, A., Brennan, P. and Mednick, S. (1997) 'Interaction between birth complications and early maternal rejection in predisposing individuals to adult violence.' *American Journal of Psychiatry 154*, 9, 1265–1271.

Råkil, M. (2006) 'Are Men who Use Violence against their Partners and Children Good Enough Fathers?' In C. Humphreys and N. Stanley (eds) *Domestic Violence and Child Protection: Directions for Good Practice.* London: Jessica Kingsley Publishers.

Rayner, C. (1998) *Bullying at Work: Survey Report.* London: UNISON.

Rigby, K. (1997) 'What children tell us about bullying in schools.' *Children Australia 22*, 2, 28–34.

Rigby, K. (2002) *New Perspectives on Bullying.* London: Jessica Kingsley Publishers.

Rogers, C.R. (1995) 'What understanding and acceptance mean to me.' *Journal of Humanistic Psychology 35*, 4, 7–22.

Roland, E. (1989) 'A System Oriented Strategy against Bullying.' In E. Roland and E. Munthe (eds) *Bullying: An International Perspective.* London: David Fulton.

Rothschild, B. (2005) 'The physiology of empathy.' *Counselling and Psychotherapy Journal 15*, 9, 11–15. Rugby: British Association for Counselling and Psychotherapy.

Roy, P., Rutter, M. and Pickles, A. (2000) 'Institutional care: Risk from family background or pattern of rearing?' *Journal of Child Psychology and Psychiatry 41*, 139–149.

Rutter, M. (ed.) (1996) *Genetics of Criminal and Antisocial Behaviour.* Chichester: Wiley.

Schore, A.N. (1994) *Affect Regulation and the Origin of the Self.* Hillsdale, NJ, and Hove: Lawrence Erlbaum.

Seligman, M.E.P. (1975) *Helplessness.* San Francisco: Freeman.

Sigma Research (2000) *Prevalence of Domestic Violence among Lesbians and Gay Men.* Accessed 4/10/07 at www.sigmaresearch.org.uk/projects26.html.

Sills, C. (2007) 'Transactional analysis – A relational psychotherapy.' *Therapy Today 18*, 1, 15–17. Rugby: British Association for Counselling and Psychotherapy.

Singleton, N., Meltzer, H. and Gatward, R. (1998) *Psychiatric Morbidity among Prisoners in England and Wales.* London: Office of National Statistics.

Skinner, B.F. (1953) *Science and Human Behaviour.* New York: Macmillan.

Smith, P.K. and Sharp, S. (eds) (1994) *School Bullying: Insights and Perspectives.* London: Routledge.

Street, E. (1994) *Counselling for Family Problems.* London: Sage.

Tattum, D.P. and Tattum, E. (1992) 'Bullying: A Whole-School Response.' In N. Jones and E. Baglin Jones (eds) *Learning to Behave.* London: Kogan Page.

Thomas, J., Bouchard, T.J. Jr and McGue, M. (2002) 'Genetic and environmental influences on human psychological differences.' *Journal of Neurobiology 54*, 1, 4–45.

Thorne, B. (2002) *The Mystical Power of Person-Centred Therapy.* London: Whurr.

Toolan, M. (1988) *Narrative: A Critical Linguistic Approach.* London: Routledge.

Turkheimer, E. and Waldron, M.C. (2000) 'Nonshared environment: Theoretical, methodological and quantitative review.' *Psychological Bulletin 126*, 78–108.

Turner, J. (2000) *On the Origin of Human Emotions.* Palo Alto, CA: Stanford University Press.

Vartia, M. and Hyyti, J. (2002) 'Gender differences in workplace bullying among prison officers.' *European Journal of Work and Organizational Psychology 11*, 1, 113–126.

Velleman, R. (1993) *Alcohol and the Family.* London: Institute of Alcohol Studies.

Venter, J.C., Adams, M.D., Myers, E.W., Li, P.W. *et al.* (2001) 'The sequence of the human genome.' *Science 291*, No. 5507, 1304–1351. Accessed 10/9/07 at www.sciencemag.org/cgi/content/short/291/5507/1304.

Victoria Climbié Inquiry (2003) *Report of an Inquiry by Lord Laming.* London: The Stationery Office.

Walby, S. (2004) *The Cost of Domestic Violence.* University of Leeds: Women and Equality Unit. Accessed 4/10/07 at www.womenandequalityunit.gov.uk/research/cost_of_dv_research_summary.pdf.

Walker, A., Kershaw, C. and Nicholas, S. (2007) *Crime in England and Wales 2005/2006.* Accessed 10/9/07 at www.homeoffice.gov.uk/rds/crimeew0506.html.

Watson, J.B. (1919) *Psychology from the Standpoint of a Behaviorist.* Philadelphia: J.B. Lippincott.

West, D.J. (1965) *Murder Followed by Suicide.* London: Heinemann.

Whitney, I. and Smith, P.K. (1993) 'A survey of the nature and extent of bullying in junior/middle and secondary schools.' *Educational Research 35*, 13–25.

Whyte, J. (2006) 'A Criminal Absence of Logic.' Accessed 29/11/07 at www.timesonline.co.uk/tol/comment/columnists/guest_contributors/article704916.ece

Winstok, Z., Eisikovits, Z. and Karnieli-Miller, O. (2004) 'The impact of father-to-mother aggression on the structure and content of adolescents' perceptions of themselves and their parents.' *Violence against Women 10*, 9, 1036–1055.

Wright, R.H. and Cummings, N.A. (eds) (2005) *Destructive Trends in Mental Health: The Well Intentional Path to Harm.* London: Routledge.

Wright, R., Brookman, F. and Bennett, T. (2006) 'The foreground dynamics of street robbery in Britain.' *British Journal of Criminology 46*, 1, 1–15.

Index